# Female Sexuality in the Early Medieval Islamic World

## *The Early and Medieval Islamic World*

Published in collaboration with the Society for the Medieval Mediterranean

Society for the
Medieval Mediterranean

As recent scholarship resoundingly attests, the medieval Mediterranean and Middle East bore witness to a prolonged period of flourishing intellectual and cultural diversity. Seeking to contribute to this ever-more nuanced and contextual picture, *The Early and Medieval Islamic World* book series promotes innovative research on the period 500–1500 AD with the Islamic world, as it ebbed and flowed from Marrakesh to Palermo and Cairo to Kabul, as the central pivot. Thematic focus within this remit is broad, from the cultural and social to the political and economic, with preference given to studies of societies and cultures from a socio-historical perspective. It will foster a community of unique voices on the medieval Islamic world, shining light into its lesser-studied corners.

**Series editor**
Professor Roy Mottahedeh, Harvard University

**Advisors**
Professor Amira Bennison, University of Cambridge
Professor Farhad Daftary, Institute of Ismaili Studies
Professor Simon Doubleday, Hofstra University
Professor Frank Griffel, Yale University
Professor Remke Kruk, Leiden University
Professor Beatrice Manz, Tufts University
Dr Bernard O'Kane, American University in Cairo
Professor Andrew Peacock, University of St Andrews
Dr Yossef Rapoport, Queen Mary University of London

**New and forthcoming titles**

*Cross Veneration in the Medieval Islamic World: Christian Identity and Practice under Muslim Rule*, Charles Tieszen (Fuller Theological Seminary/Simpson University)

*Power and Knowledge in Medieval Islam: Shi'i and Sunni Encounters in Baghdad*, Tariq al-Jamil (Swathmore College)

*The Eastern Frontier: Limits of Empire in Late Antique and Early Medieval Central Asia*, Robert Haug (University of Cincinnati)

*Writing History in the Medieval Islamic World: The Value of Chronicles as Archives*, Fozia Bora (University of Leeds)

*Gypsies in the Medieval Islamic World: The History of a People*, Kristina Richardson (City University, New York)

*Narrating Muslim Sicily: War and Peace in the Medieval Mediterranean World*, William Granara (Harvard University)

# Female Sexuality in the Early Medieval Islamic World

## *Gender and Sex in Arabic Literature*

Pernilla Myrne

I.B.TAURIS
LONDON • NEW YORK • OXFORD • NEW DELHI • SYDNEY

I.B. TAURIS
Bloomsbury Publishing Plc
50 Bedford Square, London, WC1B 3DP, UK
1385 Broadway, New York, NY 10018, USA
29 Earlsfort Terrace, Dublin 2, Ireland



First published in Great Britain 2020
Paperback edition published 2021



Series design by www.paulsmithdesign.com
Cover image: Freer Gallery of Art and Arthur M. Sackler Gallery, Smithsonian Institution,
Washington, D.C.: Purchase – Charles Lang Freer Endowment, F 1946.30.



A catalogue record for this book is available from the British Library.

A catalog record for this book is available from the Library of Congress.

ISBN: HB: 978-1-8386-0501-8
PB: 978-0-7556-4469-8
ePDF: 978-1-8386-0502-5
eBook: 978-1-8386-0503-2

Series: The Early and Medieval Islamic World

Typeset by RefineCatch Limited, Bungay, Suffolk

# Contents

# Acknowledgements

The research for this book began in 2011, when a postdoctoral scholarship from the Swedish Research Council enabled me to stay at New York University as a visiting scholar. I am grateful to Everett Rowson for invaluable help in the early phase of this project. Since then, I have presented ideas from this book at various conferences and seminars and I wish to thank discussants and other attendees who gave valuable comments. I particularly benefitted from the conferences of the School of Abbasid Studies in Istanbul 2014 and Leiden 2016 and a conference in Paris 2016 on The Language of Arabic Erotica and its Translations, organized by Claire Savina and Frédéric Lagrange. I am grateful to The Swedish Foundation for Humanities and Social Sciences for financing the research project that culminated in this book.

I owe much to I.B. Tauris: to the two anonymous reviewers whose extremely helpful comments helped me clarify my ideas; to Thomas Stottor, who took an interest in my project early on and to Rory Gormley who helped me complete the book.

Many people advised, criticized and inspired me during my research and supported me during the writing of the manuscript; I can only mention a few. Jan Retsö, who supervised my doctoral thesis, has supported me and shared his extensive knowledge over the years. Long and stimulating discussions with my friend Houda El Machharawi inspired me to explore issues in more depth. Geert Jan van Gelder's meticulous reading and critical comments saved me from some errors and Reuven Snir graciously helped me with some difficult poetry. I would like to thank my colleagues at the Department of Languages and Literatures at the University of Gothenburg for their support and friendship. I am grateful, too, for the assistance of the staff at the university library, especially those working with interlibrary loans.

During the years working on this book, I have been privileged to watch my children, Julia and Alfred, grow up into young adults; they are a source of hope and encouragement. I thank my sisters, Anna and Sara, for their inspiration and my parents, Monica and Leif, for their ceaseless love. Finally, to my husband Kenneth, thank you for your wholeheartedly support and encouragement, you have made this book possible.

# Introduction

Female sexuality in the early medieval Islamic world is a subject that involves several growing fields of research, namely the history of women, gender and sexuality in Islam. The history of women and marriage is an established field, eventually merged with gender studies, with more or less well-researched publications since the first half of the twentieth century.[1] The last decades have seen several important studies on women's history limited to specific time periods, for example Fatimid, Mamluk and Ottoman, or genres and disciplines, such as early Islamic law.[2] Research on sexuality started later and is based on a more limited number of sources. Georges-Henri Bousquet and Ṣalāḥ al-Dīn al-Munajjid published books on the topic in the 1950s, but they were not followed up with substantial research until the 1970s.[3]

The early research on sexuality in Islamic literature and societies tended to make broad assumptions about sexuality in 'Islam' over considerable time periods (sometimes over a millennium). In this book, I examine attitudes towards and ideas about female sexuality in sources from different disciplines written within a relatively limited time period (if some two hundred years can be said to be limited). The sources, many of which are astonishingly unexplored, shed new light on the understanding of female sexuality during this period, not the least on attitudes to women's pleasure and right to sexual fulfilment. It is often claimed that jurists gave women the right to sexual fulfilment, but that is not entirely true for the early medieval period, as Kecia Ali has pointed out and this book confirms.[4] Yet, non-legal discourses hold largely positive attitudes towards female sexuality and women's own words and expertise were often considered. The generalizing claim that women were entitled to satisfaction in marriage is almost as persistent as the idea that premodern Islamic societies were characterized by a 'fear' of women's sexuality, embodied in the concept *fitna*.[5] Both these claims can be true, but are not meaningful as long as they are not contextualized. Newer research has been more nuanced, and have taken regard to genre and historical contexts, but this research is primarily centred on male sexuality, especially homosexual. The reason is, naturally, that there are many more sources for male sexuality, not the least homosexuality, but it is also an effect of scholars' interest in this field. There is still very little research on female sexuality in early Islamic societies, perhaps because there is a supposed lack of sources. The physiological aspects of female sexuality is an issue for medical historians, and there are, in fact, rich sources, as Leslie Peirce has pointed out.[6] Yet, these sources have generated comparatively little research so far. Moreover, as I hope to demonstrate with this book, there are other genres and disciplines that have substantial material on women's sexuality.

Most of the sources examined in the six chapters were written in the third and fourth Islamic centuries, which is approximately the ninth and tenth centuries AD, and occasionally later, even though some of them rely on and cite much earlier material.[7] The designation 'early medieval Islamic world' is not perfect. First, 'early medieval' is somewhat misleading, as it is a term based on the chronology of European history. Traditionally, a classification based on dynasties has been used for the chronology of Islamic history, but other classifications have been proposed. The early medieval period, as defined in this book, is approximately the same as the early Abbasid period, which corresponds to the late Early Islamic period and the first part of the early middle period according to another classification.[8] Second, the Islamic world encompassed a large area in the early medieval period, but I have chosen to focus on the Abbasid heartland, Iraq, where the major intellectual centres were located, at least in the beginning of this period. Many of the texts considered here were written in the capital, Baghdad, and for a time in Samarra.

The time period covered by this book begins with the 'golden days' of the Abbasid dynasty, and spans the Buyid takeover of political power in Iraq in the middle of the fourth/tenth century. This period witnessed the expansion of Islam to the majority religion in many of the regions under Islamic governance. This was the end of the formative period of Islamic law, the end of the formative and beginning of the classical period of tafsīr and the beginning of the canonization of Sunni and Shiʿi hadith.[9] Legal principles, which regulated sexuality and restricted especially female sexual behaviour, took their final shape between 740 and 800 AD, that is just before and for some decades after the Abbasid takeover.[10] Sunni Islam was established as the mainstream in the ninth century, and the Sunni and Shiʿi Schools of law took form in the beginning of the tenth century.

At the same time as the Islamic disciplines took form, there was a remarkable interest in natural sciences and philosophy. The Islamic Empire took over several important Late Antiquity centres of learning but the scholarly activities taking place there continued in some form and their production was transmitted to Arabic. Works in Greek, Syriac and Middle Persian started to be translated to Arabic in the Umayyad period, but it was the first two centuries of the Abbasid dynasty that held the most remarkable achievements.[11] The translations generated an interest in and production of books on philosophy, medicine and other disciplines in Arabic. The ninth and tenth centuries saw the birth of a systematic Islamic medicine based on Greek medical science, which is of particular interest for this book, as it transmitted and modified ideas about sexuality.[12]

The main sources used by translators into Arabic of Greek medical theory were the works of late Antique scholars in Alexandria, who wrote commentaries on the writings of Galen (second century AD) and other Greek medical scholars and collected abridged versions and paraphrases in medical encyclopaedias.[13] Galen became the main medical authority and the model Greek scholar in the Islamic world, not only for physicians but also for natural philosophers and others.[14] Hippocrates (the assumed author of a corpus of medical texts written from the second half of the fifth century to first half of the fourth century) is often referred to but the Hippocratic texts were primarily known to the Islamic physicians through Galen's commentaries. In the first centuries of Islamic medicine most medical authors in the Islamic world wrote in Arabic, therefore some scholars have preferred the term Arabic medicine. The majority of the medical authors were not Arabs, however, and therefore others prefer the term Islamic medicine, despite the fact that many, perhaps most, of them were not Muslims.[15] Neither were their medical theories particularly 'Islamic' for, as we have seen they built on medical ideas from late antiquity.[16] Nevertheless, as the medical authors lived in areas governed by Muslim rulers and many of their patrons were Muslims (often the same rulers), it is reasonable to use the term Islamic medicine.

The translations and scientific activities were patronized by the Abbasid elite and by the imperial court. The elite also supported poets and litterateurs, and the urban centres accommodated lively literary and cultural activities. Book production flourished and literacy increased, facilitated by the introduction of paper. Abbasid belles-lettres, the so-called *adab* literature, was born in this creative milieu; a vast number of anecdotes, sayings and poems were collected by late Umayyad and early Abbasid philologists, exploring the Arabic language and the rich corpus of early Arab poetry. In the third/ninth century, authors started to arrange entertaining and edifying historical anecdotes, sayings and poems in multi-thematic compendia or monothematic works and this corpus of anecdotes from the Abbasid period survived in classical Arabic literature for centuries. Although *adab* is a cultural product of high society, the anecdotes are accessible.

They make historical events and settings come alive, mostly with the focus on the verbal utterances in the form of poetry or dialogues.

Although the anecdotes are more historical fiction than history writing, historians have found *adab* useful sources for studying unofficial history, the history of women and the non-elite.[17] This is primarily due to lack of material about these groups in mainstream history books, whereas they frequently occur in *adab* compilations where there are numerous anecdotes about witty and eloquent women whose clever remarks make confronting men everything from pleasing to being dumbfounded. In the anecdotes, the socially subordinate character often plays a major role and women are often represented as particularly eloquent; they get the last word when the plot takes an unexpected turn or they turn out to be the most clever and eloquent in a verbal duel.

All fields of learning that I have mentioned here conveyed ideas about female sexuality and my aim is to show how these ideas intersected. Ideas come with people and travel with people. The Abbasid caliphate was vast and diverse; yet, the mode of financing scholarly activities through patronage fostered tight networks with clusters of scholars from different disciplines in the imperial court and other major power centres, especially in Baghdad. We can assume that the scholars who were active in the same locations exchanged ideas and read each other's works. It is the scholars from the central clusters in particular whose work lives on and is extant today. Furthermore, the ideal scholar was a polymath, who could comment on various phenomena, ethics and social etiquette alike. For these reasons, the comparison of genres is not a merely theoretical pursuit; it reflects the realities of the authors and readers. The *majlis*[18] (social gathering) was probably influential in spreading philosophical and scientific ideas to wider circles of litteratures and poets. In the words of Shawkat Toorawa: 'There seems little doubt that most of the Baghdad littérateurs (*udabāʾ*) knew one another. They were not overly numerous, they learned from the same relatively small number of teachers, they attended many of the same literary and social gatherings and salons (*majālis*), and study circles (*ḥalaqāt*), and they met in the bookshops and the Bookmen's Market (*Sūq al-warrāqīn*).'[19]

The courts of al-Manṣūr (r. 136–158/754–775) and al-Maʾmūn (r. 198–218/813–833) are often mentioned as hubs of scholarly activity.[20] Some of the scholars whose writings on women are examined in this book were connected to the court of al-Mutawakkil (r. 232–247/847–861): the influential translator and physician Ḥunayn ibn Isḥāq (d. 260/873), the physician and first author of a medical compendium in Arabic ʿAlī ibn Sahl al-Ṭabarī, and the buffoons and drinking companions Abū Ḥassān al-Namlī and Abū al-ʿAnbas al-Ṣaymarī

(213–275/828–888). Abū al-ʿAnbas is an interesting example of a polymath from this period; he started his career as a judge and then worked as a court astrologer, dream interpreter and poet.[21] He wrote some forty books on serious as well as amusing topics: astrology, *fiqh* (Islamic jurisprudence), homosexuality and erotic stories. The scholarly breadth is indicative of the intellectual climate in the early medieval Islamic world. The great intellectual al-Jāḥiẓ was still alive (he died in 255/December 868–January 869) and so were many others mentioned in this book. Another scholar who probably participated in the gatherings of al-Mutawakkil was Ibn Abī Ṭāhir Ṭayfūr, whose *Book on Women's Instances of Eloquence* (*Balaghāt al-Nisāʾ*) is a major source for Chapter 4 in this book.[22]

Islamic legal scholars in the ninth century were relatively independent from the Abbasid caliphs and did not normally participate in these learned circles, but instead opposed the debauchery and pagan knowledge taught there, although they shared some fundamental ideas about male and female nature with the natural sciences.

Abbasid power declined successively from the first half of the ninth century, and, except for a revival after the accession of al-Muʿtamid in 256/870, power was more or less in the hands of military commanders. In 334/945, the Buyid Dynasty took control over Baghdad, and became the political and military leaders of the dwindling Empire. The Buyids were Twelver Shiʿi and favoured Twelver Shiʿism but kept the Abbasid Sunni caliph. They also supported Persian and Hellenistic learning and the vast scholarly production continued. During this period, the tradition of composing large multi-thematic and sometimes multi-disciplinary encyclopaedias, which began in the ninth century, continued with legal treatises, history writing, *adab* and medical compendia, among other disciplines and genres. Abū al-Faraj al-Iṣbahānī (d. after 360/971), who belonged for a period to the circle of the Buyid *wazīr* al-Muhallabī (339–352/950–963) finished his important work *Book of Songs* (*Kitāb al-Aghānī*), which he had been working on for several decades.[23]

The earliest extant erotic compendium in Arabic, *Encyclopaedia of Pleasure* (*Jawāmiʿ al-Ladhdha*), which is an important source for this book, was probably written in this period; its author is unknown but its content seems to owe much to the relatively tolerant and cosmopolitan intellectual environment during the Buyid rule of Baghdad, with its sometime libertine outlook and eclectic attitude to religion.[24] Perhaps influenced by the Buyids, who were Shiʿites but supported a Sunni caliph, the author of *Jawāmiʿ al-Ladhdha* mixes Sunni and Shiʿi references. Although the translation movement came to an end during the Buyid era in Baghdad, the interest in translated sciences did not decrease.[25]

This interest is evident in *Jawāmiʿ al-Ladhdha*; its author apparently had an abundance of sources at his disposal, translated from Greek and Middle Persian, perhaps also Sanskrit. He collected and combined texts from the various disciplines and genres that explored human sexuality, which were written in Arabic or had been translated to Arabic in the early Abbasid era.

The name of the writer, according to most extant manuscripts and references in later erotic literature, is Abū al-Ḥasan ʿAlī ibn Naṣr al-Kātib. He might be the writer with the same name mentioned in *Kitāb al-Fihrist*, a writer who died in Baghdad in 377/987 according to Ibn al-Nadīm, who completed *Fihrist* just a few years later.[26] Ibn al-Nadīm does not mention *Jawāmiʿ al-Ladhdha*, but the other books attributed to ʿAlī ibn Naṣr in *Fihrist* confirm the interests displayed there. They are, like *Jawāmiʿ al-Ladhdha*, directed to people who wish to refine their manners and socialize with the elite: *Iṣlāḥ al-Akhlāq* (*Improving the Character*), *Adab al-Sulṭān* (*The Etiquette of the Sovereign*), *Kitāb al-Barāʿa* (*The Book of Excellence* or *The Book on Eloquence*), and *Suḥbat al-Sulṭān* (*The Book of Keeping Company with the Ruler*). Ibn al-Nadīm adds that this ʿAlī ibn Naṣr wrote more books that he probably did not finish. The title *kātib* indicates that he was a secretary of the chancery and the books ascribed to him in *Fihrist* could be directed to ambitious officials who wanted to improve their career possibilities. His father Naṣr was a physician, according to Ibn al-Nadīm, which may explain his interest in medicine, and a Christian, which means that either he or his son ʿAlī ibn Naṣr converted to Islam. However, no bibliography mentions the title *Jawāmiʿ al-Ladhdha* before Kâtip Çelebi (d. 1067/1657), who identifies the writer as 'the well-known' Abū Naṣr Manṣūr ibn ʿAlī al-Kātib al-Samānī.[27] This name is not consistent with the name of the author written on the manuscripts used in this study, which were all produced long before Kâtip Çelebi's time.[28] Nevertheless, *Jawāmiʿ al-Ladhdha* influenced later Arabic erotica and is quoted by several authors, from the twelfth-century scholar al-Shayzarī to the fifteenth-century religious scholar al-Suyūṭi.[29]

The first part of the book examines attitudes to and ideas about female sexuality in the androcentric intellectual and scientific communities of the early medieval Islamic world. Scholars and authors in the Islamic world addressed topics that reflect on the distinction between women and men. They were naturally influenced by the patriarchal traditions of earlier societies and regard women in this framework, but both their outlooks and their conclusions differ. In medical discourse, women's sexuality and bodies play a central and basically positive role, being essential for reproduction. Yet, men are described as more perfect than women, who are biologically and therefore morally inferior. In erotological discourse, women's pleasure is desirable and women's wishes regarded, yet the ideal woman is ultimately the one who pleases men. Religious discourse is strongly male-oriented and, in line with its normative project, it sets out to implement the notion of female inferiority with the help of rules that give priority to men.

The fact that these intellectual pursuits are androcentric does not mean that women did not have a voice. Women's voices is the main subject of the second part of the book, where I also discuss women's possibly agency. It is perhaps risky to use the word 'agency' in an early medieval context, but I maintain that it can be used for describing female personas' attempts to exercise influence over their own life, although this influence is sometimes extremely limited. Narrators and authors have largely ignored female views, and women were generally excluded from scholarly communities in the early medieval period, yet women play a significant role in anecdotal literature; although not as authors, they appear as speakers, oral poets and characters. Eloquence was seen as a female attribute as much as a male, in fact eloquent women were especially beloved characters in literature. Philologists and historians were fascinated by the eloquent Arab women in early Islam and used them as sources for linguistic enquiries. Correspondingly, royal women and courtesans often appear as strong and well-expressed characters with independent views in anecdotes from the Umayyad and Abbasid periods.

The first chapter discusses ideas about female sexuality and nature in medical discourse. Islamic medical authors embraced Greek medical ideas on sex differences and reproduction, in which women have a pivotal role, but one of their main achievements in the field of sexuality was the emphasis on sexual health and pleasure. Physicians believed that abstinence could cause considerable physical health problems, but they also admitted that pleasure was desirable in itself. Pharmacology, in the form of aphrodisiacs and pleasure-enhancing methods, was therefore a major topic, but mainly addressed to men. Nevertheless, physicians acknowledged women's sexual needs, not only for improving fertility, for there is an underlying conviction that women's excitement and pleasure are desirable, although not often discussed explicitly.

The second chapter addresses female sexuality as represented in the oldest extant erotic compendium, *Jawāmiʿ al-Ladhdha*, which not only covers many learned discourses on sexuality, it also educates the cultured man on how to satisfy women. Indeed, pleasing women and satisfying them belonged to the realm of refined behaviour, and knowledge about female sexuality should be part of a refined man's education. Therefore, the encyclopaedia includes sections on medical topics such as anatomy, sexual health and pharmacology, as well as chapters on sexual technique and, remarkably, a chapter on female orgasm, with classifications of women in regard to their attitudes to sex and how they reach climax. The erudite discourses in *Jawāmiʿ al-Ladhdha* are interspersed with stories about hypersexual women, who are also alleged narrators. The presence of prominent female protagonists and narrators contributes with an upgrading of female expertise and experience. At the same time, however, the stories about hypersexual women belong to a common notion that women, seen as closer to nature, have a much greater libido than men have; a notion that was confirmed by various authorities in the late Antique and early medieval world.

The third chapter addresses attitudes to female sexuality in Islamic literature from the late second/eighth to the late fourth/tenth century, a central period for the Islamic sciences. Islamic writings on female sexuality were guided by the same principle as the medical and erotological discourses, namely that women by nature are subordinate to men. The crucial issue for jurists and other Islamic scholars was that all sexual activities have to be carried out within legal bounds. This chapter discusses what normative conjugal sexual relations meant for women, as well as examining particular strategies in *hadith* and *tafsīr* for regulating female sexual behaviour. Although early jurists and traditionists did not necessarily endorse a single model, the outcome of legal discussions in the third/ninth century in particular was that legal bonds became much more restricting for women, as Islamic jurisprudence gave men the right to marry four women and have sexual relations with their female slaves.

Chapter 4 discusses women's own words about sexuality in poetry and anecdotes and verbal proficiency as a strategy to exercise agency in a male-dominated world. In *adab* literature, two types of female characters stand out; the early Islamic woman, who, intelligently and eloquently, argues against her husband and gets her way with him; and the 'anecdotal woman', often a slave, who defeats a man in a verbal duel or uses her verbal skills to get what she wants. Women's strategies in the corpus of poetry and anecdotes examined here are connected to sexuality; they rebuff unwanted attention, utilize their sex appeal in order to reach their goal and appraise men. They are experts on male sexuality and use their husbands' failures to live up to masculine ideals to their own advantages if they have to. Altogether, female sexuality is pictured as a positive force and women, albeit fictional, have their own distinct voice.

If women are portrayed favourably in many *adab* anecdotes and their active participation is appreciated, women have a more precarious role in the so called *mujūn* genre, the burlesque, often bawdy poetry that is the subject of Chapter 5. This genre was popular and women were both creators and targets of *mujūn*. In this chapter, I discuss the hazards of being outspoken for women; it was appreciated in some circles, but could be used against them or to defame their male relatives.

As an example, we will look at poems describing genitals, a typical *mujūn* motif. The chapter examines the vagina as a poetic motif; this motif is often part of misogynist descriptions of grotesque female bodies, but there are also several poems in *Jawāmiʿ al-Ladhdha* attributed to female poets who describe their own genitals in boasting terms, like male poets such as Abū Nuwās occasionally did.

The last chapter deals with a neglected topic, namely the representation of female homoerotic desire or *saḥq* ('rubbing'). A whole chapter is devoted to this topic in *Jawāmiʿ al-Ladhdha* and female homosexuality was also discussed by physicians and jurists. The chapter discusses the different explanations of *saḥq* conveyed by these physicians as well as representations of lesbian women in literature from this period. In particular, it examines women's own words about their preferences, as represented in a corpus of poems and letters attributed to women, in which they explain why they have chosen lesbianism or, alternatively, why they have rejected it.

## On translation of sexually explicit words

Classical Arabic has an exceptionally rich vocabulary for words connected to sexuality, whose nuances are difficult to find equivalents of in English. For example, perhaps the most common word for sexual intercourse in *Jawāmiʿ al-Ladhdha* is *nayk*, which has a vulgar connotation today, and is often translated as 'fucking'. It was used in bawdy poetry, the so-called *mujūn*, and could accurately be translated 'fucking'. Yet, it is also used for penetrative sex as a contrast to other sexual practices, and can simply be translated 'sexual intercourse'. I have sometimes chosen to translate it 'fucking', sometimes 'sexual intercourse', depending on the context. In *Jawāmiʿ al-Ladhdha*, the choice of word is connected to discourse, *nayk* is often used in erotology and poetry, and always used in erotic stories; the more clinical term *jimāʿ* (or *mujāmaʿa*) is used in medical discourses, and *nikāḥ* (marriage or marital sex) is used in juristic discourses. The use of these terms is not always consistent, however, and there are differences between the manuscripts.

Likewise, some scholars have chosen to translate the words *ayr* and *ḥir* as 'cock' and 'pussy', or 'prick' and 'cunt', as they are considered more vulgar than the neutral *dhakar* and *farj*. Nonetheless, when al-Jāḥiẓ discussed the word *ḥir* in the ninth century, he concluded that *ḥir* is the *ism* (name), and *farj* the *kināya* (metonym). Following al-Jāḥiẓ, it is reasonable to translate *ḥir* as 'vagina'.[30]

Part One

# Discourses on Female Sexuality

1

# Sexuality, Pleasure and Health

Burjān and Ḥabāḥib were two wise women and advisors to a king in a book written by the ninth-century author Abū Ḥassān al-Namlī, one of the 'cultured and affable' men at the court of the caliph al-Mutawakkil.[1] Al-Namlī, who was a buffoon and a drinking companion of the caliph, also wrote books on lesbianism and passive male homosexuality. The books are lost, but extensive quotations from Burjān and Ḥabāḥib in the erotic manual *Jawāmiʿ al-Ladhdha* reveal that it was a humorous and slightly irreverent exposition of different aspects of female sexuality, mixed with erotic stories and anecdotes. In the frame story, the king asks the two women questions on a variety of topics and they answer with examples from their own life. On one occasion, he asks them who has most sexual appetite (*shahwa*), women or men.[2] Their answer, 'the woman with the weakest sexual appetite overpowers the man with the strongest appetite', did probably not surprise al-Namlī's audience, as in this genre (erotic literature) women are often represented as entirely driven by their desire. They choose men based on the size of their genital organs and their performance in bed, and they love them as long as they get satisfaction. Burjān and Ḥabāḥib illustrate their claim with a dubious evidence in the crude style of *mujūn* ('sexual comedy'): 'A group of men is not necessarily enough to satisfy one woman, whereas one single woman can satisfy a group of men.' The king follows up with another question, 'Why then have women less semen than men have, when their sexual appetite is so much stronger?' The two women reply with an answer informed by medical theory and natural philosophy. The reason for this, they say, is that the female semen comes from the brain whereas the male semen comes from the back; because of the longer distance the female sperm has to flow, women have slower orgasm and lesser amount of seminal fluid.[3]

The idea that both men and women have semen was common medical knowledge at the time of al-Namlī, and some of the medical authorities whose works were translated from Greek to Syriac and Arabic maintained that the brain and the spinal cord were influential in the production of semen. According to Plato's *Timaeus*, which was available in an Arabic translation, desire is aroused when the sperm descends from the brain and passes down through the neck and the back. The earliest author of a medical compendium in Arabic, ʿAlī ibn Sahl al-Ṭabarī, maintained that the sperm comes from the whole body, but that the best sperm is produced in the brain; this sperm is white and has a balanced composition. ʿAlī ibn Sahl was a court physician of al-Mutawakkil and his ideas must have been familiar to al-Namlī, who was active in the same court. So was another influential early physician; Ḥunayn ibn Isḥāq, the most important translator of Greek works, whose circle translated Galen's summary of *Timaeus* as well as Proclus' commentary on it.[4] Al-Namlī's book about Burjān and Ḥabāḥib seems to have been written as a mocking commentary of the Greek medical ideas introduced by his peers. It was also a play with the wisdom genre; the frame story with a king and two wise individuals who advise him in various matters and answer all his questions makes it a mirror for princes in *mujūn* style on the subjects of sex and women. It might have been inspired by one of the earliest full-scale mirrors for princes in Arabic, *Kitāb al-Tāj*, which was written for al-Fatḥ ibn Khaqān, who had a high position in al-Mutawakkil's court.[5]

The example from Burjān and Ḥabāḥib illustrates the influence of Greek learning and Middle Persian literature on the cultural centres of the early Abbasid Empire. Sexuality and reproduction were topics that everybody could relate to, and the sophisticated medical ideas conveyed by the texts translated by Ḥunayn and others were probably discussed in wider circles. The emerging medical literature in Arabic was theoretical, yet the theories had impact on clinical practice and must have been at least to some extent comprehensible for non-professionals. Several aspects of sexuality were discussed by the medical authors, including topics such as sexual differentiation, fertility, reproductive and sexual health. The physical differences inspired thinkers to search for explanations for visible and imagined differences between the sexes. Greek writers offered several explanations for how some bodies become female and some male, how these bodies differ and how women and men contribute to reproduction. In this chapter, I mention these theories as long as they had impact on early Arabic-Islamic medicine. Influenced by Greek medicine, Islamic medical authors developed the field of sexual health. Compared with the former, they focused more on pleasure and contributed especially to the field of pharmacology, which they enriched with many new and complicated recipes, not the least pleasure-enhancing therapies.

## Background: Islamic medical authors

Ḥunayn ibn Isḥāq was the most prolific translator of Greek medical works, not the least by Galen, under the patronage of elite circles in Baghdad and Samarra. He was a Nestorian Christian who studied in the Byzantine Empire, and was later successful in Baghdad, where he started as a student of the court physician Yuḥannā ibn Māsawayh (d. 243/857). He served several caliphs as court physician, among others al-Mutawakkil (r. 232–247/847–861) and al-Muʿtamid (r. 256–279/870–892).[6] Among his numerous writings is a treatise on coitus, apparently based on a treatise by the Greek physician Rufus of Ephesus (fl. *c.* 100), which was translated at this time.[7] Citations from Ḥunayn's lost works are found in the medical compendium *al-Ḥāwī fī al-Ṭibb* by the later physician al-Rāzī (see below). Al-Rāzī often quotes Ḥunayn regarding aphrodisiac and other methods for stimulation.

Ḥunayn's contemporary, the philosopher al-Kindī (d. after 256/870), also wrote a treatise on coitus, and so did the younger Qusṭā ibn Lūqā (d. 298/910).[8] Qusṭā ibn Lūqā was a Melkite Christian from Baalbek who came to Baghdad around 246/860, when al-Kindī was the front figure of a circle of intellectuals.[9] Al-Kindī was close to the caliphs al-Maʾmūn (r. 218–227/833–843) and al-Muʿtaṣim (r. 218–227/833–842) and wrote almost 250 treatises, according to Ibn al-Nadīm, on a wide range of topics; apparently he was well acquainted with Greek, Persian and Indian science and wisdom.[10] His extant tract on sexuality is very short: he probably wrote more that is lost. He is, for example, credited with a medical explanation for the origin of lesbianism (see Chapter 6), although the attribution is dubious.

Later Islamic medical authors wrote large medical compendia; so did Ibn Sīnā, the most famous Muslim physician and medical theorist. One of the oldest medical compendia in Arabic was written by ʿAlī ibn Sahl Rabban al-Ṭabarī, who was a court physician and served at least three Abbasid caliphs in the then capital Samarra. He came from Tabaristan, a historical Persian province on the Caspian Sea. His father Sahl was also a physician; al-Ṭabarī quotes some of his recipes in his medical compendium, *Firdaws al-Ḥikma* (*Paradise of Wisdom*). He worked as a secretary to Māzyār ibn Qārin, who was governor of Tabaristan, until Māzyār instigated a rebellion and was executed on the order of caliph al-Muʿtaṣim in 225/840. ʿAlī ibn Sahl al-Ṭabarī was then invited to the court of the caliph al-Muʿtaṣim in Samarra, where he stayed at least until the reign of al-Mutawakkil, whose drinking companion he became.[11] According to al-Qifṭī, Sahl was Jewish, and the name Rabban was the same as the title Rabbi.[12] Nevertheless, ʿAlī ibn Sahl al-Ṭabarī was a Christian for most of his life and completed *Firdaws al-Ḥikma* in 235/850, probably before he converted to Islam. He related himself that he converted to Islam when he was seventy years old. ʿAlī ibn Sahl devoted the first part of *Firdaws al-Ḥikma* to Greek medicine; apparently, he relied on Syriac translations.[13] The second part treats Indian medicine. Both parts include sections that treat female sexuality and reproduction, women's physiology and health.[14]

The major Islamic medical author from this early period is Muḥammad ibn Zakariyyā al-Rāzī (d. 313/925 or 320/932). He was born in the city of Rayy (Rey), near Teheran in the region called Jibāl. His medical writing, especially the compendium *Ḥāwī*, relies on the many Arabic translations of Greek sources that were available at this time, but he probably also read the sources in their original language and reportedly translated from Greek himself.[15] Compared to the earlier generations of scientists writing in Arabic, he did not only give accounts of the ideas of the predecessors, he also challenged them.[16] He combined this interest in medical theory with his own clinical observations and thorough experience in medical practice.[17]

Like other medical authors, al-Rāzī was associated with the elite. He was a friend of the Samanid prince Abū Ṣaliḥ al-Manṣūr ibn Isḥāq, governor of Rayy 290–302/903–914, and dedicated a medical work to him, *Kitāb al-Manṣūrī fī al-Ṭibb* (*The Book for al-Manṣūr on Medicine*). He dedicated another work, *Kitāb Ṭibb al-Mulūkī* (*The Book on Medicine for Kings*), to ʿAlī ibn Wahsūdhān, governor of Rayy in 307/920.

*Kitāb al-Ḥāwī fī al-Ṭibb,* which became one of al-Rāzī's most important books and was translated into Latin in the thirteenth century (*Liber Continens*) is in effect his collected medical notes, edited after al-Rāzī's death for Ibn al-ʿAmīd, the *wazīr* of Rukn al-Dawla (d. 365/976). Rukn al-Dawla was one of the founders of the Buyid dynasty, and took command of Rayy and the region of Jibāl from the Samanids in 331/943. Ibn al-ʿAmīd was Rukn al-Dawla's *wazīr* from 328/940 until his own death 360/970, and was influential in making Rayy a cultural and intellectual centre. There, he supported philosophers and historians, such as Abū Ḥayyān al-Tawḥidī and Miskawayh.

Al-Rāzī was esteemed by the ruling elite, both during and after his own lifetime. He belonged to the intellectual elite, with knowledge in Greek and ancient sources, and frequented the courts. Considering his enormous written production, he must have spent a good portion of his days writing and studying ancient texts. However, he was also chief physician of the hospital in Rayy, and later in Baghdad, which gave him a broader experience and probably insight in the social conditions of a broader spectrum of the population.[18] Hospitals were charitable institutions that primarily treated poor patients, who could not afford treatment in their homes.[19] Al-Rāzī's case studies reveal that he also received various patients in his home.[20]

One of the most prominent physicians during the fourth/tenth century was ʿAlī ibn al-ʿAbbās al-Majūsī, who belonged to a Persian Zoroastrian family from Ahwaz. He was a court physician of the most successful Buyid sultan, ʿAḍud al-Dawla (324–372/936–983), son of Rukn al-Dawla, and known for supporting scholars and poets. ʿAḍud al-Dawla's education had been supervised by the *wazīr* Ibn al-ʿAmīd, the one who ordered the edition of al-Rāzi's medical notes and perhaps inspired his interest in medicine. The sultan established two hospitals, one in Shiraz, where he started his career as a ruler only thirteen years old, and another in Baghdad, which he conquered from his cousin in 367/978.[21] Al-Majūsī was active in his court in Shiraz, but does not seem to have moved with ʿAḍud al-Dawla to Baghdad. Only one work by al-Majūsī is known, *Kitāb Kāmil al-Ṣināʿa al-Ṭibbiyya*, also called *Kitāb al-Malakī*, a medical work that was widely used later in the middle ages and translated into Latin.

A contemporary with al-Majūsī, from the western part of the Islamic world, Ibn al-Jazzār (d. 395/1004–5), worked as a physician in Kairouan, the then capital of Tunisia.[22] He wrote about sexual diseases in his medical compendium *Zād al-Musāfir wa-Qūt al-Ḥāḍir* (*Provisions for the Traveller and Nourishment for the Sedentary*).

The most famous medieval Islamic physician and medical author is Ibn Sīnā (370–428/980–1037), who also was a philosopher, known in Europe as Avicenna. As the other physicians mentioned here, he belonged to the elite of the society, and served, in periods, rulers and their families. As a teenager, Ibn Sīnā worked as a physician for the Samanid ruler in Bukhara. He continued to work for different rulers the rest of his life, with high positions in administration, but as the political situation was turbulent, he sometimes had to flee and move from court to court. He never ceased writing, however, and the result was some of the most famous medical and philosophical treatises in Arabic. His main medical work, *Kitāb al-Qānūn*, was completed in Hamadhan, were he was also appointed as *wazīr* by the Buyid ruler Shams al-Dawla (r. 997–1021). His work as a physician seems to have been mainly theoretical, however, as indicated by the lack of case studies in his works.[23]

## Sex differences in Greek and Islamic medical theory

Some of the most prominent scholars who translated Greek medicine and philosophy into Arabic wrote about sexuality, inspired by a substantial body of writings on human sexuality in Greek, which deals with topics such as male and female contribution to reproduction, sex differentiation and genital anatomy. Fertility was not only a problem for anyone who tried, unsuccessfully, to have a child; it was also part of an intellectual pursuit, which engaged the educated community. How does conception occur? What is the contribution of the father and the mother? How does a child become female or male? Sex differentiation became a significant subject for medical theory and natural philosophy alike, linking the visible differences between women and men to physiological processes.

Greek medical theory was based on humorism, the idea that health is affected by the four humours, blood, phlegm, yellow and black bile, and that a balanced humoral composition is a condition for good health. Islamic medicine was also guided by the idea of the classical elements, fire, water, air, and earth underlying the constitution of everything found in the physical world, also human beings According to Aristotle, each of these elements possesses two of four qualities: fire is hot and dry, water is cold and wet, air is hot and wet and earth is cold and dry. These qualities never occur in their pure form; in living bodies, they are manifested in specific combinations called temperaments. Already the Hippocratic writings supported the idea of balance as a fundamental concept for health, a notion that is relative as what constitutes balance fluctuates with sex, age, geographical place and time of the year.[24]

Galen's typology of human temperaments was pivotal for Islamic natural philosophers and medical authors. According to it, there are nine possible temperaments, called *mizāj* in Arabic. Only one of these combinations was seen as perfectly balanced (and therefore ideal). All others are imbalanced, four with one dominating element and four with two dominating elements. As in the Hippocratic notion of balance, the temperaments are individual for human beings, but also depend on factors such as sex, age and the climate in the land where the individual was born.

Early Greek thinkers assumed that modifications in the degree of moistness, dryness and temperature produce two fundamentally different bodies: the female and the male. Hippocratic writers maintained that female physiology is radically different from male and the reason is that women are moister due to menstruation. The female body is spongy and porous, according to their theory, in order to be able to soak up excess moistness caused by menstrual blood. Whereas everybody agreed that women are moister, there were divergent opinions as to their body temperature. Women's and men's body temperatures differ, according to pre-Socratic thinkers, but they disagreed as to which of them is hotter. Aristotle tells about one pre-Socratic philosopher, Parmenides, who argued that women are hotter than men are, and so did some Hippocratic writers. Again, menstruation makes the difference; as blood possesses hot qualities it leads to women's constitution being hotter than that of men. Aristotle did not agree with Parmenides; holding on to the dualistic view of sex differences, he maintained that women are colder than men are. One indication of their coldness is that they cannot produce semen, a complex process that requires heat.[25]

Temperature and degree of moistness were not the only conditions for sex differences, according to early Greek thinkers. The pre-Socratic philosophers connected the right to the male and the left to the female, which meant, according to the philosopher Parmenides, that female foetuses are produced in the left side of the womb, whereas male foetuses are produced in the right. As right often was valued as good and left as bad, the right–left dichotomy corresponded with the widespread belief of male dominance and female subordination.[26] Another theory, attributed to Hippocrates, suggests that sex differences originate from the quality of sperms; strong seed produces boys whereas thin and weak seed produces girls. Aristotle agreed in that the quality of the seed impinged on the sex of the foetus, but maintained that the influential factor is temperature; seed dominated by the quality of heat produces boys whereas seed dominated by coldness produces girls.

Galen adopted Aristotle's dichotomy between coldness as a female quality and hotness as a male quality. He also accepted the right–left dichotomy but explained that the reason why the origin of male foetuses in the right side of the womb is that hotter blood reaches the right side of the uterus and the right testes directly from the aorta, and this heat generates male foetuses.[27] Galen maintained that the female and male reproductive organs are originally the same but that they develop differently due to women's and men's different body temperatures. The womb corresponds to the scrotum, the ovaries to the testicles and the 'neck of the womb', the vagina, corresponds to the penis. The male's greater heat helps his organs to develop to their full potential until they extend outside the body. This is the perfect condition and an evidence for males' perfection and, consequently, women are incomplete men.[28]

Islamic natural philosophers and medical authors proposed different theories, derived from their Greek predecessors. Galen's classification of women as cold and wet and men as hot and dry was embraced by all established Islamic medical writers and natural philosophers and they usually maintained that women's bodies are moister than that of men.[29] ʿAlī ibn Sahl al-Ṭabarī mentions several possible causes of sex differences: the Hippocratic theory that a strong seed produces a male and a week seed a female; Aristotle's idea that the male is produced from seed with hot qualities and the female from one with cold qualities and a variant of the left–right theory.[30] Al-Majūsī, following Galen, describes the womb as having two cavities, with male foetuses generally produced in the right cavity whereas females are produced in the left.[31] Galen's anatomical model of the female reproductive organs as inverted male organs was more or less emphasized by Islamic physicians. ʿAlī ibn Sahl al-Ṭabarī, who owes less to Galen than other Islamic physicians, only mentions in passing that the womb has a 'neck' with the same shape as a penis.[32] Al-Majūsī describes the womb as having a similar shape as the scrotum, except that it also has two extensions which look like horns. Following Galen, he maintains that the female genital organs bear a resemblance to the male, although 'inverted', but he does not seem to regard them as an incomplete version.[33] Ibn Sīnā is more convinced and assures that women's genitals are inverted and incomplete versions of men's genitals.[34]

All medical writers conclude that not only are the female and male reproductive organs different, so is female and male physiology. Women's and men's constitutions and temperaments are different and, what is more, these physical differences conduce to mental and intellectual differences. The assumed differences in the constitution of female and male bodies were believed to have a bearing on women's and men's moral and intellectual capacity. Typically, the outcome from observing differences in female and male physiology was that women are inferior and naturally subordinated. Many medical thinkers came to this conclusion, also when their observances and interpretations differed. According to Galen, the main reason for this is that men have a hot temperature whereas women are cold. Heat is more perfect than coldness as it is the instrument that helps nature reach perfection. There is a natural reason behind female coldness (which is the same as defectiveness); it impedes the evaporation of left-over nutriment, which instead becomes nourishment for the foetus. Temperature is not only decisive for men's superiority over women, it affects the hierarchy of all living beings. There are species that are closer to perfection than others, depending on their degree of heat and coldness, so that all living creatures are hierarchically divided according to their heat, with human beings on top. Due to their greater heat, the male is always more perfect than the female – for animals and human beings alike – the human male is therefore on top of the ladder.[35]

The idea that men are hotter than women are and therefore closer to perfection, became common knowledge among Islamic physicians. It gave them a pretext to describe male perfectness and female defectiveness, both in terms of physical constitution and moral and intellectual character. Qusṭā ibn Lūqā discussed the correlation between men's hotter quality, hairier body and stronger will, which altogether are evidence for their excellence in comparison to women.[36] More than two generations later, al-Majūsī's description of the connection between male and female body temperature and personality is perhaps the most complete and detailed:

> The males of all animals have a warmer and dryer constitution than the females, who have a colder and moister constitution than males. The sign for this is that men have more and stronger body hair, which grows faster. It is for this reason their beards grow.[37] If some women have hotter constitution, you will notice that they have more hair on their bodies, and perhaps they have moustaches and hair on their chins. Because of this, you see that the males among most animals are more resolute, fierce, and courageous than females. Therefore, men's chests are broader in order to contain the heat, and most of them have hair on their chests. Moreover, male infants starts to move quicker after birth, and they raise on their feet quicker, whereas female infants grow quicker, as their constitution is moister than that of men, and moister bodies grow up more rapidly. However, females cease to grow before males as their constitution is colder and they are weaker, while male bodies are warmer and stronger. The reason for this is that human as well as animal bodies have a natural power that makes them grow. If this power is strong, they will continue to grow, but if it is week, they will cease to grow quicker. You notice that men, in most cases, are more intelligent, knowledgeable, discerning, and considerate than women are. Their heads are therefore bigger than women's heads. They move quicker, are more aggressive and have more persistence than women have, due to the strength of their body parts resulting from their bigger heads. Furthermore, men's shoulders, arms and legs are thicker, depending, as everything that we have mentioned, on their heat. Women, on their part, lack hair on their chests, bellies, arms and legs, due to their cold constitution. They have weaker will and less courage, and for that reason their chests are thinner. You notice that most of them are less intelligent and discerning, and instead more stupid and foolish. It is for this reason their heads most of the time are smaller than the heads of men. You see also that they are more inclined to comfort and gentleness than to labour and hardship. This is due to their weak sinews, and therefore you notice that their fingers, hands and feet are more delicate. All this depends on their cold constitution. The reason why females were given moister constitution than males is the sustenance of the embryo, which is nourished by moist in the uterus.[38]

The causality as described by al-Majūsī is remarkably simple. External characteristics identified as masculine are interpreted as signs of their higher proportion of heat, and, as heat is more perfect, men are also endowed with higher intellectual and moral capacity. Hence, conveniently, sex differentiation could be used as an argument for the male-dominated society.

## Seed and reproduction

Greek thinkers developed different theories about female and male contributions to conception; the crucial question was whether women have semen or not. According to one view, both women and men emit semen during intercourse and the female and male semen have to mingle in order to produce a foetus; this is the 'two-seed theory'. Another view is the 'one-seed theory'; only men emit semen and women's contribution to conception is secondary, they contribute with their menstrual blood.[39] Most Hippocratic writers put forward the two-seed theory; they believed that women have some kind of seed, although it is not always visible the way male semen is and does not have exactly the same qualities; typically, the male semen is assumed to be stronger.[40] Aristotle supported the one-seed theory, and maintained that only male bodies have enough heat to produce semen.[41] Galen took an ambiguous middle position; he embraced the idea of a female sperm, produced in the ovaries, which he suggested were the female testes. Yet, he was influenced by Aristotle's dualistic model. As a compromise, Galen maintained that female and male seeds are different; although both male and female semen contribute actively, the female seed is thinner and cooler, and therefore less perfect.[42]

As Ursula Weisser shows in her seminal work *Zeugung, Vererbung und Pränatale Entwicklung* the early Islamic physicians unanimously adopted the two-seed model of generation but they had different views of the composition and the role of the female seed.[43] Most followed Galen and believed that the female and the male seeds are different and contribute differently. The ambiguity that sometimes appears in Galen's texts as to the role of the female seed was inherited by al-Majūsī, whereas Ibn Sīnā, who was both a philosopher and a physician and closer to Aristotle than to Galen, seems to side more with Aristotle's one-seed theory. As Weisser points out, he could not totally abandon the notion of a female seed, as Galen's conviction that women can produce semen was indisputable for scholars in this period.[44] All writers took for granted that the semen of the man and the woman have to mingle in the womb in order for conception to take place. In order to do so, both the man and the woman have to ejaculate. What we today label orgasm is therefore called *inzāl* (ejaculation) for both women and men.

The different views regarding whether women have semen or not were connected to how semen is produced, the origin of semen. The encephalogenetic theory, proposed by the Pytagoreans and Plato, recognized the brain, being the central organ, as the origin of semen, and the spinal cord as the passage way for semen before ejaculation. The pangenetic theory, sustained by most Hippocratic writers, assumed that semen (female as well as the male) was derived from 'the whole body', that is from vessels containing the four body fluids (the humours in Greek medical theory: phlegm, blood, yellow and black bile).[45] Later, Aristotle developed the haematogenous theory; namely the idea that the male sperm is produced from blood in a process in which the heat in men's bodies converts blood to white sperms. According to this theory, female bodies are too cold to convert blood to semen and women instead contribute to conception with their menstrual blood. Galen supported the haematogenous theory developed by Aristotle but combined it with the notion of female semen, which Aristotle rejected.

The Arabic version of the Hippocratic treatises *On Generation* and *On the Nature of the Child*, which in Arabic was called *Kitāb al-Ajinna li-Buqrāṭ* (*The Book on Embryos by Hippocrates*), seems to combine the encephalogenetic and the pangenetic theories. Its explanation of the origin of semen is more ambiguous than that of the Greek version; whereas it states that 'the sperm derives from all healthy members' it affirms more than once that the sperm 'descends from the brain'.[46] The text in the Arabic version is often faulty and some parts are more accurately paraphrases and commentaries of the Greek text; yet, this version was influential in early Islamic medicine and used by, among others, ʿAlī ibn Sahl al-Ṭabarī and al-Rāzī.[47]

In ʿAlī ibn Sahl al-Ṭabarī's explanation of the origin of semen, he mentions all three possible origins – the brain, the whole body and blood. He states that seed is produced by transformed blood, which comes from the whole body and that the best seed, which is white and balanced (*muʿtadil*) is produced in the brain. If produced elsewhere, the seed is thinner or thicker or has another colour – this seed is corrupted (*fāsid*). He describes the male and female reproductive organs as connected with vessels and veins to the brain and the heart, the womb is also connected to the liver. When the male body is heated up from sexual excitement, seed comes from the whole body and is pushed to the spines, from there to the two kidneys, and further to the two testicles and by way of the penis to the womb. Finally, the male and the female seed have to mingle in the womb in order to produce a foetus.[48] Al-Ṭabarī does not describe how female seed is produced or the role of female excitement; probably it should be understood in analogy with the process that takes place in men's bodies.

Islamic medical writers convey all three theories about the origin of semen. Although the haematogenous theory of Aristotle and Galen was by far the most common, it was sometimes combined with the pangenetic theory or, occasionally, the encephalogenetic theory.[49] The encephalogenetic theory was long since obsolete, but traces of it remained in the Hippocratic corpus, and then combined with the pangenetic theory. Al-Ṭabarī's contemporary, al-Kindī, writes that 'semen comes from the brain and the spines'.[50] One century later, the North African physician Ibn al-Jazzār holds on to the belief that the brain, heart and liver are central organs for sexual intercourse, as the power to arouse comes from the heart, the semen from the brain and sexual appetite (*shahwa*) from the liver.[51] Ibn al-Jazzār's contemporary al-Majūsī, following Galen closely, maintains that semen is converted blood.[52] Both men and women emit semen that has to mingle in order for conception to take place, but female semen is different; it is thin and has a cold temperament, whereas men's semen is thick and hot.[53] The two seeds complement each other, as the coldness and thinness of the female semen temper the hotness and thickness of the male semen, which otherwise risks spoiling the substance of the foetus. Due to its thinness, female semen has also the advantage of being able to reach parts of the womb that the male semen cannot reach.[54] There is therefore a natural and even beneficial cause behind women's 'defectiveness': Nature – or God – has seen to it that female coldness and male hotness complement each other.

Ibn Sīnā adopted a more complex, and indeed contradicting, view, influenced by the fact that he followed Aristotle in his philosophical works and Galen in his medical works. In the section on gynaecology and reproduction in *Qānūn* he presumes that women have semen, whereas in his philosophical work *Shifāʾ*, his view is closer to that of Aristotle. While he does not reject the idea of the female seed, he suggests that it does not contribute the same way as the male seed does. In any case, he agrees with earlier Islamic medical authors in that female and male seeds have to mingle in order to conceive, a view that underscores the importance of female orgasm.[55]

## Sexual health in Islamic medicine

Currently the most adopted definition of sexual health is that of the World Health Organization (WHO), which identifies sexual health as follows:

> a state of physical, emotional, mental and social well-being in relation to sexuality; it is not merely the absence of disease, dysfunction or infirmity. Sexual health requires a positive and respectful approach to sexuality and sexual relationships, as well as the possibility of having pleasurable and safe sexual experiences, free of coercion, discrimination and violence.[56]

This definition is unmistakably modern, yet it bears a remote resemblance to the understanding of sexual health in medieval Islamic medicine. The common denominator is the insistence that sexual health is not only about physical health, but also about emotional and mental wellbeing.

Islamic medical sources discuss reproductive health, the connection between sexual activity and general health, and are more or less filled with remedies of medicine for sexual dysfunctions. In addition to these pertinent issues, medical authors address sexuality from a broader perspective and provide recipes for contraceptives and aphrodisiacs as well as pleasure-enhancing methods and preparations. This medicalization of sexuality is interesting in itself, but it also involves questions about women's agency and pleasure, which are of particular interest for this chapter. For the Islamic physicians, sexual health was a central health issue with impact on the general state of the body. It was generally considered that sexual intercourse with moderation is necessary for good physical and mental health. Excessive sexual activity is not good, but neither is abstinence. ʿAlī ibn Sahl al-Ṭabarī, who writes relatively little about the benefits of sex in his *Firdaws al-Ḥikma*, still mentions that abstinence as well as excess has negative effects and is especially precarious for women, as will be discussed below, whereas moderate sexual activity gives energy, happiness, appetite and brightness to the face.[57]

The notions of benefit and harm of sexual activity are derived from Greek medicine. In humoral theory, the individual body temperament is assumed to be relative to the person's sex, age, season and climate of the place of birth, and disorders can be adjusted by things like diets, exercise, bath and sexual activity. Intercourse is thus a means for adjusting humoral imbalances; it can also create new imbalances if not used with caution. Islamic physicians in general put somewhat more emphasis on the benefits. In his treatise on coitus, al-Rāzī refers to Galen in particular, but cites more authorities in his edited notes, *Ḥāwī*, not least Rufus of Ephesus by way of Oribasius.[58] The overall physical benefit of sexual activity, according to al-Rāzī's sources, is the strengthening of the body. Intercourse relieves the body by means of eliminating repletion, which makes it grow and produce new skin. Among the mental benefits are relaxing of the mind and soothing of anger, as well as curing melancholia and madness. Intercourse is especially good for phlegmatic illnesses and it restores the patient's appetite but Oribasius warns that sexual intercourse can also cause injury to certain bodies, especially if they are dry. Conversely, intercourse is good for people with an abundance of sperm, blood and heat. People with a dry constitution should be precautious but can practice intercourse normally, with the help of diet and exercise.

The subfield of medicine called *ʿIlm al-bāh* (science of coitus) treated the effects of sexual activities on physical and mental health, as well as issues such as sexual dysfunction. Several works were written in this field, inspired by various chapters on the subject in Greek medical compendia. The primary model was a monograph on sexual intercourse by Rufus of Ephesus (fl. *c.* 100) that was translated into Arabic under the title *Kitāb al-Bāh* (*The Book on Coitus*).[59] In the late ninth and early tenth centuries, several treatises on coitus were written in Arabic by authors close to the Abbasid elite: the philosopher and polymath al-Kindī, the translators Ḥunayn ibn Isḥāq, ʿĪsā ibn Māssa al-Baṣrī and Qusṭā ibn Lūqā.[60] The eighth century alchemist Jābir ibn Ḥayyān is credited with a book on coitus and so is the early Abbasid court physician Jibrīl ibn Bukhtīshūʿ.[61] In the tenth and eleventh centuries, al-Rāzī as well as Ibn Sīnā wrote on the topic. The long title of al-Rāzī's treatise *Kitāb al-Bāh wa-Manāfiʿihi wa-Maḍārrihi wa-Mudāwātihi* (*On Sexual Intercourse, Its Harmful and Beneficial Effects and Treatment*), reveals the primary themes of the genre.[62] Most treatises in the genre contain sections on health benefits of coitus (*manāfiʿ al-bāh*), its damages (*maḍārr al-bāh*), when (*awqāt*) and under which circumstances (*aḥwāl*) it is healthy to practice it, in addition to remedies for sexual problems and aphrodisiacs.[63] The medical encyclopaedias usually included similar sections.

The section on health benefits of sex in the medical compendia is sorted under preventative health care, as sexual activity was seen as a method of preserving health (*tadbīr al-ṣiḥḥa bi-l-jimāʿ*). Notably, the sections on preventative health care are more concerned about men's health than that of women. Women's sexual health is mostly viewed as belonging to the realm of reproduction, and thus it is discussed in the section on female reproductive health. The medical compendia by al-Rāzī, al-Majūsī and Ibn Sīnā separate between sexual health (belonging to preventive health care) and reproduction. In al-Rāzī's compendium *Al-Manṣūrī fī al-Ṭibb*, the chapter 'Benefits and Harms of Sexual Intercourse' (*manāfiʿ al-jimāʿ wa-maḍārruhu*) is primarily directed to male readers and includes general advice to men on how to keep oneself healthy, clean and handsome.[64] In *Ḥāwī*, the section 'Benefits of Coitus' is sorted together with treatments of men's genital organs (chapter 10). The chapter begins with a discussion of the harmful effect of abstinence for men, such as loss of appetite and melancholy.[65] The possible consequences of women's abstinence, which were generally considered more immediately dangerous than those of men's abstinence, even life threatening, are instead discussed in 'Diseases of the Womb' (vol. 9), which deals with reproduction. Al-Majūsī and Ibn Sīnā make similar distinctions between men's sexual health, belonging to preventative health care, and women's sexual health, belonging to reproduction.[66] Al-Majūsī sometimes writes in general terms, but mostly loss of lust is considered only with regard to men.[67] In *Qānūn*, Ibn Sīnā has sections entitled 'Benefits of coitus' (*manāfiʿ al-bāh*) and 'Damages of coitus' (*maḍārr al-jimāʿ*) in the chapter 'Male Genital Organs', which encompasses everything that has to do with coitus and obviously addresses male patients.[68] Women's health is discussed in a separate part in connection with reproductive health and embryology.[69]

There are exceptions, however. In the longer version of the *Book on Coitus* by Qusṭā ibn Lūqā, he discusses women's health more than men's health in the section on the benefits of intercourse, whereas the shorter version hardly mentions women at all.[70] Treatises on coitus and sections on intercourse in medical compendia often discuss patients in general terms, and the few examples are almost exclusively about men. The greater emphasis on men's sexual health is partly due to audience expectations, as readers and patrons were mostly men, and sexual health was a typical topic a wealthy patron would like to support. The medical authors thereby followed genre conventions while at the same time satisfying the requests of their patrons. Yet, women's sexual health was considered an even more precarious issue than that of men, as women's abstinence could cause serious diseases and even death.

## Women's sexual health

Women's sexual health was addressed already by the earliest Greek medical writers, who suggested that regular sexual intercourse helps keep the female body healthy. According to the Hippocratic writers' theory of 'the wandering womb', excessive dryness forces the womb to wander around in search of moisture and this ailment can be prevented by regular sexual intercourse, which moistens the womb. Keeping the womb moistened is thus a main benefit of intercourse for women, but there are other health benefits as well. According to the Hippocratic treatise *On Generation*, 'the women's bodies become healthy when linked with the bodies of the men'.[71] This is partly because the male semen keeps the womb moistened, but also because intercourse warms up the blood in the body and facilitates the menstrual flow. Without intercourse, menses are stuck in the body, and cause pain and disease. The writer of the treatise *Diseases of Young Girls* describes the suffering of adolescent girls who do not get married; abstinence causes accumulation of blood in their bodies, which makes them violent and confused. It is not intercourse per se that cures them, however, but pregnancy.[72]

The Hippocratic writers claimed that the wandering womb can cause serious disorders to women, especially if it raises and blocks the respiratory tract. Treatment is necessary, as the pressure of the wandering womb on the internal organs can cause suffocation; therefore the disease was termed 'hysterical suffocation' (uterine suffocation), from the Greek word for uterus, *hystera*.[73] They suggested a range of therapies to put the womb in place; such as different kinds of scent therapy or both inhalation of foul odour and application of fragrant oils on the lower parts by means of pessaries or vaginal fumigation with sweet-smelling herbs, which could 'lure' down the womb that had moved upwards.

Galen rejected the idea of a wandering womb but agreed that certain diseases are caused by uterine 'suffocation', which in turn is caused by retention of blood or female seed. It particularly afflicts widows, as semen can be dammed up due to lack of sexual intercourse. The purported 'movements' of the womb, described by the Hippocratic writers, are in reality contractions, according to him, which cause a slight upward movement. Yet, in spite of his rejection of the idea of a wandering womb, he recommended some of the Hippocratic remedies, such as scent therapy.[74] Even if Galen did not explicitly recommend intercourse as a therapy, he hints occasionally that a suffering woman can be cured by orgasm that helps her to dispose of excessive fluid. He once heard about a midwife who administrated a sort of sexual therapy when she told a widow afflicted with suffocation how to cure herself by rubbing the customary remedies on her vulva. This would make her feel pain and pleasure together as she was releaved of excess semen.[75]

Late antiquity medical writers and encyclopaedists, such as Oribasius (326–403 AD), Aetius of Amida (flourished middle of sixth century) and Paul of Aegina (seventh century), kept the notion of uterine suffocation as a life-threatening disease and standardized the remedies: scent therapy, making the woman sneeze, injection of fragrant oils in the womb and bloodletting, among other things. They also proposed noise-making, which meant shouting at the patient in order to arouse her.[76] These encyclopaedias were significant for the Islamic medical writers who unanimously accepted the variants of the diagnosis proposed by Galen and the late antiquity authors and, furthermore, they combined it with the Hippocratic notion of the wandering womb.[77]

Most Islamic authors of medical compendia devoted a section to gynaecology, including reproductive health and pregnancy. Medical works also included topics such as theories of conception and the anatomy of the reproductive organs. The curiosity was fuelled by the existing scholarly discussions on the subject in gynaecological literature in Greek, and physicians writing in Arabic in the ninth and tenth centuries interpreted and elaborated on parts of this literature. The main Greek gynaecologist, Soranus of Ephesus, was rarely cited, as pointed out by Monica Green; instead medical writers in Arabic relied on the more theoretical work by Galen, often combined with Hippocratic ideas. The field of gynaecology was less prominent in Islamic medicine than in Greek, however, and less innovative than other aspects of sexual health. Nevertheless, the Islamic physicians emphasized women's satisfaction as a health issue and strengthened the focus on mutual pleasure.

Almost all Islamic physicians bring up the serious disease called 'suffocation of the womb' (*ikhtināq al-raḥm*) or uterine suffocation; some describe it in detail whereas others mention it in passing. Early Islamic physicians held on to the remedies proposed by Galen and the late Antiquity encyclopaedists, but most of them also recommended sexual therapy and intercourse as remedies. ʿAlī ibn Sahl al-Ṭabarī's description of uterine suffocation is the earliest extant in Arabic. Noticing similarities between women and men, he remarks that women can feel the same intense desire that men can and suffer from the same ailments if they are deprived of sex. In addition to these shared ailments, there are more dangerous diseases that only afflict women.[78] He is careful to point out that excessive intercourse can afflict women's health, by causing the womb to rise and block the diaphragm. This serious condition leads to asphyxiation with possible mortal effect.[79] Sexual abstinence, on the other hand, is equally dangerous, as it produces damned-up semen from which vapours develop and escape. Al-Ṭabarī specifies the dangerous effects of these vapours, peculiar for women: apnoea, corruption of liver and stomach, palpitation, weak cognitive ability, headache, uterine suffocation, miscarriage, tumours and vomiting.[80] He identifies sexual abstinence as its cause, but does not explicitly recommend intercourse as a remedy in this case. Instead, he recommends the remedies that were by then ordinary: scent therapy, using oils with hot qualities for massage of the thighs and on vaginal pessaries, steam therapy for the vagina, phlebotomy, potions and fumigation.[81] Influenced by the Hippocratic writers, al-Ṭabarī recommends intercourse for preventing disorders when the woman is pregnant as intercourse ensures a balanced temperature and keeps the womb moist and warm, which is essential during pregnancy as an imbalanced temperature and too much coldness can cause miscarriage.[82] The same advice is later given by al-Rāzī, who cites 'a book' claiming that intercourse is especially good for pregnant women, as it facilitates childbirth, an idea that he had also heard from a friend who had tried it himself with his partner who was near delivery, with good result.[83]

Other medical writers agreed with al-Ṭabarī about the particular danger of abstinence for women, and the dangers of uterine suffocation were to become mainstream knowledge among Islamic physicians. Qusṭā ibn Lūqā follows al-

Ṭabarī's description of the lethal symptoms of the vapours produced by women's abstinence closely in the longer version of his *Book on Coitus*.[84] In the shorter version of this book, he mentions especially the two diseases uterine suffocation and apnoea, referring to the Greek physician Rufus.[85] A section is devoted to uterine suffocation in the medical compendium *Kitāb al-Dakhīra* (*The Book of Treasure*), attributed to the mathematician and polymath Thābit ibn Qurra (219/834–288/901)).[86]

*Ḥāwī*, which is a particularly rich source, devotes a relatively long section to this peculiar disease, relying on numerous ancient and late antique Greek and Syriac authors, many of whom recommend sexual therapy as a remedy.[87] Al-Rāzī attributes to Galen the assertion that there is no more useful remedy against uterine suffocation than intercourse.[88] Galen himself instructed a midwife to perform sexual therapy on a patient, by rubbing her vagina with her finger.[89] Al-Rāzī attributes the same instruction to several earlier authors – Ahrun, Māsarjawayh and Sābūr ibn Sahl, sometimes directed to a midwife, sometimes without an addressee.[90] Ahrun, a priest and physician who lived in Alexandria after the Arab conquests and wrote a medical handbook in Greek, transmitted Galen's explanation of uterine suffocation caused by excess semen or retention of menses.[91] Māsarjawayh, a Jewish-Persian physician who lived in Basra during the Umayyads, and was probably the first translator of Syriac medical texts into Arabic, instead conveyed the Hippocratic idea that suffocation is caused by motions of the womb.[92]

There is an ambiguity in al-Rāzī's rendition of these medical authors. Ahrun, for instance, maintains that retention of menses and semen causes an 'upward contraction' (*tashammur ilā fawq*) of the womb which blocks the respiratory tract. The 'upward contraction' is Galenic, which means that the womb is not really moving, but the wording is sometimes 'raise upwards' (*irtafaʿ*), and consequently the Galenic description becomes Hippocratic, as in the case of Māsarjawayh.[93] In *Manṣūrī*, al-Rāzī first recommends the ordinary remedies, such as scent therapy and fumigation. Addressing midwives, apparently the caretakers of diseased women, he instructs them to expose the sick woman to unpleasant odorous, such as castoreum (beavers' secretion) and sulphate, which supposedly causes the uterus to discard the semen. Shouting in the woman's ear and smearing her belly with aromatic oil made of musk and ambergris (*ghāliya*) can also be effective, as well as bloodletting in the thighs. If all this does not help, he recommends a procedure that looks like a simulation of orgasm; the midwife smears her finger with aromatic oil and tickles or rubs the orifice of the uterus for a moment, until the supressed semen is released.[94]

Al-Majūsī, who usually followed Galen, still accepted the Hippocratic idea of a moving womb. Suggesting the by now commonplace therapies, he explains that one effect of scent therapy is making the uterus move downwards towards the pleasant smell in order to escape the foul odour.[95] He also quotes many remedies and recommends sexual therapy. Like al-Rāzī and his sources, he instructs the midwife to rub the orifice of the uterus to simulate intercourse; this procedure warms up the suffocating semen and softens it, which enables it to flow out. He concludes that sexual intercourse has the benefits of discarding repressed semen. Therefore, the afflicted woman should marry, if she is a virgin, or start practicing intercourse if she has abstained for a long period.[96] Elsewhere, he clarifies that women who are used to frequent intercourse but have been deprived of it for a long period are particularly vulnerable to this disease, as are adolescent girls with a strong libido who have reached puberty. It can also afflict women who have not been pregnant due to damage of the reproduction organs, or having taken a contraceptive drug.[97] Later, Ibn al-Jazzār recommends a similar treatment as his predecessors: massage, scent therapy, making the woman sneeze, fumigation, rubbing with fragrant oils and cupping. He also instructs midwives to rub the genitals of afflicted women.[98]

We have seen how Islamic physicians relied on both Galen and Hippocrates when they emphasized the sexual nature of uterine suffocation, and clarified that abstinence is the cause and sexual stimulation the remedy. Al-Rāzī accentuates, with the help of several sources, that this disease afflicts women who are denied sexual outlet, such as widows and virgins who have recently entered puberty and not yet been married.[99] Women with great libidos are especially vulnerable.[100] Al-Rāzī's own recommendation is either medication which softens the female semen – he provides numerous recipes from several physicians – or frequent intercourse.[101] Even though the interest in women's sexual satisfication is purely medical, it affirms female sexuality as a positive force.

## Women's sexual pleasure

Islamic medical authors' adoption of the two-seed model induced them to discuss women's pleasure and satisfaction, both because retained semen could cause dangerous diseases, as we have seen, and because female ejaculation was regarded as necessary for conception. They inherited many of their concepts from Greek medical theory, but compared with their Greek predecessors, Islamic physicians tended to put more emphasis on female pleasure.

The Hippocratic writers maintained that male and female semen contribute equally to conception, nonetheless the pleasure women and men derive from intercourse is represented as different in at least one passage. According to the Hippocratic treatise *On Generation*, women feel less pleasure than men during intercourse, even if they feel it for a longer time, as men's pleasure is more intense. Women feel pleasure during intercourse due to the friction between the genital organs, which gives rise to pleasure and warmth, but if the man ejaculates before her, her pleasure ceases, as the sperm has a cooling effect and extinguishes the woman's pleasure. Reversely, if the woman is aroused before the intercourse starts she will ejaculate before the man. In both these cases, conception cannot take place as the seeds do not mingle. Therefore, it is better if the woman does not feel desire from the beginning, but that her feeling of pleasure starts when the man initiates the intercourse and it stops when they both ejaculate.[102] In this view, female pleasure is entirely mechanical, penetrative intercourse will give the woman pleasure and make her ejaculate regardless of her indisposition and previous feelings.

The Arabic version of *On Generation* puts somewhat more emphasis on women's pleasure. Like the Greek version, it concludes that men feel more pleasure than women, yet it suggests that women have two sources of pleasure. Apart for the pleasure that comes from the warmth that is produced by friction during intercourse, the woman gets pleasure from her own sperm; it descends into the womb and brings 'warmth and pleasure (*ladhdha*)'.[103] That there is a connection between a woman's pleasure and her own semen was suggested by Galen, who even claimed that without semen, a woman would not feel desire.[104] This is because the seminal fluid moistens the passageway as it flows and incites the female to the sexual act at the same time as she gets pleasure from her own emission of semen.[105] This connection was sometimes elaborated upon by Islamic medical authors, who tended to acknowledge women's greater pleasure. Al-Majūsī argued that women feel more pleasure from intercourse than men do as female ejaculation is gradual and male ejaculation is brief and intense. A woman gets pleasure both from discharging her own semen and from attaining the partner's semen. As male ejaculation is brief, the woman obtains the semen of the man all at once while she is still continually discharging her own semen. Therefore, she benefits both from the intensity of the male orgasm and of the longevity of her own, and experiences double pleasure from intercourse.[106] The connection between seed and pleasure is also suggested by the Andalusian physician ʿArīb ibn Saʿīd (d. *c.* 370/980) when he gives female pleasure as a proof for the existence of a female seed.[107]

In al-Majūsī's description it is perhaps not so much the woman who benefits from the enhanced female pleasure as her womb; female orgasm is a love affair between the womb and the male semen. The Hippocratic concept of the wandering womb had lived on despite the critique against it and was taken up by Islamic physicians such as al-Majūsī. Even more, the womb tended to be anthropomorphized and described as an independent creature. Areteaus, who lived in the second century, called the womb 'a living thing inside another living thing', or, in another translation, 'some animal living inside an animal'.[108] Al-Majūsī further animated this idea, describing the womb as 'an animal longing for semen'. The womb feels 'passionate love' (*ʿishq*) and 'longing' (*ʿishtiyāq*) for the 'essence of the semen' (*jawhar al-minan*).[109] With this terminology, the womb turns into a passionate lover (*ʿāshiq*) but unlike the typical figure of the passionate lover at the time of al-Majūsī, the passionate love of the womb is fulfilled. More specifically, the womb uses all her animal strength to satisfy her desire and attain her love. At the moment of the male ejaculation, the womb clasps the penis intensely and sucks the semen, making it flow down to its bottom and mingle with the female semen so that conception can take place. The love and passion of the womb to the male semen is thus the presumption for conception, to which the womb is a particularly active contributor.

Nonetheless, al-Majūsī does not recognize the movements of the womb as an exclusive female experience, he only mentions the male experience. When the man feels the contraction of the vagina, he knows that it is the effect of the suckling of the womb and that conception has taken place.[110] Ibn Sīnā, who relies on al-Majūsī's description of an active womb as the main contributor to conception, emphasizes instead the female experience. It is the woman who feels that conception is taking place and in his rendering al-Majūsī's lovesick womb is a metaphor; the womb appears *as if* it is longing for semen.[111] As the male semen approaches the womb, a convulsing motion follows every dose of semen and draws it to the bottom of the uterus where it mingles with the female semen. The womb's contractions draw the semen one gulp at a time – Ibn Sīnā also likens the womb to a fish breathing one breath at a time. Women are aware of these movements; they can feel the moment of conception. Moreover, the contractions of the womb attracting the male semen are a further source for her pleasure.

According to Ibn Sīnā, there are three sources for women's pleasure during intercourse: the convulsion of the uterus, the emission of female semen and the motion of male semen when it is flowing in from the entrance of the uterus to its bottom. If the man's ejaculation coincides with hers, her pleasure increases, but it is a mistake to assume, Ibn Sīnā asserts, that the woman's pleasure depends on simultaneous ejaculation. A woman feels pleasure from her own ejaculation and the emission of her semen in the uterus, regardless of the man's ejaculation. Ibn Sīnā acknowledges that conception can take place without female orgasm, but in that case, the male ejaculation has to be exceptionally forceful so that the semen can enter the womb without its help.[112]

The adoption by Islamic medicine of the idea that retention of female seed causes uterine suffocation contributed to a broader perspective on women's sexual health, which did not only focus on reproductive health, but also stimulation and satisfaction. Even if female orgasm is described as a mechanical process in the Greek sources used by Islamic physicians, and by the Islamic physicians themselves, as we have seen in the case of al-Majūsī, they often admitted that it was not that simple. Far from being derived mechanically from the penetration of the male organ, it demands more effort from the male partner. Female orgasm was seen as desirable, and as we will see in Chapter 2, a particular form of advice literature took form that emphasized the man's responsibility to helping the woman achieve it. It was not an altruistic action, as female orgasm was positive for both partners. This is a main theme in the erotic manual *Jawāmiʿ al-Ladhdha*, but its author, ʿAlī ibn Naṣr, was not the first in this regard, already ninth- and tenth-century physicians advised men how to stimulate their wives. According to al-Rāzī, Ḥunayn ibn Isḥāq gave advice on a sex position in his book on coitus (man-on-top), in order to stimulate the woman as much as the man.[113] Pseudo-Thābit ibn Qurra pays equal attention to women's and men's desire in *Kitāb al-Dakhīra* (*The Book of Treasure*). Conveying the idea that men are responsible for their partners' pleasure he teaches men how to recognize the signs that reveal that their female partners are close to climax.[114] Abū al-ʿAbbās al-Baladī (d. 990) from Egypt and ʿArīb ibn Saʿīd both emphasized that men have to stimulate their wives in order for them to achieve orgasm.[115] Al-Baladī also advises men to postpone their own orgasm until their wives have finished.

## Sexual pharmacology

If sexual technique is not enough, there is a significant number of pharmacological pleasure enhancing therapies in the earliest medical sources in Arabic.[116] The majority of the recipes are aphrodisiacs for men, in the shape of foodstuff, potions and ointments to lubricate the penis, as male impotence was seen as the main impediment for a healthy sex life, but there are also recipes aimed at enhancing women's pleasure. Early Islamic physicians prescribed some unexpected therapies, such as medications for penis enlargement and vaginal tightening, the purpose of which was the partner's stimulation. We find remedies for genital corrections in al-Ṭabarī's *Firdaws al-Ḥikma* and al-Rāzī's medical works, attributed to Greek, Indian and Arab medical experts. Eventually, this medical field became part of sex manuals and *Jawāmiʿ al-Ladhdha* is a rich source for these kind of therapies. Following a long tradition of sexual therapies in Arabic-Islamic medical and erotic literature, Ibn Sīnā recommends pleasure-enhancing remedies and even mentions genital correction in *Qānūn*. He could not disregard these kind of remedies as they were recommended by earlier well-respected physicians but apparently felt that he had to give a reasonable justification for recommending genital correction in his medical compilation.

> It is not disgraceful for a physician to discuss penis enlargement or vaginal tightening and female pleasure enhancing, as they are some of the means through which reproduction will take place. Often, the reason why a woman does not feel pleasure is that the penis is small, contrary to what she has been accustomed. As a consequence, she does not ejaculate, and if she does not ejaculate, there will be no child. This may also be a reason why she turns away from her husband and looks for another. Likewise, if she is not tight, her husband does not match her and she does not match her husband, and thus both of them need to change.[117]

Ibn Sīnā appeals to reason and attempts to give a morally acceptable motivation for enhancing women's pleasure; it is necessary for reproduction and for avoiding adultery. Moreover, pleasure enhancement leads to quick orgasm (*inzāl*).[118] If the husband's member is too small, it could lead to childlessness, which was considered a serious problem for women.[119] The idea that the female and male genital organs should match each other belongs to the notion of gender harmony, as the word for 'match' (*yuwāfiq/tuwāfiq*) also means 'to be in agreement' or 'harmony'. This is a central concept in erotological literature and here used in a physical sense – their sexual organs are not compatible – following the popular erotic literature on suitable sex positions that Ibn Sīnā refers to as a suitable reading against impotence (see p. 53).

Al-Rāzī preserves numerous therapies for enhancing pleasure during the sexual act, taken from earlier sources; sometimes he claims that they have been tested by one of his sources or himself. The male experience is the focus of his section on coitus, and most remedies aim at curing men's sexual dysfunctions and increasing their desire, though several of his aphrodisiacs and remedies could probably be used by women as well. However, a few are explicitly addressed to women to be used by them for their own benefit. Others are meant to be taken by women, but for the benefit of men.

Among al-Rāzī's sources was a 'book' by Tayādūq, or Theodokos (d. 90/709), a Christian physician who worked for the Umayyad governor of Iraq, al-Ḥajjāj (d. 95/714).[120] Tayādūq provided some remedies for tightening the vagina, one with the double effect of arousing the woman. The latter is made by extract of Yemeni alum (*shabb Yamani*) dissolved in water mixed with cyperus rotundus (or sedge, *su'd*), Chinese cinnamon (*salīkha*), and gallnut (*'ufṣ*) pounded with kohl. A piece of cloth is steeped in this mixture and given to the woman to wear as a pessary two hours before intercourse. She could also simply use pounded sorrel seeds (*ḥummāḍ*), which, according to Tayādūq, makes women 'become like virgins'.

Al-Rāzī also quotes the early Abbasid court physician Ibn Māsawayh and his student Ḥunayn ibn Isḥāq, who provided remedies for making vaginas more pleasant in order to enhance men's pleasure. Ibn Māsawayh relates that women use cardamom for warming their vaginas and he adds that it is very effective.[121] Al-Rāzī took several recipes of aphrodisiacs and remedies for the vagina from Ḥunayn's lost book on coitus as well as another book by him on the stomach. For tightening the vagina and eliminating excess moisture, Ḥunayn prescribes a mixture of pine bark (*qushūr al-ṣanawbar*), alum (*shabb*), and cyperus rotundus, cooked with aromatic herbs (*sharāb rayḥānī*) and gallnut until thickened. After that, pieces of linen cloth (*kuttān*) are dipped in the beverage, stored in a sealed glass bottle, and used as pessaries when needed. In a series of recipes, substances such as gallnut, cyperus rotundus, alum and pepper are used against excessive moisture and coldness in the genital area.

Other treatments for vaginas in *Ḥāwī* are al-Rāzī's own. He provides remedies for warming up the vagina with the help of substances with hot qualities; it can also be done by warming up the back. The heat is supposed to stimulate desire and enhances the pleasure of both partners. Al-Rāzī suggests a remedy which, at the same time, excites the woman and warms up her vagina, by letting her insert honey and ginger in her vagina and pressing her back with hot soft compresses.[122]

The linguistic choices in *Ḥāwī* and other medical literature give agency to the men and make women objects, as in phrases such as 'give the remedy to her before intercourse'. Many of the vaginal therapies suggested by Tayādūq and others are used to enhance men's pleasure, and thus reflect a view of women as an object of men's sexual enjoyment. Even when they provide remedies for enhancing women's excitement, it could be argued that the ultimate motif is to increase men's pleasure, as a lustful woman was generally considered more exciting. Nevertheless, the underlying conviction in medical discourse on sexual health is that women's excitement, pleasure and satisfaction are desirable, although it is not often discussed explicitly.

Sometimes the focus on women's pleasure is clearly expressed, as when al-Rāzī remarks that heat stimulates the pleasure of both partners and occasionally assures that a particular recipe is especially stimulating for women. For instance, he prescribes an anointment made of pounded asafoetida in jasmine oil, which is anointed on the penis before intercourse in order to enhance the pleasure of the man and the woman.[123] Al-Rāzī also cites a source recommending eating celery (*karfas*) as an aphrodisiac for both men and women.[124] Furthermore, he provides several remedies for enlarging the penis, such as massaging the penis with fat and warm oils, and daubing it with milk from sheep or mountain balm (*bādharūj*) extract, or smearing it with pitch before intercourse.[125] Other active ingredients in this regard are dried and pulverized leeches (*ʿalaq*) and earth-worms (*kharāṭīn*), which are rubbed on the penis, the latter after being mixed with sesame oil.[126] Al-Rāzī does not go into details as to the benefit of penis enlargement, but as we saw above in the quotation from Ibn Sīnā, the goal was obviously the pleasure of the female partner.

## Women's secrets

Women's concerns are addressed in remedies attributed to 'an Indian woman', quoted by ʿAlī ibn Sahl al-Ṭabarī in *Firdaws al-Ḥikma*.[127] The treatments are early examples of remedies that were taken up in later medical literature, such as eliminating excessive moisture and odour and tightening of the vagina. The Indian woman's patients were women who wished to use their sexuality to be successful with their husbands, masters or lovers. They were supposed to administer the remedies themselves, which was not always the case in later literature, where, as we have seen, men are supposed to control and administer remedies intended for their wives or concubines.

The Indian woman's recipes have multiple ingredients and the preparations are complex. One remedy, a fumigation that ensures the love of the husband, contains numerous substances, among others spikenard (*sunbul*), costus (*qusṭ*), wild spikenard (asarabacca, ar. *asārūn*), yew (taxus baccata, ar. *zarnab*), cyperus rotundus, pomegranate flowers (*jullanār*), cinnamon (*qirfa*), aloe wood (*'ūd al-anjūj*), musk and amber.[128] Other compound drugs prescribed by the Indian woman are mixed with oils and used with pessaries, such as a set of remedies that promise to make a woman like a virgin again (on at least one occasion she addresses middle-aged women who want to tighten their vaginas). One of these remedies contains a mixture of gallnut, mouse fat and aubergine mixed with sesame oil. Another is a complex recipe with many substances, such as pepper, long pepper, ginger, Myrobalan plum, saffron, gallnut, myrtle leaves, pomegranate flowers, citrus leaves, olive leaves and musk. The mixture is cooked slowly with sesame oil and cow milk, and applied on a pessary, morning and evening. The preparations of these remedies were time-consuming and most probably costly, and are obviously directed to elite women, enslaved or free, who had to compete for their husband's attention in polygamous households, or perhaps directed to elite courtesans.

Women's concerns were again explicitly addressed in a treatise attributed to Galen and presumably translated by Ḥunayn ibn Isḥāq, called *On the Secrets of Women*, followed, in one extant manuscript, by *On the Secrets of Men*.[129] There are reasons to doubt the authenticity of this treatise as the attribution to Galen is certainly wrong and Ḥunayn's name could have been added to provide authenticity, as he was the main translator of Galenic works. It is interesting nonetheless, the subject is pharmacology but the form is popular literature. It even has a frame story, in which a queen named Fīlānūs asks Galen to write a book for her with remedies for 'improving her body', and, for each remedy, a therapy with the opposite effect that she could inflict on her competitors and opponents.[130] Galen answers her request and gives her two remedies for each condition; one that cures it, to be used by the queen, and one that causes it, to be used on her rivals. Some of the conditions are medical, others have to do with beauty and sexuality, exemplified by the two first pairs of remedies; the first for fattening and emaciating the body and the second for making women shun sex or love lesbian sex (*saḥq*). The latter not only renders enemy women attracted to lesbian sex, they will 'not think about anything else'.[131]

For her own benefit, the queen requests a remedy that 'makes women dislike sexual intercourse (*mujāmaʿa*) to the extent that they can be without it'. The remedy to be inflicted on the enemy instead 'excites the sexual appetite of women so that they leave their houses looking for sex and threw themselves before men'. In the queen's worldview, it is better for women to have less sexual desire, but they should still be sexually attractive; the queen asks for a remedy that makes the pubic area smell so good that 'the one who comes close to it wants to return to it' while its opposite makes it smell so bad that no one can come close to it. A similar pair of remedies prevents or causes bad smell from the mouth. Another remedy makes the face shiny, clean and beautiful and the skin white, while the enemy is afflicted with the reverse. In all, the queen's wishes indicates the power of her sex appeal; her sexuality is an asset as long as she has control over it, and is not possessed by it.

The queen's wish list contains the annihilation of annoyances connected to the female body, some of them petty, as the remedy that will afflict the queen's enemy with pubic hair so rough that it is impossible to pluck and if she shaves it she will not be able to remove the roots, which will remain rough.[132] Its opposite prevents the growth of pubic hair if taken by girls who have not reached puberty and helps the pubic area stay soft and white. Other remedies quicken or delay puberty or modify the menstrual cycle so that it is regular or irregular. Some conditions are recognizable from early Islamic medical theory: one remedy puts the womb in place and another increases and strengthens female semen. One prevents or causes itching in the genital area, another helps the queen to control her bladder, while her enemy is affected by incontinence, a third prevents or causes flatulence; and a fourth prevents or causes white hair.

Among the secrets of women we find a remedy for restoring the hymen of young women, and some of its ingredients are the same as those used in the Indian woman's recipes (gallnut and pomegranate flowers) while others are used in recipes in *Jawāmiʿ al-Ladhdha* or elsewhere for tightening vaginas (such as pomegranate peel and Boswella serrata). There is of course also a remedy for rupturing hymens, without sexual intercourse, a gruesome curse on the queen's young female enemies. Remedies intended for women who want to conceal that they have been deflowered are also found in serious medical treatises. Al-Rāzī quotes Ḥunayn ibn Isḥāq, the purported translator of *On the Secrets of Women*, who also prescribes gallnut together with lemon grass flowers for this condition, obviously directed to women.[133]

## Women's agency in Islamic medical discourse

Like all fields of early Islamic science and learning, medical writing is principally addressed to and assumes the male body as the norm for general medical discussions.[134] There were no female medical authors and female physicians are largely excluded from written sources, although there is evidence that midwifery was a recognized profession for women in the eighth and ninth centuries.[135] This certainly reflects the interests of the scholarly elite, who were exclusively male. Gynaecology, obviously, concerns women's health, and women are required to handle medications pertaining to their bodies. The choice of wording in the medical discourse, however, gives the impression of male domination also in the field of women's medicine, an ostensibly private sphere. The medications are prescribed by male physicians and some writers choose wordings that authorize the male reader to be the administrator of the female patient's remedy, such as 'give the medication to the woman' or 'make her use it with a pessary'. Possibly, the medical authors in these cases address a physician or a male kin of the woman. In other cases, such as in *Kāmil* by al-Majūsī, the administration of drugs to women is described in the passive voice; they are given a potion to drink and medicine is prepared for them. It is possible that instances such as these are formulaic phrases, without any correlation to the real situation. Although the intended reader of medical literature is primarily a man, there must have been female readers, and we know about a few female patrons. For instance, one of al-Mutawakkil's concubines commissioned Ḥunayn ibn Isḥāq to write about children who are born in the eighth month of pregnancy.[136] The first woman to commission a hospital was al-Mutawakkil's mother Shujāʿ and later the royal concubine Shaghab, mother of the caliph al-Muqtadir, endowed a hospital in Baghdad.[137]

Birth control was permitted in medieval Islamic societies and its practice was discussed by Islamic scholars as well as medical authors.[138] Whereas Islamic scholars sometimes had doubts on moral grounds, medical authors saw only the benefits and were equally positive towards abortion. The preventive method considered by the jurists is coitus interruptus (*ʿazl*), which is obviously administered by the man, but other methods were used by women. Numerous such methods are described in the medical literature; Basil Musallam provides lists of methods and medical substances in some major medical works in his seminal work from 1983, *Sex and Society in Islam: Birth Control before the Nineteenth Century*.[139] Many, even most, of these methods were used by women. The most common method was to insert suppositories or pessaries smeared with contraceptive substances while other methods such as potions were also for female use, but they were less common.[140] Only a few were used by men, primarily by smearing the penis with contraceptive substances in addition to coitus interruptus. Of the fifty contraceptive prescriptions in al-Rāzī's *Ḥāwī*, counted by Musallam, only three were taken by men; in al-Majūsī's *Kāmil*, two out of seven prescriptions were for male use and in Ibn Sīnā's *Qānūn* four of twenty were for men.[141] Yet, although most contraceptive methods were used by women, physicians and jurists prescribed that they should be prepared and handled by men.[142] Al-Majūsī, for example, warns that women could mishandle contraceptives and remedies for retention of menses, and use them for feticide and abortion.[143]

The medical authors put different weight on women's experience and needs: some take it into serious consideration, others more or less disregard it. It is not only a question about the priorities of individual authors, however, the differences are also motivated by genre conventions. The subgenre of *ʿIlm al-bāh* and similar sections in medical compendia, are, as we have seen, almost exclusively concerned with men's sexual health and dysfunctions, so much so that it seems that 'bāh' is a male activity. Women's sexuality is instead mentioned in other sections, such as those on reproduction.

It has been argued that Islamic medical authors in general had no direct experience of examining women's genitals, but relied on the works of their predecessors and that their writings therefore are more or less exclusively theoretical. Manfred Ullmann, relying on the Andalusian physician al-Zahrāwī (d. 1013) claims that modesty prevented physicians from examining women's private parts, and that this was instead was the work of midwives.[144] But, as Weisser points out, the attitudes towards appropriate examination of the female body must have varied between different societal classes, regions and epochs.[145] In certain times and contexts, there might have been less anxiety against examining women.

Occasionally, medical literature mentions female informants and patients. Al-Ṭabarī had a few female informants for *Firdaws al-Ḥikma*, in addition to the Indian woman, who conveyed information about issues relating to women. He describes several magical healing procedures and mixtures, which were probably common in popular medicine and practiced by women, not the least in connection with pregnancy and childbirth. He had been told by women in his native Tabaristan, for instance, that pregnant women in Gilan (a region by the Caspian Sea), used a certain stone for protection of the foetus. He also recounts that the chief physician at the hospital in Gondeshapur had told him about a stone carried by women in a family in Ahvaz to protect the foetus. Its magical power was so great that if a woman with the stone met another pregnant woman, the latter miscarried.[146]

From al-Rāzī case studies, we know that he treated female patients, and was therefore familiar with women's personal experience of bodily illness.[147] He and other physicians sometimes mention female healers and practitioners, often deemed as amateurish and largely incompetent. Nevertheless, he admits that patients often prefer to consult female practioners; he even wrote a medical tract on the subject (now lost): *Why ignorant physicians, common folk, and women in the cities are more successful than scientists in treating certain diseases—and the physician's excuse for this.*[148]

## Conclusion: Women's health and pleasure

The early medieval Islamic world saw the birth of a systematic Islamic medicine based on Greek medical science written in Arabic. Many physicians were not Muslims but their work and writings were financed by Muslim patrons, often rulers, from the translators and physicians at the courts of the Abbasid caliphs to the great philosopher and physician Ibn Sīnā, who lived in the eastern part of the Islamic world and worked for Samanid and Buyid rulers. The early physicians were influenced by a treatise on coitus by Rufus of Ephesus (fl. *c.* 100), which was translated into Arabic with the title *Kitāb al-Bāh* (*Book on Coitus*) and apparently treated the possible health benefits and of sexual activities. The subject was developed by Islamic physicians from the late ninth to the early tenth centuries and 'the science of coitus' was established as an independent medical discipline. Some wrote treatises with the same name, others included chapters on the benefits and possible harm of sex in their medical compendia. The physicians advised against abstinence on health grounds and provided numerous recipes for remedies against sexual dysfunctions and pleasure-enhancing therapies.

As we have seen in this chapter, although medicine as a learned subject was male dominated, the Islamic physicians put emphasis on women's pleasure and satisfaction, apparently more than their Greek predecessors. All Islamic physicians adopted the two-seed theory, even if Ibn Sīnā had some doubts, and the notion of female semen reinforced the emphasis on women's pleasure. In this notion, female ejaculation is essential for conception, as the male and female semen have to mingle in the womb in order for a foetus to be produced. Moreover, abstinence was considered particularly precarious for women, as they have to discard semen in order to avoid several serious ailments. According to ʿAlī ibn Sahl al-Ṭabarī, dammed-up semen could cause apnoea, corruption of the liver and stomach, palpitations, weak cognitive ability, headache, miscarriage, tumours and, in particular, the life-threatening disease uterine suffocation. This means that female orgasm is not only necessary for reproduction but also for women's health. Influenced by their Greek predecessors, Islamic physicians identified other benefits of sex for women, for example, it facilitates childbirth and is therefore especially good during pregnancy. Some women are more vulnerable to the dangers of abstinence than others; al-Rāzī mentions girls who have reached puberty but are not yet married, widows and women with great libidos as especially exposed to abstinence-related diseases. In many cases, he, al-Majūsī and other physicians prescribe intercourse or sexual therapy as a remedy for ailing women.

In contrast to their Greek predecessors, some Islamic physicians conclude that women get more pleasure then men during intercourse. According to them, women have two or three sources for pleasure, all connected somehow to semen. Al-Majūsī maintains that as a woman gets pleasure from discharging her own semen and from attaining her partner's semen, she benefits both from the intensity of male orgasm and the longevity of her own. Ibn Sīnā takes the idea one step further and adds a third source of female pleasure, namely the convulsions of the uterus, and maintains that a woman does not need male ejaculation for feeling pleasure.

In Hippocratic writings, a woman's way to climax is sometimes described as a mechanical process. Islamic physicians admit that it is not that easy and men are advised to pay attention to their wives, and later physicians especially give advice on concrete methods. There are a significant number of pleasure-enhancing therapies in medical compendia in Arabic. Many of them are directed to men or are not gender-specific, but some are explicitly directed to women. Some of them certainly rely at least to some degree on female experience. In the beginning of the eleventh century, the highly regarded physician Ibn Sīnā recommended 'penis enlargement' when women cannot reach orgasm because the genitals do not 'match' each other. Women's satisfaction is not only necessary for reproduction, he explained, but also for avoiding adultery. Admittedly, many recipes addressed to women are intended to help them manipulate their sexual assets in order to gain men's love, attention and attraction, as for women their sexual attraction could be a strategy for gaining advantages. Nevertheless, the underlying conviction in medical discourse is that women's pleasure and satisfaction are desired by their male partners and essential for their own well-being and for the future of humanity.

2

# A World of Pleasure

Scholarly interest in sexual health merged with intellectual interest in human behaviour in a field of learning that emerged in Arabic Islamic literature in the ninth century, namely erotology. Parts of the *Kāma Sūtra*[1] were translated into Arabic together with other erotological texts that are now lost. Some of them are preserved in the erotic compendium and sex manual *Jawāmiʿ al-Ladhdha* (*Encyclopaedia of Pleasure*), which was probably written in the late tenth century and covers many aspects of human sexuality. The main theme of this book is sexual knowledge and behaviour as a mark of distinction; the knowledge is not accessible to everybody and only after having adopted the methods of this knowledge is it possible to behave in line with it. The reward is greater pleasure, more love and an amazing sex life. The intended readers of the book are refined men (*ẓurafāʾ*) but female sexuality is at its centre; only when men know how to please women are they truly refined and the highest pleasure is reached only when the female partner is satisfied. Men want to be beloved by women, and their love is obtained when they are sexually satisfied. The author advises:

> Know that women prefer a man who knows how to behave well in all circumstances and how to be in harmony with them. They reject a man who has no knowledge about women and do not love him even if he is exceptionally handsome and rich. Then again, they love a poor and disgraced man who is devoid of praiseworthy manners as long as he is well-informed about women and knows how to be in harmony with them. Therefore, the man has to endeavour so that her orgasm (*inzāl*) coincides with his at their first meeting. That will make her heart favourably disposed to him and it is the most powerful way of strengthening love between them. If it happens in the beginning [of their relationship], their love will last and their affection be complete.[2]

Though it is not clear from the beginning what it means 'to be in harmony' it turns out that it is the same as simultaneous orgasm. To put it differently, the key to women's love is a harmonious relationship, which is achieved by mutual sexual satisfaction, and it is the men's responsibility to make this happen. They have to have knowledge about women and it is exactly this knowledge that the author of *Jawāmiʿ al-Ladhdha* intends to give them. This book, the author writes in the introduction, presents the sexual sciences (*ʿulūm al-bāh*) that a sophisticated man needs in order to make love with his beloved in a civilized manner, in line with Socrates' saying that 'sexual intercourse without cordiality is crude'. When the man unites with the one he loves he should 'use good manners and polite speech' in order to distinguish himself from animals and common people who are driven by their 'animal nature'.[3]

To be in harmony is *muwāfaqa*, 'to be in agreement' or 'to match', the same term that Ibn Sīnā used when pointing out that genital correction can be appropriate in certain circumstances (see Chapter 1). There are several ways of reaching harmony in *Jawāmiʿ al-Ladhdha*; one is sexual technique, another is sexual pharmacology and the author provides similar recipes as in the mainstream medical compendia. In all circumstances, however, the refined man has to 'have knowledge about women'. He has to know her body type and other physical characteristics in order to know how she best reaches climax. He also has to take into consideration her age and social situation; whether she is married or not, is free or is a slave.

The advanced knowledge presented for the sophisticated reader includes medical topics such as anatomy, sexual health and pharmacology taken from medical sources, some of which convey mainstream Greek and Islamic medicine but others more obscure (or perhaps, the author's or his informants' misinterpretations of) conventional medical knowledge. The encyclopaedia is arranged by topics, of which some are purely medical or pharmacological but most are combined with ethics and erotology and almost all are peppered with poetry and anecdotes and some with hadith and wisdom. There are also ample examples from the occult sciences, from magical recipes for arousing desire and attaining love to physiognomy as a means to detect people's sexual capacity. The author devotes several parts of the encyclopaedia to sexual etiquette and the typology of women, some of it adapted from the *Kāma Sūtra* and other sources, Persian and Arabic. The *Kāma Sūtra* linked pleasure to other matters relevant for a sophisticated elite, which is also a recurrent theme in *Jawāmiʿ al-Ladhdha*.

The knowledge about women conveyed to the readers of *Jawāmiʿ al-Ladhdha* is the subject of the first part of this chapter, which discusses especially its representation of medical and erotological sources. The presupposition of ʿAlī ibn Naṣr's advice to men is that women are driven by sexual instinct; they abstain from beauty and wealth and choose the man who can satisfy their libido. Women's great libido (*shahwa*) is an underlying theme in *Jawāmiʿ al-Ladhdha* and confirmed by erotic stories with female protagonists. These erotic stories are the subject of the second part of the chapter, which also discusses the spread of the notion of women's increased libido in the ninth and tenth centuries. It shows that although *Jawāmiʿ al-Ladhdha* conveys ideas about women's defective nature, in line with medical discourse and natural philosophy, female experience and authority are central in the book.

## Medicine in the *Encyclopaedia of Pleasure*

Harmony is essential for good health according to Greek and Islamic medical theory, as a healthy body and mind depends on the balance of humours and temperatures. Harmony is also essential in *Jawāmiʿ al-Ladhdha*, but here it is more or less the same as sexual harmony; the sign of being compatible is simultaneous orgasm.

As we have seen in Chapter 1, medical monographs on sex (*kutub al-bāh*) as well as medical anthologies usually contained a chapter on 'the benefits and harms of coitus'. ʿAlī ibn Naṣr was naturally inspired by medical discourses on sexual health, but he went even further when he described the benefits of coitus; accordingly, he entitles a similar chapter 'On the merits and benefits of marital sexual intercourse' (*fī faḍl al-nikāḥ wa-manāfiʿihi*). In line with the intention of the encyclopaedia, he is not interested in possible harm. What he actually does is amalgamate two different discourses: the medical, which identifies benefits (*manāfiʿ*), and the religious, which defines merits (*faḍl*); the term *nikāḥ* (marital sex) also belongs to the religious discourse rather than the medical. The following benefits are recognized by his medical sources, the 'predecessors in the science of coitus', a group he often refers to:

> The predecessors in the science of coitus (*al-mutaqaddimīn fī ʿilm al-bāh*) explained that coitus gives fire to the soul, joy to the heart and renewal of affection and intimacy. It effects increase in the body, gives consolation to the eye, sharpness to the mind, brightness of the intellect, assurance and permanence of the pledge, solidity of love, continuance of friendship, and the recovering of disunion. Acquiring a woman gives happiness for the hearts, pleasure for the souls, treatment for the chest, the calming of passion and the heat of the man.[4]

This exceedingly positive view of sex is typical for *Jawāmiʿ al-Ladhdha*; it not only results in a healthy body and mind, it is also good for the intellect. The merits and benefits are seen from a male point of view in this citation, but it is evident from the rest of the book that the author believed that women attain similar benefits from sexual union.

The majority of the medical explanations differ from or are simplified versions of the established medical theories, as probably ʿAlī ibn Naṣr was not a trained physician or educated in medical theory. His sources were possibly Late Antique medical compendia translated into Arabic, which he either misunderstood or which were corrupted, perhaps in translation. The description of the womb in the chapter on anatomy relies on Galenic sources and has resemblances to that of al-Majūsī, although it is considerably simplified and misunderstood. Galen described the womb as being 'sinewy and hard'; al-Majūsī maintained that the nature (*jawhar*) of the womb is close to the nature (*jawhar*) of sinews, as it is able to expand during pregnancy. ʿAlī ibn Naṣr merely states that 'the womb is sinews (*ʿaṣāb*)'.[5] He adds that as sinews are cold and dry, and the womb affects the female body, women's constitution is cold and dry; contrary to the Greek authorities and all established Islamic physicians, who maintained that females are cold and moist. The moistness, otherwise described as a female quality, is instead inherent in the male reproductive organ, which therefore is soft while the womb is dry to the extreme. The dryness affects the female body so much that its genitalia are inverted. Here, ʿAlī ibn Naṣr presents a reversed model of that of Galen. Galen claimed that the female body, with its internal genitalia, is the first stage, and only men have the heat which is needed to move on to the second, perfect stage: the male body with its external genitals.[6] In ʿAlī ibn Naṣr's model, the external genitals is the first stage, but the extreme dryness of the womb forces it inwards, so that it becomes inverted. In this, he is somewhat close to the Hippocratic idea that excessive dryness forces the womb to wander.

One of the Greek medical authors referred to by ʿAlī ibn Naṣr is Soranus, who is rarely quoted in Arabic; the citation includes statements remotely similar to his work on gynaecology, with a description of the anatomy of the womb, its size and its characteristics during intercourse (when it swells as the womb creeps closer to the vagina, eager to attract the sperm).[7] The chapter ends with a rather bizarre attribution to Galen, who is supposed to have claimed that women have five wombs. Of these wombs, two are situated on the right side, facing the liver, and two are situated on the left side, facing the spleen. On the right side, the upper womb produces female foetuses and the lower male; on the left side, the locations are reversed. The fifth womb, finally, is affixed to the other four and produces hermaphrodites.[8] The reference to several 'wombs' here is perhaps a corrupt reading of the 'cavities' or 'cells' of the womb, described by Galen, or the Hippocratic writers' use of the plural of the word womb. Al-Majūsī, following Galen, claims that the womb has two cavities. However, the model also conflicts with the mainstream medical theory that male foetuses are produced in the right side of the womb, where the proximity to the liver makes it warmer, whereas female foetuses are produced in the left side as the spleen makes it cold. A similar theory was known in medieval Europe, namely the doctrine on the seven-cell uterus, which claims that the womb has as many as seven cells.[9] Albeit curious, this theory followed the conventional right–left origin of male and female foetuses, as the three cells to the right produce male foetuses and the three to the left produce female ones. The seventh cell in the middle produces hermaphrodites, due to the location midway between the heat generated by the liver and the cold generated by the spleen.

The main medical field in *Jawāmiʿ al-Ladhdha* is pharmacology, especially aphrodisiacs, and several chapters are devoted to pleasure-enhancing methods and remedies. Most recipes are designed to help men, as they are more likely to have sexual dysfunctions. The description of the features of the opposite sex that triggers arousal represents women as less complicated and easier aroused; when a woman looks at a penis a physical reaction is instigated, her vagina 'quivers', when she touches it beneath the clothes, her body becomes lax; and when she takes it in her hand, her body is ready for intercourse.[10]

Many of the numerous recipes for stimulating desire and enhancing pleasure are therefore intended for men, in the form of ointments to be smeared on the penis for example. Others, such as foodstuff, are not gender-specific and a few are explicitly directed to women (or both sexes). ʿAlī ibn Naṣr also provides recipes for enlarging the male organ and make it smell good and numerous recipes for tightening and beautifying the vagina. Many of the substances are the same as those used by the established physicians mentioned in Chapter 1.

Besides increasing pleasure, the desired outcome for men is to be adored by women. An electuary made of pearls, with several benefits, makes the penis harder, prolongs erection, strengthens the nerves in the brain and eyes, fattens the body, increases pleasure and makes the woman love the man.[11] Several ointments are to be used for penis enlargement, with active ingredients such as Arabica gum (*ṣamagh ʿarabī*), squill bulbs (*baṣal al-faʾr*), anacyclus pyrethrum (*ʿāqirqarḥā*) and rocket (*jirjīr*).[12] At least some of the substances mentioned by ʿAlī ibn Naṣr were recommended by established physicians; al-Rāzī had, for example, recipes with pulverized leeches (*ʿalaq*) and earth-worms (*kharāṭīn*) mixed with sesame oil, to be rubbed on the penis.[13] Others are less conventional and sometimes unnecessarily cruel (involving torturing of live birds). While some of the substances may seem unappealing, ʿAlī ibn Naṣr adds a few ointments (with substances such as the fat of a young bird and the gall of a bull) with the additional effect of improving the appearance of the penis; this, as well as the enlargement, are evidently to the benefit of women (who are supposed to prefer large penises). For the pleasure of the woman, he provides remedies for perfuming the male genital organs after bath, with rosewater as a main ingredient.

There are other recipes for warming up the vagina and reducing vaginal fluid, some with the exact wording as al-Rāzī's *al-Manṣūrī fī al-Ṭibb*; including substances such as *kirm-dāna*, pepper and cyperus rotundus, which are supposed to warm up the genital area, and alum and kohl, which help against excessive fluid.[14] A few of ʿAlī ibn Naṣr's remedies for enlargement can also be used for the vagina, in case it needs to be enlarged. Tightening is more common and there are several recipes in the standard medical compendia, but ʿAlī ibn Naṣr's remedies are more versatile and detailed. He even gives a justification based on equality: 'Just like women love large penises, men love when women have tight, warm vaginas.'[15] The aim of the treatments is not one-sided, however, they benefit both partners, as exemplified by a remedy consisting of, among other substances, pulverized coral (pers. *bussadh*), mouse-ear (pers. *marzangosh*), mace (*basbāsa*), peel from pomegranate and citron (*utruj*), celery (*karfas*), lupine (*turmus*), Boswellia serrata (*kundur*) and lemon-grass (*idhkhir*). The ingredients are to be kneaded with ben oil (*bān*) and inserted with a pessary to be worn by the woman during the day and taken out at night, with versatile benefits:

> This remedy has seven benefits: it strengthen the labia, protects the uteral orifice, makes the vagina smell good, tightens the neck of the womb and protects it, quickens male ejaculation and amplifies female semen. Increased female semen makes the intercourse more pleasurable for men.[16]

Other remedies that promises to tighten the vagina contain ingredients familiar from mainstream compendia, among other things Arabic gum, cinnamon, Yemenite alum, gallnut and pomegranate flowers. The remedies are prepared, ʿAlī ibn Naṣr explains, in order to tighten vaginas after childbirth or frequent intercourse, or to restore virginity. He also provides some recipes for birth control. As often, his remedies have several benefits, for example an electuary to be taken by the man with cassia (*salīḥa*) as one of the main ingredients of many, which, at the same time, prevents pregnancy, makes the woman love the man and increases the man's sexual capacity.[17] Some medical recipes border on magic, and others are definitely magic. Among the former are several recipes of ointment with peculiar ingredients to be used by men (normally rubbed on the penis) in order to make the female partner adore him and enhance her pleasure.[18]

## Seed and harmony

Like all medical writers in the early medieval Islamic world, ʿAlī ibn Naṣr accepts the idea that women emit semen during intercourse and that this semen has to mingle with male semen. He is not interested in theories of conception however; instead, he argues that the mingling of semen strengthens love in a relationship: 'when his and her fluids coincide and mingle, their love and mutual affection are strengthened as much as possible; their love is proportionate to the degree they coincide and mingle'.[19] It is as if he credits the seminal fluid with magical properties; its role is to create the ideal harmony between a woman and a man. Instead of using the Arabic term for seed, *zar*ʿ, or sperm, *minan*, the common terms in early medieval medical texts, he uses the less technical word 'water', *mā*ʾ, which is the term for seminal fluid in jurisprudence.[20]

He connects semen with the legal discourse in another instance, using a term for sperm from the Qurʾan, *nuṭfa*, the drop of sperm from which God created the pair, male and female, according to Qurʾan verse 53:45–6. Warning men that their wives will ignore their legal rights in marriage as long as they are not satisfied, he claims that a wife attends to her husband's right (*ḥaqq*) and a concubine to her master's right in proportion to the degree of harmony (*muwāfaqa*) and pleasure of the sperm (*nuṭfa*) she attains from him. He warns of a troublesome time ahead if men do not meet these requirements, there will be 'a foundation for dispute', 'life will be bitter', 'the bed will be abandoned', 'the women will part' and so on, until there is nothing left but divorce.[21] With the expression 'pleasure of the sperm', using a Qurʾanic term for sperm, he connects his idea of love caused by the mingling of sperms with Qurʾanic discourse.

As we have seen in the previous chapter, the two-seed theory and the notion of female ejaculation was mainstream but there were those who did not agree; ʿAlī ibn Naṣr refers to the discussion about the nature of women's orgasm among Indian philosophers, some of whom did not adopt the idea of female semen and ejaculation. He quotes Auddalaki, an authority in the *Kāma Sūtra*, saying that female orgasm is continuous, like an itch, without a climax.[22] Nevertheless, in *Jawāmi*ʿ *al-Ladhdha*, the notion of female semen is essential for harmony between the couple as sexual harmony is first and foremost the simultaneous ejaculation of the female and male.

ʿAlī ibn Naṣr has found various sources that help him to further his argument. One of them is a spurious attribution to Aretaeus of Cappadocia, a physician who was rarely mentioned by Islamic medical writers, which discusses the genital organs, simultaneous orgasm and the qualities of semen.[23] The text attributed to

Aretaeus underlines the importance of the agreement between the sex partners in ways of achieving orgasm. The time and rhythm of movements during intercourse differ between individuals, and it is essential, he argues, to synchronise them. The speed and intensity of movements of each of them have to be in agreement with each other during the stages of intercourse, as agreement between the couple is essential for their happiness and love. If the man, for instance, is quick in the beginning and slow in the end, his female partner may be deprived of her orgasm. This is a severe condition, as it risks inducing hatred and misery in their relationship. On the other hand, if the man is slow in the beginning and quick in the end, the woman may ejaculate before him, and as her fluid dries up, the movements of his penis will hurt her, as will the ejaculation of his semen.

The ideal condition is when the partners are compatible (*muwāfaqa*), which is when they attain harmony (*ittifāq*). The opposite, incompatibility (*ikhtilāf*) can be caused by variances in their movements and distribution of speed and force during intercourse, as in the example above. Another reason for incompatibility, also attributed to Aretaeus of Cappadocia, is the corruption of the male semen and incompatibility of the seminal fluids. He claims that there are three types of male sperm (*minan*) regarding their impact on the woman and their usefulness for reproduction. Here, 'Aretaeus' explains how the condition of the sperm can be examined by using smell and taste. The sound sperm is 'heavy, white, and sweet, with a smell resembling that of camphor'. It is compatible with the female seminal fluid and produces a healthy child. The next in quality contains red streaks and smells like myrtle, though slightly fetid. It is relatively compatible with the female semen. The corrupt sperm smells like aloe or myrrh and it has a bad impact on the female partner. In ʿAlī ibn Naṣr's words, attributed to Aretaeus, this is the sperm 'that the woman hates; it makes her twist and damages her womb'. This can be cured, however, by various diets; such as eating nothing except rice cooked in milk for forty days. Moreover, although the male and the female seminal fluids are visibly different, they have the same qualities in terms of flavour; they can be sweet, salty, bitter or sour. If both fluids have the same flavour, they are compatible; if not, they have to be adjusted with the help of diets. It the man's fluid is bitter and the woman's is not, for instance, intercourse is hurtful for her. If he ejaculates, it will damage her womb and she will hate him. The best combination is when both fluids are sweet.[24]

The claim about the negative impact of corrupt sperm resembles the idea held by Galen that semen containing corrupt humours aggravates the damage of retained semen in cases of uterine suffocation.[25] Ibn Sīnā also considered corrupt male semen, or the incompatibility of the female and the male semen as possible grounds for infertility.[26] It is more difficult to find influences for the second claim about the compatibility of male and female semen based on taste. 'Aretaeus' suggests testing the sperm's fertility by examining if it floats in water, a test invented by Aristotle, in addition to other curious tests to check which is its dominating flavour (bitter semen is avoided by insects, salty semen on vegetation makes the ground barren).[27] Although the attribution to Aretaeus is likely unauthentic, there is no reason not to believe ʿAlī ibn Naṣr that he found similar ideas in two books, the other attributed to an unidentified Indian author.[28] Ideas about the impact of semen on women's bodies obviously circulated in the early medieval period; in this case corrupt sperm does not only cause damage to the womb, it makes the woman dislike her male partner. It was related to the idea that intercourse (or, rather, the male ejaculation) inserts fluids into the female bodies that disturb the balance of humours.

## Erotology in the *Encyclopaedia of Pleasure*

Sexual pharmacology and sexual technique are the main methods for enhancing pleasure in the *Encyclopaedia of Pleasure*, belonging to the fields of medicine and erotology respecitvely. Several chapters are devoted to pharmacology, but Alī ibn Naṣr warns against using aphrodisiacs too often, as drugs contain substances with hot qualities that, taken in excess, may harm the body.[29] He therefore devotes an entirely chapter to a summary of all sex positions he knew about, attributing them to "wise men" (*al-ḥukamāʾ*), who recommended them as alternative to medicine. As each position is named differently by the different authors, Ibn Naṣr summarizes and presents them according to body position (standing, sitting, lying, etc.).

He does not mention his sources, but apparently at least some of the erotological sources were known among medical scholars who occasionally recommended non-pharmacological treatment of sexual dysfunctions. ʿAlī ibn Sahl al-Ṭabarī suggests imagining different kinds of sexual intercourse (*anwāʿ al-jimāʿ*) for stirring up desire necessary for healthy sexual activity.[30] In line with the almost exclusive focus on male experiences in the genre of *kutub al-bāh*, al-Kindī writes that stimulation can be assisted by the eyes when looking at a beautiful woman or by the hands when touching a woman's body.[31] His student, Abū Zayd al-Balkhī (*c.* 235–322/850–934), builds on this basic observation and adds that, except for looking at beautiful women, desire can be stirred by reading books on coitus that contain descriptions of women and sexual intercourse.[32] Ibn Sīnā recommends reading erotic stories and books about 'the conditions and types of sexual intercourse'.[33] It is possible that they believed that women's desire can be explained in analogy, or that they thought that women's desire was unproblematic.

Only ʿAlī ibn Naṣr states explicitly that women are similar to men in this regard, they get aroused by watching sexual activities and it could be a good idea to use this kind of incitement for chaste or shy women. Once, he relates, a man married a shy young woman who resisted his attempts to have sex with her. He endeavoured in different ways to persuade her, but to no avail. Then, he got the idea to give her a beautiful dove couple and encouraged her to look at them. She did, and when she saw them mating, her natural instinct arose.[34] The erotic stories in *Jawāmiʿ al-Ladhdha* also have a therapeutic purpose as they can help readers with sexual dysfunctions to obtain healthy sex.

Earlier medical authors warned about negative health effects of certain positions. The woman-on-top-position was considered harmful for men, and Quṣṭā ibn Luqā warns against it in his book on coitus. So also did al-Rāzī, who instead recommends the man-on-top position out of concern for men's health.[35] In line with the physicians' recommendations, Ibn Naṣr recommends using unconventional positions with precaution, but not because of health; his main concern is women's feelings. Free women tend to be shy, he writes, and showing their naked body is a disgrace for them. Therefore, persuading them to engage in unconventional sex may be humiliating for them and should be avoided. This is not the case with slave concubines, he states conveniently, they are more robust and enjoy unconventional sex.[36]

Nonetheless, ʿAlī ibn Naṣr does not discriminate between free and enslaved women in regard to the necessity to give them pleasure, nor are 'free' and 'enslaved' parameters in his typologies of women. In *Jawāmiʿ al-Ladhdha*, female pleasure is desirable in itself and as a means to enhance men's pleasure. In the chapter on women's sexual appetite, he proposes different categories of women based on biological and sociological factors, such as age, body type and marital status. His typologies aim at giving the male readers knowledge of women, which is the first step towards gaining their love. Men have to know to which category a woman belongs, so that they can reach harmony by means of simultaneous orgasm, the ultimate goal. The physical categories borrowed from the erotological tradition are sketchy and unsubstantiated, even improbable, and it is possible that they were never meant to be anything than pleasant reading.

In one long account, arranged in diagrams in the oldest extant manuscript, Ibn Naṣr divides women into fifteen types with regard to their appetite, depending on age, body type, appearance and marital status.[37] The fifteen types are divided into three groups. The first group consists of women who do not like vaginal intercourse, but prefer embracing and kissing, playful chatter and conversation. They are five types: girls who have not reached puberty, short women, fleshy women, white-skinned women and women who are always together with their husbands. The next group consists of seven types of women who love sexual intercourse: women who are between youth and middle age, women whose nipples are slightly inverted, long women, slender women, thin brown-skinned women, and finally, unmarried women. The third group consists of three types who vary as to their degree of lust: adolescents, women in their twenties and women between these two age groups.

ʿAlī ibn Naṣr identifies eight types of women in terms of the nature of their orgasms, depending on their length and physical constitutions.[38] A basic typology is that tall and thin women have quick orgasm but the short and plump have slow orgasm. But there are other considerations to take into account, as each of these types can be divided according to two variables. The first variable is marital status: a woman can be married, unmarried, or married with an absent husband. The second variable is the strength of her desire for intercourse.

The categorizations are rough and the numbers in each group vary between the different manuscripts. The purpose of the typologies are probably to display knowledge in the sophisticated erotic sciences rather than being used for identifying women. The author makes continuous and divergent claims about women's desire throughout the book, such as noting that adolescent girls can feel a slight aversion to sex, whereas women in their twenties are affectionate, as they have understood the impact they have on men. He also makes divergent claims about the reason for the uneven distribution of sexual appetite in women, more or less astonishing, as when he claims that there are two reasons why some women have more desire than others: that they need the man and his money, or that they are fat, as body flesh increases desire. The first incentive is psychological and the other physical, but both have the same effect: increased longing for sex. Elsewhere, he claims that there are three reasons for the incitement of women's appetite: some desire a man out of love for him, some hope for sex and others want a noble man so that their children can inherit his lineage. He repeats several times that appetite in women is governed by age, in that while men's appetite is at its height when they are adolescents, women's appetite grows with age.[39]

A similar and more established method for identifying women and determining their degree of appetite was physiognomy, which was a recognized discipline at this time. Physiognomy was, at least in theory but probably also in practice, a tool for evaluating slaves.[40] A specific branch of physiognomy evaluates women's pleasurability – the degree of pleasure a man can obtain from her – called 'the physiognomy of women' (*firāsat al-nisā'*).[41] According to Ibn Naṣr, and he was not alone in this regard, it is possible to determine from a woman's physical constitution, complexion, colour of eyes and preferred food whether her orgasm is quick or slow.[42] He devotes a chapter to physiognomy containing various lists of traits that reveal lustfulness in men and women and the size and shape of their genitals, especially concerning women.

The focus on women's desire and differences, albeit sketchy and spurious, communicates to the male reader that he has to work hard in order to understand the constitution of his female partner, so that he reaches the goal: her orgasm. The result is an exceptional emphasis on women's desire and pleasure. Some of the instructions are less categorical and more realistic, and rather amusing. Declaring that women's sexual appetite and love are either manifest or concealed, Ibn Naṣr acknowledges some women express their desire and are likely to let the man know what they want. As to the aim of simultaneous orgasm, he puts some effort into teaching men some tricks to achieve it. Instead of considering the categories mentioned above, they can begin with estimating the degree of their female partner's libido. Some women, he claims, 'do not want the penis to leave their vagina', and if a man has a partner of this type, he has to distract her with pleasant and amusing activities, in order to keep up with her.[43] Ibn Naṣr suggests that the man should engage his partner in romantic conversation, and entertain her with beautiful poetry and singing. He can also play chess (*shaṭranj*) with her and take her for a walk in a garden, if she is one of the women who go out. If she instead is slow in coming, he can carve a wooden sandal into the shape of a penis, and either arouse her with this or his fingers before intercourse. Apart from the dildo, he has other realistic instruction of stimulating the vagina.[44] He also gives a telling instruction of how a man can manipulate ejaculation; if he is too quick, he can slow down the pace by imagining corporeal punishment and prison, perhaps reflecting the uncertain career of a high official.

Some guidance offered in *Jawāmiʿ al-Ladhdha* seems to be made by the author himself, but he also relies on a number of unidentified sources. One of the main sources for Indian erotology is someone called al-Hindī (the Indian), who was the author of a *Book on Coitus* (*kitāb al-bāh*). Al-Hindī was mentioned a century or so earlier by al-Jāḥiẓ, who attributes to him a statement about the size of the genitals of male elephants and deer.[45] In *Jawāmiʿ al-Ladhdha*, al-Hindī is the authority of a paraphrase of the first part of book two in the *Kāma Sūtra*, on sexual typology based on the size of the genitals and degree of sexual appetite.[46] He is an expert on physiognomy, providing information on how to recognize a woman in love, as well as sexual etiquette and seduction, addressed to both women and men. Apart from the *Kāma Sūtra*, al-Hindī's sources might be other Indian erotological texts. One of the earliest Indian erotological works after *Kāma Sūtra* is Nāgarasarvasva, which is difficult to date and according to Daud Ali was written between 800 and 1300.[47] This later tradition introduced more methods for defining love couples and types of women, including body type and physiognomy, inspired by works on, among other things, divination, bodily prognostication and physiognomy that developed in India in the first millennium CE.[48] These works, like *Jawāmi ͑ al-Ladhdha*, included characteristics of men and women suitable for marriage, including body type and walking style. It is possible that Indian texts like these were collected in anthologies in Middle Persian and later translated into Arabic, or they could have been translated directly from Sanskrit into Arabic in the early Abbasid era, as were some medical texts.[49]

Other texts cited or paraphrased in *Jawāmi ͑al-Ladhdha* might have a Persian origin as some are attributed to 'al-Fārisī' (the Persian) and others to Bunyāfis al-Ḥakīm (Bunyānnafs in *Firhrist* by Ibn al-Nadīm). The latter is a jester and libertine, and discusses, among other things, which penises women prefer (large and long).[50] The author of *Jawāmi ͑ al-Ladhdha* also cites from the book on Burjān and Ḥabāḥib, which in turn might be inspired by Indian erotology, perhaps from Middle Persian sources.

## Women's *shahwa* and female nature

Tiresias, the blind prophet in Greek mythology who was transformed to a woman for seven years, once was involved in an argument between Zeus and Hera, according to the *Bibliotheca*, a compendium with myths and legends from the first or second century AD. The subject of their argument was whether women or men have more pleasure from sex. Tiresias, who had experience from both genders, was asked to determine. His answer, which displeased Hera, was that 'if the pleasures of love be reckoned at ten, men enjoy one and women nine.'[51]

Tiresias' conclusion was, in some form, transferred to Arabic literature, but without the setting from Greek mythology. It appears in some variants in two traditions that seemingly are poles apart, namely hadith and erotic fiction, but instead of pleasure, they measure women's sexual appetite (*shahwa*). As a hadith, it circulated in both Sunni and Shi ͑i traditions. The Andalusian Maliki scholar ͑Abd al-Mālik ibn Ḥabīb (d. 853) attributes to the Prophet the claim that God created ten parts of *shahwa*, and then made nine parts in women and one part in men.[52] By giving the saying the status as a Prophetic tradition, it became an authoritative saying about female and male libido.

The Twelve Shiʿi scholar al-Kulaynī (d. 328/939–940) devotes a section to women's nine shares of appetite in the book on marriage in the hadith collection *Kitāb al-Kāfi*. Here, he quotes a tradition from ʿAlī ibn Abī Ṭālib, which he got from Aḥmad ibn Muḥammad ibn ʿĪsā (d. after 274/893), a scholar in Qumm, one of the most important Shiʿi hadith transmitters and authors in the end of the third/ninth century.[53] The tradition specifies that God gave women ten times as much appetite than men, but adds that he also gave them bashfulness, which enabled them to control it:

> God created ten parts of *shahwa*, and then made nine parts in women and one part in men. Had God not given them bashfulness (*ḥayāʾ*) in proportion to their appetite, every man would have nine women clinging to him.[54]

In *Kāfi*, subsequent comments by Imam Jaʿfar al- Ṣādiq (148/765) accentuate women's endurance (*ṣabr*) rather than their bashfulness; they were, according to him, given the libido of ten or twelve men, together with the endurance of an equal number of men. In any case, bashfulness or endurance is a strength God gave women, without which female libido would create chaos.

The traditionalists did not agree on the ratio of women's *shahwa*. According to a version attributed to the Prophet by the Sunni traditionalist al-Kharāʾiṭī (d. 327/938) in his book on love, *Iʿtilāl al-qulūb*, the ratio is much higher: 'Women were given ninety-nine times as much more appetite than men, but they were overcome by bashfulness.'[55] The hadith is included in a section on chaste women who resist men's advances or resist their own desire to unite with their beloved. The purpose of the hadith is probably to elucidate the difficulties women who want to stay chaste face, and the inner strength that they need to resist their natural drive to commit fornication. This makes the gendered emotion of bashfulness perfectly rational.

The hadith is occasionally referred to in the Sunni tradition after al-Kharāʾiṭī. Al-Ṭabarānī (d. 360/971), who, according to Jonathan Brown, 'took pride in gathering rare hadiths found nowhere else',[56] quotes a hadith with a similar content as the one attributed to ʿAlī ibn Abī Ṭālib by al-Kulaynī, except it starts with Muhammad bragging over his own potency:

> I was given the strength of forty men in sexual intercourse while every believer has been given the strength of ten. Sexual appetite was divided in ten parts; nine was given to women, one single part to men. If they were not given bashfulness together with appetite, every man would have nine lustful women.[57]

At the same time as the hadith about women's enormous libido was transmitted by hadith scholars, a similar saying was part of an erotic story attributed to a Persian woman called Bunyāndukht; or rather, Bunyāndukht was the protagonist of a book with this title. The book is mentioned in *Fihrist* by Ibn al-Nadīm, where she appears together with a man, Bunyānnafs and another woman, Bahrāmdukht; all three are titles of erotic stories. The titles hint at a Persian origin, and, consequently, they are arranged under the heading 'Titles of Books composed about Coitus, Persian, Indian, Greek, and Arabic, in the form of stimulating discourse.'[58] Bunyāndukht is one of the titles mentioned here that are cited extensively in *Jawāmiʿ al-Ladhdha*. Ibn al-Nadīm died 385/995 or 388/998, so we know that the story about Bunyāndukht circulated at this time, but it might of course be older as the book on Burjān and Ḥabāḥib with a similar content was written one century earlier at the court of al-Mutawakkil.

Bunyāndukht was a wise woman and sex expert, like Burjān and Ḥabāḥib, and people came to her and asked her questions about sex. When asked why women are inclined to desire men other than their husbands and love them with stronger passion, her explanation is similar to the hadith on women's nine shares of *shahwa* but from another religious context, apparently Zoroastrian. She answered that that is the plan of 'the creator of sexual appetite' (*khāliq al-shahwa*) and that it is 'a great benefit'.[59] In this way, women's great *shahwa* is understandable; it is the foundation for producing new generations. Bunyāndukht reminds the questioner that without desire for intercourse, this earth would not be populated. Then the 'holder of power over carnal desire' (*sulṭān al-ghilma*[60]) made women's appetite so strong that a woman is inclined to desire someone else than her husband as he does not care if the creation is ruined by passion. After this allusion to divergence between the creator of *shahwa* and the holder of power over *ghilma*, Bunyāndukht continues: '*Shahwa* is divided into eleven parts. Of these, humans were given ten parts and animals one. Then the ten parts were divided; women got nine parts and men one part.' When a man finds a woman submissive and tender, Bunyāndukht explains, it turns him on and, finding the woman desirable, his lust (*ghilma*) is aroused and his *shahwa* ignited. If a man (who has much less appetite than women) still can be so easily aroused by a woman, it is no wonder that women can find strange men desirable.

Bunyāndukht illustrates her statement with an anecdote about a man who brought his wife to a judge and claimed that she was mad – apparently, he wanted to have the marriage annulled. The judge asked him what was wrong about her, and he answered: 'She faints when I have intercourse with her so that I believe she has died.' The judge answered: 'You are not worthy of this woman.' The reason behind the judge's critical assessment of the husband is implicit; a wife who enjoys intercourse to the degree that she faints is desirable. The opposite, a man who faints when he reaches climax, is not heard of, and for this reason, ʿAlī ibn Naṣr remarks, people believe that women have stronger appetite than men have. He objects to this belief, however, because as far as he knew, very few women faint under this condition.[61] Instead, men are more excited and passionate during intercourse. This is one of the instances when the author of *Jawāmiʿ al-Ladhdha* explicitly or implicitly criticizes the notion of the hypersexual woman; this notion is explained as a male erotic dream. ʿAlī ibn Naṣr has investigated the case, he tells us, and has not come across one single man who is not wishing for a woman who is so passionate that she faints when she reaches climax. Perhaps he is right, because this kind of woman was even given a name in Arabic; she is a *rabūkh*.[62]

Another citation from Bunyāndukht is more cynical, but although it borders on misogyny it should rather be read through the eyes of 'sexual comedy' (see Chapter 5). When Bunyāndukht is asked the by now familiar question who has more *shahwa*, men or women, she answers:

> We, women, value sexual intercourse so much and have so strong desire that when God had created us and let us choose between eternity and sex, we chose sex. We feel the greatest pleasure from intercourse and enjoy its taste. Men get just a nibble of it, just as if someone dips his finger in honey and then licks it; it is the mouth that feels the sweet taste of the honey, not the finger.[63]

This and similar allegations can be regarded as offensive and distasteful, which is precisely the comical point of *mujūn*; the offensive and distasteful is thought to be humorous. Bawdy humour reduces both sexes to their bodily functions and impulses, even if women are the main targets in these examples.

Bunyāndukht maintains that *shahwa* is part of a divine plan for the best of humankind. Ibn Naṣr expresses a similar view in the introduction to *Jawāmiʿ al-Ladhdha* where he explains women's greater *shahwa* within a religious discourse; it is part of God's plan for procreation. God used *nikāḥ*, 'marital, i.e. legal sexual intercourse', for breeding the animal population and populating the world with worshippers. Then, he gave women a greater share of *shahwa* so as to make them compliant with men's sexual advances and, by their consent, produce offspring.[64] Ibn Naṣr's introduction also acknowledges Galen's explanation of the motivation behind the procreative organs, and is similar to other Islamic physicians' introductions, but women's greater share of *shahwa* is his own addition.[65]

## Women's expertise in the *Encyclopaedia of Pleasure*

There is no book in the Arabic erotic tradition that contains so many poems and sayings attributed to women as *Jawāmiʿ al-Ladhdha*. In this, it reflects not only the available books at the time of the author, but also the expectations of the readers. Many of the women in *Jawāmiʿ al-Ladhdha* are fictional characters, not historical personalities, yet, the focus is on female experience, and women (fictional or not) are considered experts on their own sexuality. Later books, also those that to some degree rely on *Jawāmiʿ al-Ladhdha*, such as *Kitāb al-Wishāḥ fī Fawāʾiḍ al-Nikāḥ* by al-Suyūṭī, only contain a fraction of this material and female experience plays a minor role in these books. Many of their examples are instead taken from the body of anecdotes about early Umayyad women and Abbasid slave courtesans that lived on for centuries. None of them cite Bunyāndukht and only a few refer to Burjān and Ḥabāḥib.

In the books of Burjān and Ḥabāḥib and Bunyāndukht, the female protagonists are sex advisors and experts, and at least Bunyāndukht retells stories that could have been based on female experience. In both cases, however, women are sometimes depicted as having an enormous libido, which, at least implicitly, is connected to a misogynist discourse, according to which women's assumed imperfect physiology generates moral and intellectual defects. This is especially true for the story about Burjān and Ḥabāḥib, which, apparently, was written in the tradition of sexual comedy (see Chapter 5). This does not necessarily mean that they are representations of female defectiveness, rather, they are there to stimulate the readers' erotic fantasies. The hypersexual woman is presented as a male erotic dream although the border to misogyny is not sharp.

Even though Abū Ḥassān al-Namlī seem to have had some medical knowledge and Burjān and Ḥabāḥib are portrayed as medical experts, his book is directed to readers who want to be amused rather than educated. It is written as a mock mirror for princes, but instead of being instructed about rule and good manners, the king acquires knowledge about women and sex. The two wise, and apparently, elderly women inform him about female desire and how it is expressed by different types of women; each of which has a name that the king is encouraged to study. He also learns how to measure women's sexual appetite based on the size of their vaginas and other characteristics.

Furthermore, Burjān and Ḥabāḥib teach the king how to be beloved by women. Although women dislike bad-mannered, stingy and poor men, according to these experts, good manners are not a requirement for gaining their love. Instead, women's love is proportional to the size of the male member and the most effective way of winning their heart is simultaneous orgasm. This is ʿAlī ibn Naṣr's message throughout *Jawāmiʿ al-Ladhdha*, and it is possible that he edited the story written by al-Mutawakkil's courtier Abū Ḥassān al-Namlī, and added his own ideas about the power of seed. If not, the idea that simultaneous orgasm is crucial, not only for procreation but also for love, evidently circulated long before ʿAlī ibn Naṣr wrote *Jawāmiʿ al-Ladhdha*.

The setting of the story about Bunyāndukht is, like Burjān and Ḥabāḥib, a question and answer session. Various anonymous people ask her questions and her expertise comprises topics such as the physiognomy of sexually potent men and the difference between women's and men's *shahwa*. In a few cases, her answer borders on misogyny, as seen above; in others, she is an advocate of women's agency. She addresses women directly, for example, when she gives advice to women 'who want to gain pleasure from having intercourse with a young man'. These women, she continues, must do the following things, after which she gives detailed advice of seductive conduct, personal hygiene, perfume, and the preparation of aphrodisiacs.[66] Everything is on the woman's terms. Her desire is the prerequisite for the seduction to take place to begin with, and she is the one who chooses the man with whom she wants to have sex.[67] Although the advice turns into soft pornography, stimulation is not necessarily its only purpose. The setting is upper class, the perfume and clothes are exclusive and the woman sophisticated, which indicates that the protagonist could be a upper-class courtesan. It is assumed that women know how to prepare and apply cosmetics, fragrant oils and aphrodisiacs. This belongs to the sphere of Persian wisdom, according to the author of *Jawāmiʿ al-Ladhdha*, which is associated with refinement and sophistication. Bunyāndukht is called *al-Fārisiyya* (the Persian woman) and the story is included in a chapter entitled *Fatāwā al-Bāh*, as an example of the words of Persian experts on sexual techniques (*kalām al-furs al-ʿulamāʾ bi-ṣināʿat al-bāh*).[68] The soft pornography is in line with the title of the section in *Fihrist* where Bunyāndukht is mentioned – titillating stories (*al-ḥadīth al-mushbiq*) – but, as the focus of the erotic description is female pleasure, it is possible that it was written for a female audience. It seems to be an extract from a courtesan's handbook on how to seduce men, but the purpose of the seduction is explicitly that of pure pleasure, not monetary or other rewards.

In a more cynical response, Bunyāndukht describes how a woman can get the best out of her husband. When someone asks her how a woman should behave towards her husband, she answers: 'There are three types of husbands, the spouse (*zawj*), the master of the house (*rabb bayt*) and the wittol (*dayyūth*).' Of these men, only the spouse is worthy of sincere love, respect and loyalty from his wife, while the wife is free to take advantage of the husband who is too lenient and to dupe the one who is too strict.[69]

In another long and more explicitly pornographic narrative, Bunyāndukht tries to persuade a mother to let her daughter have sex with the man she loves. The account begins with a girl *(jāriya*[70]) who comes to Bunyāndukht and complains about her strict mother, who has no sympathy for her, despite her suffering from unfulfilled desire.[71] The girl's desire is so strong that she contemplates killing her mother if she will not allow her to be with the object of her desire. Bunyāndukht feels sympathy for the girl, and reproves her mother for restraining her daughter, who she likens to a mare who should be allowed to roam freely in the meadows. She reminds the mother that she was once a young woman like her daughter and desired young men like her. Bunyāndukht then visualizes an encounter the mother once had with a young man and describes their intercourse in detail with explicit words. The driving force in this act is the mother's words, quoted by Bunyāndukht to make her remember how much she once wanted sex and how much she enjoyed it. Her words are dirty and gratifying at the same time, sometimes tender, sometimes violent, following the rhythm of the intercourse. She eulogizes her beloved's penis in order to arouse and stimulate him, which will make him proceed in a way that is stimulating for her.

The setting of this narrative is intriguing: an elderly or middle-aged woman, Bunyāndukht, interprets the desire of a young girl by visualizing her mother's sex life. The visualization is pornographic, as the sexual act is described in detail, but it is also somewhat empowering. The reader of this pornographic story is supposed to find women's desire and erotic fantasies arousing. For possible female readers, even though the strength of the daughter's desire is connected to the notion of women's defective nature, the story can be read as an account of female experience and solidarity between generations.

Bunyādukht's erotic narratives display luxury, perfume, fine clothing and polite behaviour, all alluding to Persian refinement. This refinement is explicitly contrasted to the wisdom of the old Arabs (*al-qudamā'*) and the Bedouins, which is represented by another woman, Ḥubbā al-Madīniyya, a famous Umayyad woman from Medina. By the time of the early Abbasids, she had become the subject of humorous anecdotes, where she talks about her sexual appetite to her daughters and gives advice to her son and his friends as well as the young women of Medina (see Chapter 5). In *Jawāmiʿ al-Ladhdha*, Ḥubbā stands for tradition, and perhaps that is why she is an ardent defender of heterosexuality against lesbianism which she accuses the slave-girls in Medina of being involved in.[72] She is an expert on women's favourite men, anal heterosexual intercourse and the importance of snoring *(nakhīr)* and sighing (*zafīr*) during intercourse, which she describes as part of a woman's *ghunj*, lustful and coquettish behaviour.[73] This is sought-after in women, ʿAlī ibn Naṣr remarks, and some commentators even described the Houris of Paradise as possessing *ghunj*.

The motif of Ḥubbā's expertise in lascivious sounds is derived from the anecdotes that were made famous by al-Jāḥiẓ and Ibn Abī Ṭāhir Ṭayfūr mentioned in Chapter 5. It fits in well with the notion of the insatiable woman in *Jawāmiʿ al-Ladhdha*.[74] Here, Ḥubbā figures in a long, explicit narrative in which she give advice to her daughter before she escorts her to her husband on the wedding night.[75] She instructs her daughter to use dirty language and initiate the act by showing her husband what she wants him to do with her. After she has instructed her daughter, she goes to her son-in-law and instructs him how to please his wife and enjoy himself. The mother who instructs her daughter and son-in-law became a popular frame for erotic stories, and occur in different versions for centuries; in one variant, the mother instructs her son how to please his wife. In *Jawāmiʿ al-Ladhdha* the mother is Ḥubbā, who was extensively used by Ibn Naṣr's contemporaries for this type of female character. Together with Bunyāndukth, she is an advocate for female agency in sex; both emphasize the importance of manifest desire, and instruct young women to show the man what they want (or what they are expected to want). Women are encouraged to display *ghunj*, a term that includes lustful sounds and movement during intercourse.

As pornographic accounts, the erotic stories in *Jawāmiʿ al-Ladhdha* presuppose readers who are aroused by women who display desire and take command. As accounts of women's agency, however, they are slightly different. Whereas Bunyāndukht emphasizes that the goal is the woman's own pleasure, Ḥubbā seems more concerned about her daughter's relationship with her husband. Both Ḥubbā's and Bunyāndukht's narrations are products of elderly women's erotic imagination, they visualize other women's sexual encounters. Bunyāndukht fantasizes about 'the mother's' sex life when she was young and Ḥubbā imagines the coming sex life of her daughter. As narrators, although their narratives are fictional, they may well express their own wishes and desires. They are at the same time in a pact with the male readers, who are supposed to be stimulated by stories about women with great libidos.

## Conclusion: Women in an erotic compendium

The *Jawāmiʿ al-Ladhdha* (*Encyclopaedia of Pleasure*) is the oldest extant erotic compendium and sex manual in Arabic and was probably written towards the end of the tenth century. Although its origin is unknown, it relies on sources translated to or written in Arabic in the third/ninth and perhaps fourth/tenth centuries. It confirms that Indian erotology was transmitted into Arabic in the third/ninth century, as was other erotic writings, some of them perhaps Persian. It reveals the content of books mentioned by Ibn al-Nadīm in *Fihrist*, a number of which were composed at the court of al-Mutawakkil. The author of *Jawāmiʿ al-Ladhdha* presents erotology in an Islamic context; he uses a legal vocabulary and confirms his theses with Islamic authorities, both from Sunni and Shiʿi traditions.

*Jawāmiʿ al-Ladhdha* is informed by contemporary medical theory and adopts the notion of female seed and the importance of orgasm, but the author, ʿAlī ibn Naṣr, takes the idea one-step further. He claims that the mixing of semen is pivotal, not for reproduction, which he says nothing about, but for love and affection, which are the outcomes of mutual satisfaction. Just as in medical theory, harmony is what one should strive for, but even here, harmony turns out to be, or at least leads to, intense pleasure. ʿAlī ibn Naṣr relies on obscure sources that confirm his idea of love and harmony and presents somewhat bizarre theories, such as the compatibility of the female and male sperm based on their taste, which he attributes to Aretaeus, who also maintained that divergences of movements during intercourse could cause hatred and misery in a relationship.

The bibliographic encyclopaedia *Fihrist* by Ibn al-Nadīm mentions several erotic stories with female protagonists, some of which are quoted in *Jawāmiʿ al-Ladhdha*. The favourite female character in stories that were popular in the third/ninth and fourth/tenth was a woman, young or old, with strong libido and entirely driven by sexual desire. She talks explicitly about her sex-life and sexual preferences, or describes those of other women. The hypersexual woman is an erotic fantasy but sometimes also a scholarly construction, related to the notion of female defectiveness in medical theory and natural philosophy. Nevertheless, the author occasionally challenges this representation on empirical grounds: as when he states that women are different just as men are and that sexual appetite differs between individuals, that women are different, just as men are, and some have more appetite, others less. The erotic compendia relies on diverse and sometimes conflicting sources, and it is therefore difficult to distinguish a single worldview or a single notion of female sexuality. However, an 'empirical track' runs through the book, and this track is always pragmatic. Eventually the theories have no practical bearing in the erotic compendium. They are conflicting and often obscure and seem to display sophisticated knowledge as a way for the refined readers to distinguish themselves from the commoners. The world in which ʿAlī ibn Naṣr lived was highly hierarchical, and so was the worldview of the intellectual discourses he related to, something that naturally affected his view of class and gender.

ʿAlī ibn Naṣr has a distinct message that he maintains all through the book: sexual intercourse is a mutual act and the cultured man who wants to enjoy it must behave well towards women and be sure that they get pleasure from it. He explicitly addresses men who want to be sophisticated and distinguish themselves from the common people, and sophisticated men should be beloved by women, regardless of their supposed defective nature. Only when men know how to please women are they truly refined and the highest pleasure is reached when the female partner is satisfied.

# 3

# Women and Sexual Rights

In the introduction to the chapter on slave concubinage in *Jawāmiʿ al-Ladhdha*, ʿAlī ibn Naṣr addresses a critical question. After having stated that 'anything in excess is bad, except for women', which is proven by the fact that God has permitted men to be intimate with slave concubines, he presents a possible objection:

> People may be eager to know why men are allowed to have intercourse with their female slaves when women are not allowed the same. Likewise, why is it allowed for a man to have intercourse with four wives, when a woman is not allowed to have intercourse with two men or with her slave, although she needs it more, considering that women have nine shares of sexual appetite whereas men only have one share?[1]

There is a rational reason for this discrimination, he continues:

> Even if a man has intercourse with one hundred females, lineage will not be corrupt, heritage will not be mixed up and juridical decisions concerning kinship will not be confused. Then again, if one woman has intercourse with two men at the same time, it would not be possible to know the father of the child, and thus lineage becomes corrupt as well as the heritage.

Ibn Naṣr's justification exposes the contradiction between a fundamental notion underpinning his erotic encyclopaedia, namely the importance of female sexual gratification, and legal jurisdiction, which granted men legal access to multiple women and enhanced male privileges. He is aware of these contradictions and expects objections from his audience. The erotic stories in his book presuppose that women have more sexual appetite than men have, something that he disputes himself on empirical grounds, but which his audience may not forget. At the same time, the core of his sexual ethics is the intimate meeting between one man and one woman, before which the man has to prepare greatly in order to achieve the goal – simultaneous orgasm – which 'secures love and makes it endure'. In theory, a man is perhaps able to satisfy an unlimited number of women, but hardly in practice. Many women would instead risk going mad and become sick out of abstinence, in line with medical and erotic discourse.

Formulating the legal principles, early jurists considered the two conditions in Ibn Naṣr's discussion above. First, that the Qur'an gave men the right to marry four wives and keep slave concubines; and second, that 'lineage' may be corrupted if women have sexual access to more than one man at the same time, which would be detrimental to society. Therefore, they ask women to give up their right to sexual autonomy to their husbands, and focus instead on the sexual rights and pleasure of men. This tendency in Islamic writings from the early medieval period is discussed in this chapter regarding the notion of sexual availability in marriage, exemplified with exegesis of verse 2:223 in the Qur'an.

As we have seen in the two previous chapters, ideas about female sexuality were not uniform and this is reflected by a certain ambiguity in the body of recognized Islamic texts. Some accounts, considered Prophetic traditions by a number of scholars, maintain that women have much more sexual appetite than men have, and others emphasise men's moral duty to please their wives. However, the jurists chose to largely disregard this moral duty when they outlined the legal marriage system and divided men's and women's conjugal rights and duties. As Prophetic hadiths developed into an important legal source in the course of the third/ninth century and fully implemented as Sunna and the second most important source, after the Qur'an, during the fourth/tenth century, some hadiths were elevated that gave explicit priority to men's privileges in general, and sexual needs in particular.[2]

The aim of this chapter is not to examine the legal stances or theological understandings of female sexuality in the early medieval Muslim society. The focus is instead on the development of certain themes concerning female sexuality in Islamic writings that interconnect with other disciplines and therefore with the cultural and intellectual environment at large. The question is how the scholarly community understood certain traditions, regardless if these traditions were considered authentic by authoritative scholarship. Fabricated hadiths might reflect ideas current in the early Abbasid society, but so could hadiths that were considered authentic, not the least as they were used for enforcing certain ideals.

## Female sexuality and marriage

Male-dominated marriages were not an invention by Islam; they were the norm in all written legal systems in the region before the Islamic caliphate, as well as in the societies surrounding it, even though the exact arrangement of conjugal relations differed between legal systems. In the Qur'an the word for marriage, *nikāḥ*, originally signifying sexual intercourse, implies a marriage with a marriage contract, which became the prerequisite for an Islamic marriage.[3] A basic marriage regulation was already outlined in the Qur'an, and these rules were probably implemented in the Muslim community from the beginning. The principles for a more elaborate marriage system were formulated during the legal discussions that ended with the completion of the Islamic law in the middle of the fourth/tenth century.[4] In this system, the payment of a marriage gift gave men authority (*milk*) over the wife's sexual availability.[5] The Arabic word *milk* is one of many legal terms in marriage law taken from the semantic field of commercial transactions; it means ownership and is likewise used for ownership of slaves. It was the *milk* over a woman that made sex with her lawful, whether she was a wife or a slave concubine. In *Marriage and Slavery in Early Islam*, Kecia Ali uncovers the consistent exploitation of the analogy between marriage and slavery during the formative era of three schools of law: Māliki, Hanafī and Shāfiʿī. The jurists did not always agree and some interpretations gave somewhat more rights to women than others, yet they were all governed by the same central norm and used the same analogy to slavery.

In *Sexual Violation in Islamic Law*, Hina Azam elaborates on the notion of women's sexuality as a commodity that can be sold and bought, in connection with attitudes to sexual violation. She identifies two conceptions of sexuality that were current in the Late Antiquity Near East and influenced Islamic legal writers. The first, the 'proprietary approach', was embraced by many ancient societies. In this conception, a woman's sexuality is regarded as a commodity, belonging to the male kin or husband. When a woman was married off, the groom typically paid a bridewealth to her father or other male kin. Bridewealth was the price for her sexual, and thereby reproductive, availability. According to the second conception, the 'theocentric approach', sexuality is governed by divine law. Each individual, regardless of gender, is a moral agent accountable to God for her or his actions. Consequently, the woman, not her kin, is also the 'owner' of her sexuality, as she is accountable to God for what she does with it. The theocentric conception came to the Near East with the monotheistic religions, especially Christianity, and was embraced by Islam. In the Qur'an, bridewealth is instead understood as a compensation for the rights of having sexual intercourse and this compensation should be paid to the woman herself.[6] According to Harald Motzki, this is an innovation brought into the region by Islam. A woman's sexual capacity is her own property and, accordingly, the bridewealth becomes her property and she has the sole right of disposal of it.

In Late Antiquity Arabia sexual violation of women was predominantly treated as a property crime. When Islam came with the theocentric perspective, it led to a reframing of sexuality. The proprietary approach regarded a woman's sexuality as property, as it could be exchanged with money in marriage or sale transactions, and sexual violation was therefore liable to monetary penalties. The penalty was not paid to the woman herself, however; as her sexual availability belonged to her father or other male kin, it was he who received the compensation.[7] Furthermore, the punishment was unrelated to the woman's consent. A sexual relation before marriage was seen as a sexual violation, regardless of if she went into it willingly. The crime was a crime against the 'owner' of her sexuality, her father or close male relative. The theocentric ethics instead regarded sexual violence as a violation against God. It divided between licit and illicit sex, and sexual violence was only punished if it occurred in illicit relations.[8]

As an example of the 'theocentric reframing of sexuality' in early Islam, Azam describes the attitude to sexual violation. In the main, early Islamic jurists adopted the theocentric ethics, as the attitudes towards sexual violation changed from regarding it as primarily a usurpation to primarily a violation against God. However, the proprietary sexual ethics was not altogether discarded, as we have seen in the example of the bridewealth. The proprietary sexual ethics was still alive, not the least noticable in the practices of marriage and slave concubinage.[9] There was an ambiguity in the emerging Islamic law in regard to free women, as their sexual availability was seen as a commodity at the same time as they were regarded as individual moral subjects. As a woman cannot contract a marriage herself, her father or another close male relative must be her guardian and marry her off. If she is a virgin, her consent is not needed, which means that her father can legally marry her off against her will. Thus, as expressed by Ali, 'sexual experience gave the bride a voice'.[10]

The practice of *mahr* (marriage gift) is an indication of the survival of the proprietary sexual ethics, as it is a transaction of a woman's sexual capacity, even if the price is paid to the bride and not her kin. A monetary compensation to the wife gives the husband exclusive right to her sexual capacity and the progeny. Furthermore, Ali points out that the exchange of monetary compensation for the wife's sexual capacity does not end with the *mahr*. The husband's maintenance of his wife during marriage – paying for food, clothes, and other needs in accordance with her social standing – is obligatory only as long as she is sexually available to him.[11] Ali shows that for these early jurists maintenance was linked to the wife's sexual availability, that is, her willingness to submit to sex if the husband so wished. For example, the wife was not obliged to do household chores and the husband could not withdraw their maintenance if she refused.

The proprietary conception of female sexuality is most obvious in regard to female slaves, as ownership gave men the legal right to have intercourse with them, as long as they were not married. Yet, even in the case of marriage the owner had some propriety rights to the female slave's sexual capacity, as the owner had the right to marry off a slave without her consent. Moreover, the *mahr* became the property of the owner, not the slave.[12] The owner also had property rights to any child that was born in the marriage, regardless if the father was a slave or not. The male slave had somewhat more rights than the female slave: they were not obliged to consent to sexual activities with their owners and they had the right to divorce their wives. Early on, Islamic authorities gave owners the right to dissolve their slaves' marriages, but in the ninth century, reflecting the general strengthening of male conjugal authority, the consensus was that divorce (*ṭalāq*) was the exclusive right of the husband, slave or free.[13] The owner of the female slave received the monetary compensation, however, as was the case with the *mahr*. The female slave could not contract the wife-initiated divorce (*khul*ʿ) that was otherwise possible for women in certain circumstances. The *khul*ʿ divorce was instead contracted by the owner, who also received the monetary compensation.[14]

Islamic jurists considered sexual intercourse outside marriage or concubinage (*zinā*) a transgression against the boundaries (*ḥudūd*) set by God, or a transgression against the society as a whole, as it blurs the patrilineal descent and therefore creates social chaos.[15] Children born from *zinā* unions have no one to inherit, and their patrilineal *maḥārim*, the relatives who are forbidden for them to marry, are not known. The jurists classified *zinā* as a *ḥadd* crime, which meant it is a violation against God and that offenders should be subjugated to corporal punishment. Corporal punishment was meant to be both a redemption for the transgression of the sacred boundaries and a purification for the offender.[16] The Qurʾan specifies different punishments for this transgression, in one sūra (4:15), women who commit *zinā* are to be confined to their houses until death, whereas another sūra (4:16) stipulates a lighter punishment, which is revoked if the offenders repent. According to most interpreters, these verses were abrogated by Qurʾan 24:2, which orders that offenders are punished with one hundred lashes, if there are four approved witnesses. Later jurists established that this rule applied only to individuals who have never been married. Based on hadiths, they fixed a much more severe punishment for married or previously married individuals, namely stoning to death.

By the time of al-Bukhārī (256/870), the allotment was clear: flogging for unmarried and death by stoning for married and previously married offenders; slaves should receive a lighter punishment.[17] The requirement of four witnesses approved for testimony and legal protection against false accusations, made the realization of the punishment for adultery difficult. These witnesses had to be men, although Shiʿi jurists accepted female witnesses.[18] Scholars tried in different ways to propose behaviour that would minimize the risks of engaging in illicit sex. Wives were restricted from going out and had, ideally, few chances to do so, but men were subjected to many temptations: prostitution, for example, and engaging themselves in relations with slaves of both genders.[19] It is against that background that we can understand the appeal to wives to be sexually attractive and making efforts to seduce their husbands.

## Men's rights, women's duties

When jurists developed the legal foundations for marriage in the second/eighth and third/ninth centuries, they stipulated that the husband has almost unconditional right to sex and linked the wife's right to maintenance to her sexual availability. According to them, the husband has right to sex whenever he wishes; that is part of his marital rights and the wife is legally prohibited from rejecting him or doing anything that prevents sexual intercourse, such as performing the voluntary fast.[20]

Sexual compliance hence became an essential component of female marital obedience, together with the prohibition to leave the house without the husband's permission. The husband's sexual claim on his wife was proved by Prophetic traditions; she has to submit to him sexually whatever she is doing, even if it demands a great effort on her part. The examples of the efforts the wife has to undertake, if her husband orders her to, range from the mundane – she has to agree to sex even if she stands at the oven – to the imaginary – she has to obey if the husband commands her to travel from a red mountain to a black mountain, and then back again from the black mountain to the red mountain.[21] Evoking the Bedouin past, a common hadith that is quoted by Sunni as well as Shiʿi authorities asserts that a wife has to submit to her husband's sexual demands even if she is sitting on a camel's saddle.[22]

Sexual availability was not only a wife's conjugal duty, it was a religious obligation and part of her religious practice according to both Sunni and Shiʿi scholars. Several hadiths collections in the third/ninth and fourth/tenth centuries stress that women's marital obedience is commanded by God, which means that disobedience against the husband is a sin against God. In the Shiʿi collection *Kāfī*, al-Kulaynī quotes a hadith attributed to Jaʿfar al-Ṣādiq about a man who forbad his wife to visit her dying father and to attend his funeral. The Prophet urged her to obey her husband and stay in his house, after which both the obedient woman and her father will be awarded by God.[23] If the wife refuses to come to her husband's bed, she will be cursed by the angels as long as her husband is angry with her.[24] In a variant, her prayer will not count as long as her husband is angry with her.[25] Implicitly, this refers to a woman's willing submission to her husband, as he had the right to force her to have sexual intercourse. Paradise is promised to women whose husbands are pleased with them and hell to those who refuse their husbands. Consequently, the husband plays the decisive role for where his wife will end up after death – heaven or hell.

What is more, jurists maintained that men have not only the right to have sex with their wives whenever they wish, they also had the right to pleasure. The legal term for the husband's sexual claim on his wife is *istimtāʿ*, meaning 'enjoyment', and was used specifically for sexual enjoyment.[26] The sexual claim on the wife could also be phrased *istimtāʿ bihā*, meaning to 'derive pleasure from her'. Implicit in this legal term is the husband's right to enjoy her the way that gives him pleasure. Women are therefore instructed to make an effort to enhance their husband's pleasure and make him feel beloved. Among men's rights, al-Kulaynī specifies, on the authority of Jaʿfar al-Ṣādiq, is women's duty to use pleasant perfume and put on their most beautiful clothes and finery. They should make sure that they appear before their husbands in this condition early in the morning as well as late in the evening.[27] Conversely, a woman should not make herself beautiful for a man other than her husband. If she does so, al-Kulaynī warns, her prayer will not count until she cleanses herself and performs the full-body ritual purification.[28]

Men were allowed to force themselves on their wives if the wives refused to have sex with them.[29] Ideally, however, a woman should not only submit to her husband and obey him, she should also do it willingly. Whether this was a possible claim or not was debated. For example, Muhammad ibn Jarīr al-Ṭabarī (d. 310/923) argued that men cannot command their wives to love them, even if they wish; women are only legally bound to obey them.[30]

## Your women are a tillage for you: the interpretation of Qurʾan 2:223

Wives' submission to their husbands' sexual demands became a topic in scholars' interpretations of the first part of Qurʾan 2:223: *nisāʾukum ḥarthun lakum fa-ʾtū ḥarthakum ʾannā shiʾtum*. In modern English translation, this sūra is rendered 'Your wives are as a tilth unto you; so approach your tilth when or how ye will'

(Yusuf Ali) and 'Your wives are as fields for you. You may enter your fields from any place you want' (Muhammad Sarwar). The verse, according to most Qur'an interpreters, granted men the right to have sex with their wives not only when but also *how* they wished. Most of them agreed that there are limits to how men can have intercourse with their wives, but these limits have nothing to do with the wives' possible objections. Instead, they argued that only vaginal sex is allowed, as anal sex is against the notion *ḥarth*, which means that the wives are 'the place for sowing', and the sowing in this case does not lead to children.

The early Qur'an exegesis (*tafsīr*) by Muqātil ibn Sulaymān (d. 150/767) offers an explanation of the origin of this verse that, in a slightly different form, reappeared in many later exegeses.[31] In Muqātil's interpretation, the Jews' suspicion against the customs of the new inhabitants in Yathrib was the motif behind the revelation of verse 2:223. When the Muslim emigrants (*muhājirūn*) settled down in Medina, the Jews in Medina told them that the only permitted sexual position is the man-on-top position with the woman lying on her back, maintaining that God's book forbids all other ways of having intercourse. The Muslims went to Muḥammad complaining, as they were used to having more freedom in this matter. Then came the revelation of this verse and gave them permission to have vaginal sex the way they wished. Muqātil's interpretation is above all a polemic against the Jews, and he positions Islam as a more sex-positive religion than Judaism, with easier rules for conjugal relations – at least for men.[32]

In the somewhat later *tafsīr* by the Yemenite scholar ʿAbd al-Razzāq al-Ṣanʿānī (d. 211/827), a similar origin is outlined, with the difference that the Jews did not try to forbid the Muslims to use a bigger variation of sexual positions; instead they attempted to frighten them by spreading the superstition that it makes the offspring cross-eyed.[33] A hadith claiming that the verse was revealed because the Jews in Medina spread the superstition that unconventional sex – or vaginal sex from behind – made the offspring cross-eyed was considered sound by the authoritative Sunni hadith scholars, al-Bukhārī, Muslim (d. 261/875), al-Tirmidhī (d. 279/892), Ibn Māja (d. 273/887), Abū Dāwūd (d. 275/888) and al-Nasāʾī (d. 303/915).[34] ʿAbd al-Razzāq also introduced a variant that reappears frequently in later exegesis. According to this version, the Prophet Muhammad's wife Umm Salama was involved in the revelation of Q 2:223 and Ḥafṣa bint ʿAbd al-Raḥmān spread the word. The verse was revealed after Umm Salama had asked the Prophet if it was permissible for a man to have intercourse with his wife when she is prostrating.[35]

The explanations of the revelation of verse 2:223 given in the two early Qur'an exegeses are repeated in hadith collections and *tafsīrs* from the middle of the third/ninth century onwards. At this time, an important addition was introduced that became the perhaps most wide-spread account, namely that the authority to choose sex position was given to men after their wives had refused to consent to their sexual wishes. This explanation is told on the authority of Ibn ʿAbbās who heard it from Ibn ʿUmar, and it circulated in some variants.[36] According to the major version, the people of the book allowed only the traditional sex position, which was the man on top position. As the Jews were respected by the polytheist clans living in Yathrib/Medina because of their learning, they had been able to influence them in this direction. When the *muhājirūn*, who were used to 'enjoying their women' in various ways, face-to-face or from behind, entered Medina, they settled down among people who were more conventional in their sexual behaviour. Hence, when one of the *muhājirūn* married a woman from Medina and attempted to have sex with his new wife the way he wanted, she refused. She told her new husband to approach her the conventional way or keep away from her. The Prophet heard about the woman's refusal, and the verse was revealed to him, giving all Muslim men full authority to choose sex position regardless of their wives' wishes. Consequently, the divine revelation in these interpretations gives men explicit right to have sex with their wives the way they want, even against their wives' will.

Another version of this explanation is fused with the two explanations given in ʿAbd al-Razzāq's *tafsīr*, one referring to the Jew's superstition and the other tracing the origin to a question from Muhammad's wife Umm Salama. In this version, Ḥafṣa narrates that she heard from Umm Salama that the inhabitants in Medina (the *anṣār*) never practiced sex from behind with the woman kneeling down before the Muslims came, as they were afraid their offspring would become cross-eyed, which the Jews claimed. When the *muhājirūn* settled down in Medina and married women from *anṣār,* they tried to have sex with their new wives this way. One woman refused to obey her husband, and said, 'I will not do this before you ask God's Messenger about it.' She went to Umm Salama and told her about the matter and Umm Salama, in turn, asked the Prophet, who came and recited the verse to her.[37] The implication of this hadith is that the wife was motivated by piety; she would not obey if her husband asked her something sinful, yet the consequence is the same: women have to agree to their husbands' sexual demands.

The verse was vividly discussed in later *tafsīr* as already around the year 900, al-Ṭabarī quoted thirty-two hadiths and reports about the first part of the verse, *nisāʾukum ḥarthun lakum fa-ʾtū ḥarthakum ʾannā shiʾtum,* and several of them involve reluctant wives. In one hadith attributed to Ibn ʿAbbās, feminine plural is used, indicating that *all* women from Medina who were married to Qurashites from Mecca refused their husbands' sexual demands.[38] Al-Ṭabarī reports an important discussion with consequences for conjugal relations about the meaning of *ʾannā shiʾtum*; opinions differed as to whether it connotes 'when you want' or 'how you want'. The first, 'when you want' was generally recognized by legal scholars, but the second, 'how you want', was possibly more controversial. Those who prefer the interpretation of *ʾannā* as 'how' are often concerned about proving that 'how they want' does not include anal sex. The majority interpretation was that the word *ḥarth*, which is commonly interpreted as 'sowing place', indicates that only vaginal sex is allowed, as this is where the human seed is placed. The interpretation of the verse has further implications than condoning or prohibiting anal sex. It concluded that men have not only the right to satisfy their sex drive, but also to perform the act the way that is most gratifying for them (except for anal sex, according to some): that is, the right to pleasure. Women have to submit to their husbands and they have to agree to intimate acts that they may not like. For the exegetes, women's feelings were irrelevant.

Qur'an interpretations with alternative theological outlooks do not offer significantly different explanations for this verse. The ʿIbāḍī exegesis by the North African Hūd ibn Muḥakkam (d. towards the end of the 3rd/9th century), is chiefly interested in the prohibition of anal sex and so are the Shiʿi exegeses by al-ʿAyyāshī (d. *c.* 320/932) and al-Qummī (d. end of 4th/10th century).[39] Al-ʿAyyāshī quotes imam ʿAlī al-Riḍā censuring anal sex for the harm it could cause women. When he was asked about a man who had anal sex with his slave concubine, he criticized the practice with the words. 'the woman is a doll (*luʿba*), she should not be harmed'.[40] This is actually the only interpretation I have found that considers women's feelings; here the reason why anal sex is not permitted is not that it does not 'sow' in the right place, but that women may not like it. Interestingly, 'doll', used as a metaphor for 'woman', implies that women should be treated well and their feelings be considered. A doll is beautiful, fragile and non-mobile, but, as a metaphor, evokes the image of a totally dependent and powerless creature. This metaphor is used in later marriage manuals as an instruction to women to please their husbands by obeying them. Al-Tijānī (fl. 1300), for instance, quotes a hadith stating that women are men's dolls (*luʿab*), and men decide how they want their dolls to be adorned.[41]

Finally, the first part of verse 2:223 is discussed at length in the extensive tradition-based exegesis by al-Suyūṭī (d. 911/1505), *Al-Durr al-Manthūr fi-l-Tafsīr bi-l-Maʾthūr*. He quotes as many as 101 hadiths and reports on this sentence alone, which is only the first part of the verse.[42] This is to be compared with an average of two to three hadiths per verse in the sample from *al-Durr al-Manthūr* analysed by

Stephen Burge.[43] Many of these hadiths lack setting and merely assert that God only permits vaginal sex (the majority), as long as the woman is not menstruating, or that God also permits heterosexual anal sex. Others historicize the verse and give the background of the revelation. The background is described differently, but most interpretations involve the Jews in Medina, the *anṣār* and the *muhājirūn*. The Jews' criticism or superstition is, as we have seen, the earliest motif in exegeses. In some variants, the Jews had been able to influence the *anṣār* in this matter, and the latter criticised the *muhājirūn* for their more permissive attitude to sex positions. The underlying motif of several hadiths is thus the Jews' negative influence on the *anṣār*, and their delusion in matters of sexuality. However, as many as 36 hadiths out of 101 in *al-Durr al-Manthūr* by al-Suyūṭī involve one or several women who dislike their husbands' sexual behaviour. According to these hadiths, as we have seen, the verse gave men the right to have sex with their wives the way the men want, without caring about the wives' desires. This makes obliging women submit to their husbands' sexual wishes, even when they feel aversion, a major theme in the corpus of interpretations of this verse. Consequently, the divine word states that women's possible aversion for certain sexual acts is insignificant. Instead, they are supposed to submit willingly to sexual activities they may dislike.

## Do Women have sexual rights?

Considering the widespread belief in women's superior sexual appetite, surprisingly few Islamic scholars from this period bring up women's claims to sexual satisfaction in marriage. One early hadith, quoted by ʿAbd al-Razzāq al-Sanʿānī, appears to teach men sexual etiquette and to implicitly stress the importance of women's satisfaction: 'When the man has intercourse with his wife he should give her *mahr*, and if he accomplishes his want (*qaḍā ḥājatahu*) but she has not accomplished her want, he should not hurry her (*fa-lā yuʿjilhā*).'[44] As we saw above, the *mahr* is linked to sexual intercourse in that the wife is entitled to it in full after consummation of the marriage. The hadith seems to argue that when the woman commences sexual relations with her husband, he is not only obliged to give her monetary compensation, he should also consider her sexual satisfaction.

ʿAbd al-Razzāq, whose *Muṣannaf* is one of the earliest collections and is regarded as a valuable and reliable source by Motzki, had the hadith from Ibn Jurayj (d. 150/768), one of his main informants, who attributes it to Anas ibn Mālik (d. 93/712).[45] This means that this brief 'sex education' to men at least stems from the middle of the second/eight century. Later, the hadith was included in the *Musnad* of Ibn Yaʿlā (d. 307/919) and in Ibn ʿAdī's collection of hadiths with weak transmitters.[46] Both variants found in the printed editions of these books have a clarifying addition after 'he should not hurry her', namely 'until she accomplishes her want', and, Ibn ʿAdī continues, 'like he wants to accomplish his want'.[47] The addition makes it clear that the aim of the hadith is to urge men to make sure their women are sexually satisfied.

This hadith did not make it into the canonical collections, however, and did not guide legal writing on marriage in the formative era of Islamic law. Instead, men's right to satisfaction was confirmed by hadiths and exegesis and guaranteed by legal rulings. Wives were encouraged to commit to their husbands' pleasure and if they refused their sexual advances, they lost their maintenance. As Kecia Ali shows, the second/eight and third/ninth century jurists hesitated to make sexual satisfaction a legal claim for women.[48] All jurists agreed that consummation of the marriage is obligatory; if it was not consumed within a year, the marriage should be annulled. After consummation, the jurists from the different law schools had somewhat different opinions about women's claim to intimate relations. Al-Shāfiʿī (d. 204/820) denied wives any such claims, whereas early Māliki jurists acknowledged that total deprivation of sex could be harmful for the wife, and that it was a ground for divorce on her initiative. Still, early Māliki jurists did not set up a minimum frequency for the husband to have sex relations with her before she could ask for divorce.[49] Later, many, but not all, jurists set a time limit for women to be deprived of sex before they could ask for divorce; commonly four month.

Nevertheless, although the jurists did not give women the same rights as men to sexual satisfaction, they at least granted them some rights in regard to conjugal relations; they required men to spend time with their free wives and to divide it fairly between multiple wives. To spend time was not the same as having sex, though; and fair division of time did not mean that men were obliged to treat multiple wives fairly in regard to sex. Slave concubines did not have this claim and therefore their owners could spend as much or as little time with them as they wished. Ali calls attention to al-Shāfiʿī's justification for allowing men to treat their wives unfairly in regard to sex: 'intercourse is a matter of pleasure and no one is compelled to it'.[50] This did obviously not apply to women, who could be compelled to intercourse regardless of their pleasure. It is possible that al-Shāfiʿī meant 'erection' rather than pleasure. If not, the statement reveals a profound male bias and neglect of women's needs in marital law.

Connected to sexual rights is birth control and whether women could use or refuse to use contraceptive methods against the will of their husbands. Legal literature discusses birth control; the normal contraceptive method here is coitus interruptus, which is obviously administrated by men. Most jurists required men to have their wives' consent before they practice coitus interruptus, whereas slave concubines lacked any agency in this question; they were not allowed to refuse. According to Musallam, most jurists motivated the requirement of a free woman's consent with her right to children and 'complete sexual fulfilment', and those jurists who denied women the right to children still did not overrule her right to sexual fulfilment.[51] Musallam makes this assumption based on later sources, however, as for legal writings from the formative period these views are difficult to find. The earliest legal compendia do not refer to women's right to sexual fulfilment, only to free wives' right to children. The main impetus for the rules about coitus interruptus in, for example, the *Muwaṭṭa*ʾ by Mālik (d. 179/795), the *Muwaṭṭa*ʿ by al-Shaybānī (d. 189/805) and *Āthār* by Abū Yūsuf (d. 181/978), is men's right to enjoy their female slaves without making them pregnant.[52] Hence, it is men's right to pleasure that is the first motivation, besides preserving the monetary value of their slaves. According to al-Shaybānī and Abū Yūsuf, who were disciples of Abū Hanīfa, men need permission from their free wives before practising coitus interruptus with them or, if the wives were enslaved, permission from their wives' owners. The argument was that free wives were entitled to children, whereas enslaved women's children were the property of their owners. In this case, later authors elaborated the legal discussion in an indicative manner, giving some room for women's claim to sexual fulfilment. According to the twelfth-century Hanafī jurist al-Kāsānī (d. 587/1191), al-Shaybānī and Abū Yūsuf argued that although enslaved women do not have the right to their children, they have 'right to satisfy their desire' (*qaḍā al-shahwa ḥaqquhā*).[53]

According to Bauer, early Qurʾan interpretation was more open for favourable opinions about women's sexual rights. In contrast to the interpretation of Q 2:223, which we have seen did not take into account women's wishes, a few interpreters of Q 2:228 concluded that women have equal rights to intimacy and sex. The words in question, *lahunna mithlu 'lladhī ʿalyhinna*, translated 'And they (women) have rights similar to those (of men)' by Pickthall and 'And women shall have rights similar to the rights against them' by Yusuf Ali, mean according to some, that women have the same rights as men have to sexual satisfaction, contrary to the majority interpretation that women have rights just as men have, but not necessarily the same rights.[54] Al-Zajjāj (d. 311/923), maintained that verse 2:228 gives women not only the right to sex, but also to pleasure (*al-ladhdha*) from their husbands, just as men achieve pleasure from their wives.[55] Bauer cautions against presuming that this interpretation reflects a legal opinion, rather it was 'a recommendation for behaviour that is not guaranteed in the law'.[56] According to Bauer, a few others of al-Zajjāj's contemporaries and later interpreters also mentioned mutual sexual rights in their exegesis of 2:228. She quotes al-Naysābūrī (d. 458/1065), who attributed to al-Shāfiʿī the opinion that the verse gives wives the right to sex, which, if true contradicts his legal writing.[57]

## Female seed and purity

Islamic sciences adopted ideas about female nature that circulated in Late Antiquity; ideas that were considered common knowledge among the scholars. From the field of medicine and natural philosophy, the belief that both men and women emit sperms that contribute to conception (the 'two-seed theory') was adopted by Islamic scholars. This idea, as Kathryn Kueny points out, is already present in the Qur'an, which also appears to supports the idea that the sperm is produced in all parts of the body (in effect the pangenetic theory, see Chapter 1).[58]

Purity was an important concept in the major religions before Islam, with various manifestations in the different purity laws and other rules for purification in ritual and ordinary practice. Marion Katz has found that at least some jurists in early Islam appear to have considered women inherently impure and that touching women was polluting for men, due to a literal interpretation of the phrase 'if you have touched women' (*lāmastum al-nisāʾ*) in verse 5:6 of the Qur'an.[59] The majority interpretation of this phrase was that it refers to a figurative understanding of 'touch', meaning sexual contact. Sexual acts and natural processes connected to sexuality and reproduction were considered polluting for the bodies involved in these acts and natural processes. These bodies had to be purified or else avoided by pure bodies.[60]

The assumed existence of female seed had impact on purity laws, as the full-body ritual purification (*ghuzl*) has to be performed after intercourse and ejaculation other than during intercourse. Therefore, canonical collections include hadiths stating that rulings concerning ejaculation also apply to women, most of them on the authority of the prophet's wives ʿĀʾisha and Umm Salama.[61] One of the earliest collections of authoritative statements, *Muṣannaf* by ʿAbd al-Razzāq al-Ṣanʿānī has a section on women's nocturnal emission.[62] Several of the hadiths in this section are variants of the same motif, a woman asks the prophet about female nocturnal emission and he answers that it must be followed by full-body ritual purification. Stating that women can have nocturnal emission (*iḥtilām*) just as men have, they presuppose that women ejaculate semen just as men do. One explanation quoted by ʿAbd al-Razzāq on the authority of ʿAlī ibn Abī Ṭālib affirms, 'If the woman has a nocturnal emission and ejaculates seminal fluid, she has to perform the *ghusl*.' In a variant of the hadith, one of the Prophet's wives objects to the idea of female emission, but is countered by the Prophet, 'how else could the child resemble her?'[63] According to Motzki, ʿAbd al-Razzāq's works are valuable sources for information about the development of Islamic jurisprudence and Qurʾan exegesis in the centres of religious learning at Mecca, Medina and Basra from at least the beginning of the second/eight century.[64] Considering that, the idea that the female sperm and ejaculation was necessary for conception entered Islamic thought early on, even if the objections to it by female authorities indicate that it was not entirely uncontroversial.

## What happened to women's *shahwa*?

We have seen in Chapters 2 and 3 that some ideas inherited from Late Antiquity were widespread in the early medieval Islamic world: namely that women have more sexual appetite than men have and female nature is inferior to that of men, resulting in less moral and intellectual capacity. This supposed combination of a strong libido and inferior nature was seen as inducing women to commit adultery and fornication. This belief may have been behind female genital cutting (*khitān*), which was practiced in early medieval Islam. Already the Byzantine physician Aetius of Amida, who described female genital cutting in Egypt in the sixth century, explained that it was practiced in order to reduce women's desire.[65]

Male circumcision was likely performed in Arabia before Islam, but there is little evidence that female genital cutting was practiced in Mecca and Medina.[66] Still, al-Jāḥiẓ maintained that pre-Islamic Arabs practiced female genital cutting, and gave a similar reason as Aetius of Amida, uncircumscribed women are more likely to fornicate as they get more pleasure from sex than circumscribed. Al-Jāḥiẓ had heard from a judge called Janāb al-Khashkhāsh that he had registered all uncircumcised and circumcised women in a village, and concluded that most of the pious women there were circumcised whereas the fornicators were not. Indian, Persian and Byzantine women were not circumcised, according to him, and therefore more likely to be adulterers; they have more desire for men as their sexual appetite is greater.[67] Female genital cutting is also mentioned in *Jawāmiʿ al-Ladhdha* where the author remarks that Jewish women are not circumcised. The aim of the cutting, Jāḥiẓ continues, is to achieve moderate *shahwa*, not to erase it, and therefore the Prophet told a female circumciser not to cut too much, as that is better for the girl's beauty and more pleasing for the husband. If it is removed entirely, 'the pleasure is gone and the husbands' love diminish'.[68] This reasoning suggests that al-Jāḥiẓ and his sources took for granted both that women have a naturally greater libido and that their moderate libido is pleasing for men. If the woman is beloved by her husband and sexually satisfied, she is less likely to commit adultery. Therefore, a noble man 'at our place', al-Jāḥiẓ relates, probably alluding to Basra where he lived, used to tell the female circumciser not to cut off more than what is visible.

Al-Jāḥiẓ's claim that genital cutting had been practiced for ages by the Arabs primarily informs us about local customs in the ninth century.[69] An uncircumscribed woman was called *baẓrāʾ*, meaning 'having a clitoris', a word that was used as an invective for a fornicating woman in poetry and historical narratives from the early Islamic period. Especially insulting was the epithet *ibn al-baẓrāʾ*, son of the uncircumcised woman, which meant that the man called so was a bastard, as his mother likely was a fornicator, due to her uncontrollable *shahwa*.

Yet there are only a few hadiths that mention female genital cutting, which may indicate that the practice was not common. Or, as Jonathan Berkey suggests, the fact that traditions about this practice are uncommented in the early Islamic sources might mean that it was taken for granted. Female genital cutting was performed by women in an environment of which male jurists and writers know little.[70] Both Sunni and Shiʿi jurists recommended the practice but did not regard it obligatory; 'circumcision is a sunna for men, and a noble deed (*makrama*) for women'.[71] It seems to have been a local custom (*ʿurf*), however, which meant that it could be practiced in some are as in the Islamic world, but not in others.

## Chaste and lustful: the ideal wife

In the book on women in *The Book on Choise Narratives* (*ʿUyūn al-Akhbār*) the judge and philologist Ibn Qutayba (d. 276/889) quotes a tradition attributed to ʿAlī ibn Abī Ṭālib: 'The best of your women is she who is chaste with her vagina (*al-ʿafīfa fī farjihā*), but lustful to her husband (*al-ghalima li-zawjihā*)'.[72] This is one of a handful of early traditions that explicitly endorse female sensuality and wifely seductive behaviour, attributed to religious authorities or tribal lore. Ibn Qutayba underpins this claim with several Arab proverbs collected by the philologist al-Aṣmaʿī (d. 213 or 216/828 or 831).[73] In the fourth/tenth century, we find a similar tradition attributed to the Prophet in *Kāfī* by al-Kulaynī, stating that 'the best of your women is she who is chaste (*ʿafīfa*) but lustful (*ghalima*)'.[74]

Al-Kulaynī also cites the hadith about women's nine shares of sexual appetite, which is controlled by means of her bashfulness, discussed in Chapter 2. Taken together, these two hadiths claim that the ideal woman is not only able to control her excessive lust, she is also able to master her natural bashfulness when alone with her husband. Another hadith in *Kāfī* stresses that the ideal woman gives her husband what he wants and she does so willingly (*badhalat la-hu mā yurīd min-hā*).[75] Willingness is thus an important notion here. The hadiths are included in a section on 'the best women' in *Kāfī*, where other ideal female characteristics are enumerated, such as being obedient, beautiful and fertile. A Prophetic hadith with similar wording in the book on weak transmitters by Ibn ʿAdī (d. 365/975–6) circulated among Later Sunni scholars.[76]

The chaste and lustful woman as a female ideal is evoked in third/ninth and fourth/tenth century exegesis of Qurʾan verses on feminine companions in Paradise. In the Qurʾan they are sometimes called houris (*ḥūr*) or wives with wide, beautiful eyes (*ḥūr al-ʿayn*), but they are vaguely described and Nerina Rustomji points to the obscurity surrounding them.[77] They are not defined with a single term, not all female companions are called houris. It is not even clear if *ḥūr al-ʿayn* refers to a feminine being at all, and if it does, whether this being is a male believer's earthly wife transformed after death or belongs to a separate category.[78] While especially the mystic tradition interpreted these verses metaphorically, many hadith scholars chose a literal – and explicit sexualized – interpretation. They depicted the houris not only as sexualized female beings, but also as ideal wives to the believers in Paradise; extraordinarily beautiful, sensual, always content and never angry.[79] Their sensuality is exclusively directed to their husbands, whom they are entirely devoted to, as expressed in writing on their breasts according to the early ninth century scholar Ibn Ḥabīb. 'You are my love, I am your love, my eyes are only for you and my soul leads to you.'[80]

A few epithets are used in the Qurʾan to describe them: they are virgins (verse 56:36), beautiful (38:70), with swelling breasts (*kawāʿib* 78:33) and equal in age (*atrāb*, 38:52, 56:37, 78:33). One of these epithets is *ʿuruban* (56:37), an obscure word that provoked many comments in later *tafsīr*. In English translation the word is rendered 'lovers' (Pickthall), 'chastely amorous' (Arberry), 'beloved (by nature)' (Yusuf Ali) and 'loving (their husbands only)' (Mohsin Khan). These are in fact only a few of the meanings suggested by Qurʾan exegetes. Al-Ṭabarī gives more than twenty reports from authorities who interpreted the word *ʿurub* (s. *ʿarūb*): some maintained that they are the houris, a separate category, others that they are the believers' earthly wives, transformed in Paradise to young virgins.[81]

Al-Ṭabarī begins with a description of the wives transformed to houris. First, besides being virgins, they are *ghanijāt*, meaning displaying *ghunj*, which is, approximately, the same as sensual behaviour. Second, they are *mutaḥabbibāt ilā azwājihinna*, meaning 'loving towards their husbands'. Third, they *yuḥsinna al-taba* ʿʿ*ul*, 'do well in obeying their husbands'. This single word, hence, accommodates three ideal female characteristics; the wife who is ʿ*arūb* is affectionate, obedient and lustful towards her husband.

Almost all authorities agree that ʿ*urub* refers to females who love their husbands, but the strength of their love is expressed differently, with a creative use of Arabic forms and synonyms for love. A few interpreters maintain that they are 'women who are affectionate towards their husbands' (*mutawaddidāt*), but most agree that their love is more passionate. This is most often expressed as 'women who are passionately in love with their husbands' (ʿ*awāshiq li-azwājihinna, muta*ʿ*ashshiqāt*, and ʿ*ashshaqna li-azwājhinna*). Another expression is 'they love their husbands violently' (*yuḥbibna azwājahunna ḥubban shadīdan*). The sexual component of their love is expressed in 'they desire their husbands sexually' (*yashtahīna azwājahunna*) and 'a desirous woman' (*al-mushtahiya*). Other explicit words for being lustful and behaving sensually are also used, such as *maghnūja* and *shakila*. Finally, stressing that this passionate nature and sensual behaviour are solely for the benefit of the husband, many interpreters add that they are obedient, using the specific terms *ḥusn al-taba*ʿʿ*ul* and the verb *ḥasanat al-taba*ʿʿ*ul*.

The majority opinion of al-Ṭabarī's sources is that the female companions in Paradise (whether they are the earthly wives transformed to young virgins or the houris) love and obey their husbands, feel sexual attraction for them and act affectionately towards them. Other early exegeses provide the same interpretations; most maintain that the women so called are loving, even passionately loving to their husbands. Hannad ibn al-Sarī (243/857), Saʿīd ibn Manṣūr (d. 227/841–2), ʿAbd ibn Ḥamīd (d. 249/863-4), Ḥamīd ibn Zanjawayh (d. 251/865–6) and Ibn al-Mundhir (d. 318/930–1) maintain that the women called ʿ*urub* desire their husbands sexually.[82] Hannad ibn al-Sarī, Ibn al-Mundhir and Ibn Abī Ḥātim (d. 327/938–9) assert that a wife who is ʿ*arūb* is sensual and lustful (*ghanija/maghnūja*). ʿAbd al-Razzāq, Saʿīd ibn Manṣūr, ʿAbd ibn Ḥamīd and Ibn al-Mundhir, also use a word for 'lustful' (*ghanima*).[83]

There are only a few divergent interpretations. Two of al-Ṭabarī's sources claim that ʿ*urub* signifies eloquent women (*ḥasanāt al-kalām*), probably based on the shared root ʿ*rb* with the word ʿ*arab*. Yet another interpretation is suggested by the Shiʿi scholar al-Ṭūsī. He bases his interpretation on the shared root ʿ*rb* with the word *ʿarab*, but also keeps the sexual connotation. The women who are *ʿurub* are, 'passionately loving to their husbands and give them noble children'.[84] The nobleness is related to the Arab origin. More precisely, a woman with this epithet is 'playful (*laʿūb*) with her husband as she is cheerful in his company (*unsan bihi*), and desires him passionately (*rāghiba fihi*). She is sociable like an Arab and speaks Arabic.'

The feminine ideal as expressed in these interpretations resembles the wifely model summarized in the hadith 'the ideal wife is lustful and chaste', that is a combination of the erotic and pious ideals. The ideal female creature is created for the enjoyment of men, and whether she is a houri or an earthly wife, she is sexy and lustful, but directs her lust and displays her sexiness only to her husband, entirely devoted to him. The houris as described by most early Qurʾan interpreters are remarkably similar to the female characters in erotic stories, except that the latter are not necessarily obedient and chaste. The words *ghanijāt* and *maghnūja*, commonly attributed to the houris, are connected with the word *ghunj*, which is invoked as a female ideal numerous times in *Jawāmiʿ al-Ladhdha*, denoting lustful behaviour during intercourse. As we saw in Chapter 2, the Umayyad society woman Ḥubbā explained that *ghunj* means lustful sighing during intercourse. Interestingly, al-Ṭabarī informs that the word *maghnūja* is from Medina, which confirms Ḥubbā's expertise, as she lived in Medina and is called 'the Medinese Ḥubbā" (Ḥubbā al-Madīniyya).[85]

## Towards women's sexual rights

The number of Prophetic traditions increased dramatically from the beginning of the second/eight century and Basra and Kufa in Iraq seem to have been centres for many fabrications. In the third/ninth century, the corpus of hadiths exceeded half a million, and from them, traditionists identified some four or five thousands as sound.[86] These 'sound' hadiths became increasingly important for the Islamic sciences; during this period Prophetic traditions became the second authoritative source (after the Qurʾan) for legal scholars and were also used in Qurʾan exegesis. As we have seen in this chapter, only a few Prophetic traditions that were recorded in early hadith collections defended women's right to sex and pleasure, while there were several traditions that accentuated men's right to pleasure and wives' duty to be sexually available. Jurists chose to disregard the few hadiths that supported women's sexual rights and gave explicit priority to men's rights. In this, they also disregarded contemporary medical authors who highlighted the importance of sexual gratification for women, for health reasons and for conception, although they adhered to the notion of female seed.

Women's right to pleasure is somewhat accentuated in later legal literature, however. Early legal discussions of contraceptives, which is here the same as coitus interruptus, justify the practice primarily as men's right to have sex with their slaves without begetting children while mentioning in passing that they need free wives' consent. Only later jurists required men to get permission from their wives with justification that free women have the right to children and to 'satisfy their desire', as stated by the sixth/twelfth century Ḥanafi jurist al-Kāsānī. The Hanbali jurist Ibn Qudāma (d. 620/1223), for example, wrote that coitus interruptus with free wives is *makrūḥ*, because it results in less progeny and 'cuts the pleasure of the woman'.[87] The Shāfiʿī jurist al-Shīrāzī (d. 476/1083), instead maintained that men do not need free wives' consent, because they have 'right to pleasure' not to ejaculation (i.e. children).[88]

From the twelfth century onwards, a few traditions circulated that supported women's right to sexual fulfilment. These hadiths parallel ʿAlī ibn Naṣr's advice in *Jawāmiʿ al-Ladhdha* and appear to be influenced by the erotological tradition. Abū Ḥāmid Muhammad al-Ghazālī (d. 505/1111) and Abū Manṣūr al-Daylamī (558/1162) both quoted the following hadith: 'The Prophet said: "Let none of you come upon his wife like an animal, but let there be a messenger between them." He was asked: "What is the messenger, messenger of God?" He said, "The kiss and words."'[89] Indeed, the message in this hadith is similar to that of the erotic compendium *Jawāmiʿ al-Ladhdha*, which devotes a chapter to 'talking and kissing' and gives the same advice, but attributed to 'al-Hindī'. Characteristically, ʿAlī ibn Naṣr adds that it is important to talk *after* the intercourse as well; otherwise the woman may feel embarrassed and regret what she has done. In this chapter, as well as in the introduction to the encyclopaedia, ʿAlī ibn Naṣr advises men not to sleep with their women 'like animals'; he even uses the same word for animals as in the hadith quoted above, *bahīma*.

The two scholars, al-Ghazālī and al-Daylamī, convey a similar hadith with the same message: when the Prophet identifies three deficiencies in a man, the third deficiency is to have sexual contact with a slave-girl or wife without talking to her and showing affection. In addition, al-Ghazālī provides a sexual etiquette in his *Iḥyāʾ ʿUlūm al-Dīn* that is informed by medical theory and erotological tradition.

> When he has accomplished his want (*qaḍā waṭrahu*) he should slow down for his wife's sake, she has right (*ḥaqq*) to accomplish her desire. Her orgasm (*inzāl*)

> may be delayed; therefore, it is harmful for her if he excites her desire and then forsakes her. Differences in the constitution of their ejaculation causes discord whenever the husband ejaculates first. Simultaneous ejaculation is more pleasurable for her because the man is occupied with himself and therefore diverted from her, and she is probably shy. He has to visit her once every fourth night . . . more or less often depending on how much she needs for protecting her chastity (*ḥājatihā fī t-taḥṣīn*). Protecting her chastity (*taḥṣīnahā*) is his duty.[90]

Al-Ghazālī instructs men to see to that their wives are satisfied, for the sake of harmonious conjugal relations. Notably, in contrast to the erotological tradition, it is not the wife's pleasure per se that is the aim, but her chastity. Indeed, al-Ghazālī's sexual guidance appear as a more pious variant of the erotological tradition.

Part Two

# Women's Words and Preferences

# 4

# Female Strategies and Verbal Battles

The poet al-ʿAjjāj (d. *c.* 97/715) was known for his poems in the *rajaz* metre, with which he eulogized several Umayyad caliphs and high officials. He married a young woman named al-Dahnāʾ bint Misḥal from his own tribe, Tamīm, according to an anecdote in *Balaghāt al-Nisāʾ* by Ibn Abī Ṭāhir Ṭayfūr. Al-Dahnāʾ was not content with the marriage and brought her case to Ibrāhīm ibn ʿArabī, who was governor of al-Yamāma, a district east of Najd on the Arabian Peninsula. She wanted the marriage to be annulled as she was still a virgin; she told the governor that her husband behaved like a woman in bed with no experience of women. Al-Dahnāʾ was probably still an adolescent, expected to have little experience of men. The governor asked her if she did not let her husband consummate the marriage, perhaps she resisted the attempts of 'the old man'. This is what her husband claimed; he accused her for being recalcitrant; if he wanted to sleep with her he had to fight. Al-Dahnāʾ denied this and asserted that she made herself available, as was her wifely duty: 'By God, I straighten my back for him and loosen my tights.' Ibrāhīm did not believe her and decided to give al-ʿAjjāj a second chance, but he had to consummate the marriage within a year.

Al-Dahnāʾ was apparently not satisfied with the governor's decree, and her father, Misḥal, supported her, which prompted al-ʿAjjāj to justify himself in a poem:

> Al-Dahnāʾ claimed and Misḥal believed
> that the governor hasten with his decree ignoring
> my moments of impotence, but even the horse is sometimes unable
> to copulate, although he is a high breed, sturdy stallion[1]

Al-Dahnāʾ answered with a poem indicating that for her, the problem was more than a temporary impotence; the marriage lacked any kind of physical intimacy:

> I swear that he does not take me in his arms,
> nor does he kiss me or sniff me.

No passionate motion, comforting me,
Making my toe rings fly into my sleeve.[2]

After his wife's expression of yearning for intimacy, al-ʿAjjāj felt regret and recited a poem expressing his feelings for her. Even if she wished for the termination of their marriage, he was still 'not tired of being close to her' and expected to regain potency. This did not impress al-Dahnāʾ, however, who proudly declared:

By God, if it were not for my nobility and virtuousness,
for fear of the governor's punishment /and respect of the police,
I would have run from the old man of the camel's clan (*banī baʿīr*)
like a youthful she-camel, noncompliant, unruly,
striking the sides of the strapped saddle.[3]

With this poem, al-Dahnāʾ's poetic persona expresses that there is nothing al-ʿAjjāj could do to gain her affection. Regaining potency would not help him as she is turned off by his old age. She would take part in intimacies between them only unwillingly, and he would feel her disgust. Likening herself to a young camel that was ridden too early, she admitted that if she could, she would have endeavoured to shake him off. Al-ʿAjjāj was not successful as, a year later, his 'thing' was still weak and the anecdote ends with his grieving verse.[4]

The anecdote is about a failed marriage and a girl who did what she could to take command of her life; she uses her legal capacity to act in order to leave an unhappy marriage. Al-ʿAjjāj is called an 'old man' in this anecdote; as he was probably born during the caliphate of ʿUthmān (23–35/644–656) and Ibrāhīm ibn ʿArabī was governor of al-Yamāma after 69/688 until the death of the caliph ʿAbd al-Malik in 86/705, he could have been between forty and sixty years old when this incident supposedly occurred.[5] His bride al-Dahnāʾ, who was still a virgin, was probably not more than a teenager. A young girl's averseness to a much older husband was understandable, as implied by the governor's question. A big age difference was often advised against in literature on marriage, and young girls were assumed to dislike being married off to old men. It was not a ground for divorce, however, unless the husband agreed to accept compensation and allowed the wife a *khulʿ* divorce.

Al-Dahnāʾ does not only want to leave her marriage, she wants to get the best out of the divorce. The incident supposedly took place around 700, before the Islamic law was established, but later Sunni authorities ruled that the marriage was annulled if the husband failed to consummate it within a year after the case was brought to the judge.[6] At this period, there seems to have been more options for wives to initiate divorce but they had to pay back the dower. If a court instead declared the marriage annulled, due to the husband's impotence, she could keep the dower. She had to be sexually available to him, however, and not resist his advances. If she did, she was a recalcitrant wife and the husband could divorce her without paying full compensation.[7] It is hinted in the anecdote that these legal issues were behind al-Dahnā''s actions; she brought the case to the court and was eager to explain to the governor that she had fulfilled her marital obligation to make herself available to her husband. Financially, she would be better off if the marriage was annulled than if her husband divorced her, even if she had to wait a year. More importantly, however, the anecdote emphasizes her sincerity and dignity. The famous poet was not a good-enough husband for her, and she makes clear that she would have left him, was it not that she chose to follow the law. Meanwhile, she does what she can to get rid of him legally and emotionally, rebuffing her husband's attempts to mend the relationship. As such, she is the epitome of an early Islamic Arab woman as pictured in Abbasid *adab* literature: independent, clever and eloquent. Despite her young age, she is not afraid of expressing her wishes and she succeeds in getting her father's support.

The poems in the anecdote about al-Dahnā' and al-ʿAjjāj were shared by philologists and used as examples for discussing difficult words. Al-ʿAjjāj was famous for his rich vocabulary and he was one of the poets who made *rajaz* a respected metre among literary critics. His son, Ruʾba (d. 145/762), was also a poet and an important informant to the philologists in Basra.[8] According to Ibn Manẓūr (d. 711/1311–1312), the linguist Abū ʿUbayda (209/824–825) learnt al-ʿAjjāj's poem 'Al-Dahnā' claimed and Misḥal believed' from Ruʾba, and explained difficult words in it.[9] An additional poem is attributed to al-ʿAjjāj in *Kitāb al-Bayān wa-l-Tabyīn* by Abū ʿUbayda's pupil al-Jāḥiẓ, but this time the addressee is Mughīra ibn Shuʿba, not Ibrāhīm ibn ʿArabī. The same poem was quoted by Ibn Manẓūr on the authority of the philologist Ibn Barrī (d. 660/1261–2), explaining that it was part of al-ʿAjjāj's poetic commentaries on his marriage with al-Dahnā'.

> God knows, Mughīra, that I covered her like a sturdy stallion covers the mare
> and I took her like one who takes the sheep by its forelegs
> hastening to roast it for a group of guests.[10]

This report situates the events some decades earlier, which changes the story somewhat. Mughīra was governor of Kufa from 41/661 until his death between years 48 and 51 (668 and 671) and if al-ʿAjjāj really was born during the caliphate of al-ʿUthmān, he was in his twenties (or even younger) when he supposedly wrote this poem.[11] In that case, old age cannot have been the ground on which al-Dahnāʾ complained. There is something else in this poem, however. Al-Dahnāʾ's longing for 'a passionate motion' has generated a provoking, even shocking response, the image of the wife as a sheep being prepared for slaughter. In the first version, al-ʿAjjāj admitted that he had his 'moments of impotence'; here, his poetic persona is entirely aggressive, incited by the attack against his masculinity implied by the accusation of impotency.

Al-Dahnāʾ's poetic accusation, which is the most widespread of the poems in this anecdote, is transformed correspondingly. The version in *Balaghāt al-Nisāʾ*, 'I swear that he does not take me in his arms', is quoted by Ibn Manẓūr as an example of the use of the word *fatakh* (s. *fatkha*), stoneless rings. He explains that although these rings were carried on fingers as well as toes, in this poem al-Dahnāʾ refers to toe rings, implying that 'if she raised her legs, her rings would fall down in her sleeve'.[12] There are a few other versions of this verse, all with the same rhythm and easy rhyme, but with some changes in vocabulary that alter the meaning. One variant of the poem is quoted in *Balaghāt al-Nisāʾ*, in another anecdote on disputes between spouses; the poet is here called Umm al-Ward. Later commentators have assumed that Umm al-Ward and al-Dahnāʾ are the same woman, as both are said to have litigated against their husbands at the court of the governor of al-Yamāma.

The anecdote about Umm al-Ward contains fewer details and lacks legal terms, the husband and the governor are not named and only Umm al-Ward's poem is quoted.[13] The anecdote is told on the authority of the historian Hishām ibn al-Kalbī (d. 204/819 or 206/821) from Kufa, who wrote extensively on history and genealogy, and was widely cited by later scholars. This version does not depict a poetic exchange; only Umm al-Ward's poem is quoted. It serves as the justification for her appeal for divorce. The poem about her longing for intimacy and her husband's failure to satisfy her was accepted by the governor and he granted her a divorce. After the divorce, the anecdote continues, Umm al-Ward married another man who made her happy. The story did not end there, however, as her brother, who married her sister-in-law, turned out to have the same problem as her ex-husband. Umm al-Ward, therefore, recited a new, rather offensive poem lampooning her brother for his impotence. By this, she becomes one of many female characters in Abbasid literature who are experts in ridiculing men who do not live up to the masculine norms.

Another version of the poem is presented by al-Jāḥiẓ in *al-Bayān*, without mentioning the name of the complaining woman. Instead of expressing longing for intimacy in the form of 'kissing and embracing', she dismisses it, with small changes in the wording. She wants sexual intercourse, nothing else:

By God, I am not content with long embraces
or with kissing and sniffing
only with a motion that comforts me
and makes my toe rings fall into my sleeve
It is for this my mother gave birth to me.[14]

A similar poem is attributed to al-Dahnāʾ in *al-Maḥāsin wa-l-Aḍdād* by pseudo-Jāḥiẓ whereas several other authors attribute it to Umm al-Ward. According to *Jawāmiʿ al-Ladhdha*, Umm al-Ward complained about her husband's kisses:

This is not what my mother instructed me
By God, you do not own me by embracing
and not by kissing or sniffing
but with a motion that comforts me
and makes my ring fly into my sleeve.[15]

The same poem is quoted in the section on *mujūn* in *Muḥādarat al-Udabaʾ* by al-Rāghib al-Iṣfahānī (d. early fifth/eleventh century?[16]), and as an example of bad discourse in *Rawḍat al-Qulūb* by al-Shayzarī (fl. sixth/twelfth century). The reference to a mother's instruction to her daughter is in fact a common motif in erotic literature, where mothers or older women take on themselves to teach younger women 'real sex', which is, as in this case, often uninhibited and not particularly romantic (see Chapter 2).

A curious detail in the transmission of this poem is a later misreading of the line 'Making my toe rings fly into my sleeve.' Only a dot distinguishes this line from the reading 'Making my running water fly in my spathe'; *fatakhī fi kummī* becomes *fatḥī fi kimmī*.[17] Although this reading seems far-fetched, it is preferred by the editors of *Balaghāt al-Nisāʾ*, who explain that *fatḥī* may refer to vaginal lubrication from arousal. The word *kimm* is the spathe of the spadix (*ṭilʿ*) of the palm tree, and may refer to the vagina.[18] The confusion between *fatakhī* and *fatḥī* is confirmed by manuscript evidence; at least one manuscript from the sixteenth century has the latter reading.[19] The reading is perhaps exotifying; Umm al-Ward is cast as an unrefined Bedouin who likens her genitalia with the hard, oval covering (spathe) of the flowers of the date palm, which splits when the flowers mature. The date palm grew abundantly in al-Yamāma and it is expected that poets are inspired by their surroundings. Moreover, the occurrence of the word 'running water' is not so surprising considering contemporary medical theory assumed that women had seminal fluid, which they discharge during intercourse. This reading is in fact supported by a motif in early Arab poetry: the description of genitals. Considering a *mujūn* motif, especially male poets praised or eulogized their genitalia and described female genitalia in appreciating or satirizing terms. There are also some poems attributed to women who describe and praise their own vaginas, as we will see in Chapter 5.

The transformation of al-Dahnāʾ's verse illustrates a tendency in the representation of female characters in classical Arabic literature. While lexicographers like Ibn Manẓūr preserved the renderings of the early philologists, many others chose to emphasize what was probably considered the most exotic feature: not the rare vocabulary but the outspokenness of the female protagonists. Through changes in wordings or insertions of new expressions, the female characters were erotized and their words transformed to sexual comedy. This is what happened to the poem discussed above. When attributed to al-Dahnāʾ, a young woman of noble Arab origin, the poetic persona expresses longing for physical intimacy in the form of kisses and embraces as well as intercourse. When attributed to Umm al-Ward, an anonymous woman of unknown origin, the poetic persona sometimes dismisses 'softer' forms of physical intimacy and asks for rougher sex, a typical theme in erotic literature. The tendency to eroticize female protagonists and transform their words to *mujūn* is discussed in Chapter 5, which also gives examples of women's achievements as *mujūn* poets.

In this chapter, I will instead take al-Dahnāʾ's attempts to use her husband's failure to live up to the masculine norms in order to achieve her goal, the annulment of the marriage, as a starting point for a survey of verbal proficiency as a female strategy in early Arabic literature. I examine the manifestations of this strategy in two types of literature: verse and prose poems attributed to early Arab women and Abbasid anecdotes about witty women. In both cases, women's verbal proficiency is frequently displayed in a verbal battle between a woman and a man, either as a poetic duel or as an exchange of words. The positions and disagreements in the verbal battles analysed in this chapter are connected to gendered issues, as when al-Dahnāʾ and al-ʿAjjāj accuse each other of not fulfilling their marital obligations, or part of a woman's strategy to take command of the situation.

## Women's voices in poetry and prose

As far as we know, there were no female authors of literature in Arabic in early medieval society, but there were many female poets. Women's foremost poetic genre in *jahiliyya* and early Islam was the *marthiya*, the elegy, and it is often believed that female poets were confined to this genre, as it was considered respectable for women to express grief, but disreputable to express love. Marlé Hammond suggests in *Beyond Elegy: Classical Arabic Women's Poetry in Context* that the *marthiya* is 'symbolically driven by female sexuality', using tropes from the *nasīb*, the erotic prelude to the *qasida*, the beloved's eye for example, and the sensuality of the glance and the gaze.[20] In her analysis of three poems by women, the unknown Suʿda bint al-Shamardal, who probably lived during late *jahiliyya* or early Islam, and the well-known al-Khansāʾ and Laylā al-Akhyaliyya, Hammond shows their structural similarities to the *qasida*, considered a male form, and challenges the identification of women's poetry as 'mono-thematic' in comparison to the 'poly-thematic' *qasida*.[21] There are few poems by named female poets in the classical Ḥamāsa collections' sections on love-poetry (*nasīb* and *ghazal*), but Hammond argues that women created poems with erotic themes in other genres.[22] There are, however, numerous short love poems by anonymous women, not the least in *Balaghāt al-Nisāʾ*, which devotes a section to *ghazal*. During the Abbasid era, many female slaves became known as poets, and their often short poems are preserved in *adab* collections, with a few longer *qasidas* also in poetry collections. Some of their verses were parts of poetic dialogues with other poets or their owners. Most of all, they composed *ghazal*, light-hearted love poetry, which also contained accusations and laments over separation with the beloved.[23]

Conjugal relations is a central theme in many poems attributed to female poets in *Balaghāt al-Nisāʾ*; they praise their husbands or, conversely lampoon them and complain about failed marriages. Ibn Abī Ṭāhir devotes a whole chapter to this theme, called 'Women's Eloquence in Disputes between Spouses in the Form of Praise and Blame'.[24] Women's poems are occasionally parts of verbal battles with their husbands and sometimes embedded in longer anecdotes, as in the case of al-Dahnāʾ and al-ʿAjjāj. The chapter includes over eighty anecdotes covering women's monologues or dialogues between spouses, in the form of epigrams in poetry (s. *qiṭʿa*, pl. *qiṭaʿ*) or rhymed prose (*sajʿ*). The rhymed prose in *Balaghāt al-Nisāʾ* is often formulaic and stylistic, but the poetry is sometimes very expressive, and appears to reflect real emotions. The dominating emotions are disappointment, aversion, hatred and disgust. In many cases, the poems are mocking and sometimes bawdy, but far from merry.

Often, no reason or weak reasons are given as grounds for the woman's aversion, but it is sometimes stated explicitly that the reason is sexual and emotional dissatisfaction. The Arab poetic heritage includes many poems by male poets reviling or blaming women; poems satirizing or blaming wives is a common subject in Arabic literature, according to Geert Jan van Gelder.[25] The poems blaming husbands in *Balaghāt al-Nisā'* can be read as a reaction, or as belonging to the same genre.[26]

Some women express dissatisfaction with their marriages due to lack of love and respect. The lack of love may be reciprocal, as when a poet asks, 'Who will aid me against an evil husband, who looks at me and I look at him with hateful eyes?'[27] The aversion may be extremely strong and the tone utterly depressive, as in the following verse by a woman called Umayma blaming her husband: 'I wish that the fang-bearer whose poison is flowing bit me / the day they said "You are his wife" / Oh Lord, if he enters Paradise / then place Umayma, Lord of the people, in Hell.'[28]

Disappointed women complain to fathers or families who have married them off against their will to husbands who are old or below their rank. Al-Aṣmaʿī, who belonged to the leading circle of philologists in Basra together with Abū ʿUbayda, tells us about another woman who accused her father for marrying her against her will: 'Oh father, you caused me suffering and ordeal/ you placed my soul (*nafs*) in the hands of someone who degrades it.'[29] Another woman, Umm Nāshib al-Ḥārithiyya, decided to do something about her unhappy marriage with an old man. She fled from him according to the historian ʿUmar ibn Shabba (d. 262/878), reproaching her family for putting her in an awkward situation:

> Shame on the people that imposed upon Umm Nāshib
> a nightly journey, which she plunged into without a guide.
> With the garment tucked up beneath the knee I looked towards
> a waymark in a place, difficult to search.[30]

Examining women's voices in *adab* literature, we have to confront a crucial question: How should we understand women's voices in male-authored texts? We will probably never know if they were real women talking or solely fictional, fabricated by the earliest historians and philologists. The poems and prose epigrams in *Balaghāt al-Nisā'* often lack a historical setting and the poets are anonymous. Therefore, they are difficult to date, but most female poets appear to be early Islamic, whereas the narratives were written down much later. In one of the few studies of *Balaghāt al-Nisā'*, Nancy Roberts concludes from her analyses of three political speeches attributed to women that the orations are not theirs; they are nothing but instruments for the male redactor to put forward his own opinion.[31] The author of the work, according to her, makes use of the women's low status due to their gender to enhance the effect of the critique. However, although there is reason to be cautious, we should not take for granted that all poems and speeches attributed to women are fabricated. The speeches are made by named and famous women with important positions in early Umayyad society, and it is not clear why they cannot represent themselves, whereas male characters' self-representation is not usually questioned (except in cases of obvious political and religious controversy).

In anecdotes, female characters tend to be anonymous; in case they are not, the dramatis personae are limited to a rather small group of Umayyad and royal Abbasid free women and famous elite slaves. Slave women are protagonists in love stories, where they possess all sorts of good qualities, not the least fidelity, learning and intelligence. They make up what Julia Bray labels 'the urban Abbasid slave heroines', who figure in Abbasid love-stories.[32] Other dominant love narratives in Abbasid literature are located in early Islamic time. Bray identifies two types of female protagonists 'the Umayyad Bedouin heroine', who is 'forever chaste and unattainable', and 'the aristocratic Umayyad virago, who goes unveiled, taunts her admirers, and marries and divorces her way through the ranks of nobility at her own pleasure'.[33]

Early Islamic and Bedouin women were considered especially eloquent; for later readers these two groups eventually coalesced and the eloquent early Islamic Arab woman became a stock character in Abbasid literature. The complaining wife, the poetic persona of al-Dahnā''s poem, was perhaps considered exotic by later readers. Her yearning for unrestrained intercourse, which would make her toe rings fly into her sleeve, is something a noble Abbasid woman would not have been quoted as saying in Abbasid literature, at least not in the literature that has been preserved. In literary depictions of Abbasid high society, the slave courtesans have taken over the role of the female character who performs her eloquence in public. Numerous anecdotes about them in *Kitāb al-Aghānī* by Abū al-Faraj al-Iṣbahānī are formed as verbal battles where they get the last word, and famous slave courtesans also took part in a form of verbal battle, the poetic duel, as did the eighth- and ninth-century poets ʿInān and Faḍl. The standard was that a male poet initiated the duel with a short poem, to which the second poet had to improvise an answer on the same theme and with the same rhythm and metre. They continued until one of them could not come up with a new verse; according to *Aghānī*, ʿInān won most of the time. The slave courtesans were not only eloquent, they were also outspoken, and in an anecdote about the famous ninth-century singer and courtesan ʿArīb, who was contemporary with the author of *Balaghāt al-Nisāʾ* and close to the Abbasid caliphs, she borrows an image from al-Dahnāʾ's poem. When her lover Muḥammad ibn Ḥāmid, a high military commander from Khurasān, argued with her, she silenced him with an invitation to have sex: 'Make my trousers my necklace, and attach my anklets to my earrings. Write your apology on a scroll tomorrow, and I will write my apology on three. Leave those pointless concerns! As the poet said: "Stop counting faults when we meet / Come here! I will not count and you will not count."'[34]

## Women against men: litigating against and lampooning husbands

Al-Dahnāʾ was not the only woman who took her husband to court in order to get a divorce, as depicted in Abbasid literature. Ibn Abī Ṭāhir narrates about an anonymous woman who brought her case to the governor of Khurasān, Qutayba ibn Muslim (d. 96/715), a successful Umayyad commander. She was married to a man called Faḍāla ibn ʿAbdullāh al-Ghanawī, but could not stand him and asked the governor to grant her a divorce. Her aversion was her only reason, apparently she did not even try to find another, legally recognized, excuse. However, the framing of this particular anecdote does not highlight the wishes of the woman, it focuses on the male protagonist, Faḍāla. Qutayba asked Faḍāla how he could tolerate his wife's aversion, she was not his relative and he could easily divorce her. Faḍāla answered that he loved his wife, and thus had no wish to divorce her, something that did not impress Qutayba, who advised him not to love someone who did not love him back. Qutayba asked the wife why she hated her husband and she answered that she had many reasons for hating him. After that, typically, she specified her reasons in rhymed prose: 'He has little jealousy (*qalīl al-ghayra*) and is quick to become suspicious (*sarīʿ al-ṭayra*). He reprimands a lot (*kathīr al-ʿitāb*) and is very stingy (*shadīd al-ḥisāb*). From the front, his smell is horrible, but from behind, it is pleasant. His penis is soft, his eyes are staring and his legs are unsteady.'[35] Moreover, she continues, he is voracious, eats and drinks too much, and he does not wash himself properly. Her accusations were a mix of personal disgust and grievance about her husband's failure to live up to social expectations. Notably, jealousy in this context meant much more than romantic jealousy, it was considered a core masculine virtue that included the ability to protect dependants and, ultimately, preserve social stability.[36] After this affront, Faḍāla risked seriously making a fool of himself by letting his wife expose his shortcomings to the powerful governor and his entourage. Her expression of disgust and stinging words in rhymed prose were successful and her husband agreed to divorce her.

Another woman, Umm ʿAwf wanted the custody of her child after the scholar Abū al-Aswad (probably d. 69/688–689) divorced her and she brought a case against him to the court of Ziyād ibn Abīhī (d. 53/673), governor in Basra for the fourth caliph ʿAlī ibn Abī Ṭālib and later for the Umayyads. Abū al-Aswad is a quite famous figure in early Islamic history; he was active in the beginning of the Islamic sciences together with Abū Hurayra (d. *c.* 58/678) and involved in early jurisprudence (*fiqh*), and collecting Prophetic traditions (hadith). Later, for dubious reasons, he was dubbed the 'originator of Arabic grammar'.[37] Be that as it may, we are probably supposed to assume that he was a man with command of the language. There are several variants of what happened at the court, but the shortest is narrated by Ibn Qutayba:

> Umm ʿAwf, Abū al-Aswad al-Duʾalī's wife, litigated against Abū al-Aswad at Ziyād's court about a son she had with him. Abū al-Aswad said: 'I have more right to the son than she has. I carried him before she did and brought him forth before she did.' Umm ʿAwf answered: 'You brought him forth in pleasure, I did under compulsion. You carried him when he was light; I did when he was heavy.' Ziyād said: 'You tell the truth, you have more right to him.' Accordingly, he turned him over to her.[38]

Abū al-Aswad's claim that he has more right to the child, as he 'carried him before she did and brought him forth before she did', purports that he carried the child in his sperm and brought him forth at the ejaculation. Saying this, he seems to rely on the notion that the father is the sole origin of the child, which is not in line with the 'two-seed theory', which maintained that women as well as men have sperm and that both sperm are needed for producing a child. Likewise, proverbs and sayings, supposedly from the Umayyad era, convey the concept of the father as the principal origin of the child. A proverb collected by al-Aṣmaʿī, for example, which is also quoted by Ibn Qutayba, insists that women are merely 'vessels for children'.[39] The patriarchal idea that the children belong to the father and his family is reflected in Islamic law, as the father gets the custody of the child above a specific age. It is also reflected in linguistic choices, such as labelling women 'vessels', and always referring to women's children as belonging to their husbands.[40]

Whatever the case may be, the governor in this case did not care about medical theory. What convinced him was Umm ʿAwf's verbal proficiency. She gave a quick, clever and reasonable response to Abū al-Aswad's prepared argument, which persuaded the governor to give her the custody. Ziyād was himself considered an eloquent giant, his inaugural speech as an Umayyad governor has been called 'a masterpiece of eloquence'.[41] In a variant of the anecdote told by Ibn Abī Ṭāhir Ṭayfūr, the matrimonial dispute has grown to an extensive altercation, in which Abū al-Aswad's ex-wife, who is anonymous in this variant, excels in eloquence.[42] She comes alone to the court, which, in this variant, is the court of the caliph al-Muʿāwiya in Damascus, and approaches the caliph when he is sitting together 'with the notables of Quraysh and noble men of the Arabs', one of which is her ex-husband.[43] She praises the caliph in rhymed prose (*sajʿ*), and thereafter presents her case. Abū al-Aswad tries to defend himself, but whatever he says, his ex-wife has a better and more well-expressed argument. She blames him for numerous bad characteristics:

> As long as I knew him, he has been inquisitive and ignorant, persistent and miserly. When he talks, he talks evil and when he is quiet, it is with hidden spitefulness. He is a lion when he is safe and a fox when he is frightened, and stingy when he receives guests. If good people are mentioned he holds back, because of the lowliness of his ancestry. His guest is hungry and his neighbour miserly. He does not care for the neighbour and nor for his cherished goods. He does not seek and attain revenge. The most honourable person for him is the one who despises him, while the most despised is the one who honours him.

She uses the description of the female body as 'a vessel for the child' as an argument in favour of her right to the child, adding to the statement quoted by Ibn Qutayba: 'He carried him when he was light and I carried him when he was heavy. He gave birth to him in pleasure, and I gave birth to him in distress. My belly is his vessel and my breasts are his waterskin, my lap his courtyard.'[44] The caliph is much impressed by her eloquence, and exclaims, 'Praise God for the *sajʿ* of this woman!' The anecdote ends with a poem in which Muʿāwiya gives a legal decree; if a mother takes good care of her child and does not remarry, she has the right to custody. Yet, it was Umm ʿAwf's courage and superior command of rhymed prose that was behind the legal decree, not her good parenting.

It is understandable that this anecdote appealed to an author such as Ibn Abī Ṭāhir. The female protagonist is disadvantaged in several ways; she is divorced and alone, with no relatives or friends to assist her. She can only use her own talents to turn the situation to her favour, and she succeeds in doing so with the help of courage, verbal proficiency and intellectual ability. This situation must have been recognizable for an aspiring intellectual in Baghdad, who had to rely on the same skills to make himself a future, which was most easily done by attracting a wealthy patron, preferably the caliph. Al-Jāḥiẓ quotes parts of Umm

ʿAwf's words as an example of good *sajʿ*; in this version it is told by a Bedouin litigating against her son.[45] She tells her son, 'was not my belly your vessel, my lap your courtyard and my breasts your waterskin?' The son, who is no longer an infant, answers 'you have become an orator (*khaṭība*), may God be pleased with you!' Al-Jāḥiẓ explains, 'she got what she wanted by means of well-chosen words, like that which an orator achieves with his speech'.

Most of all, however, this variant of the courtroom matrimonial argument is a display of elocution in *sajʿ*. Rhymed prose was characteristic for early Arabic rhetoric, and was widely used in literature preserved from the pre-Islamic and early-Islamic periods. In the pre-Islamic period, it was used in speeches, oracles, lamentations, war cries, curses and magical utterances. After Islam, the use of rhymed prose in official speeches declined, due to its association with pre-Islamic magic, but *sajʿ* continued to be used for arguments, to which we can count the debate between Abū al-Aswad and his ex-wife.[46] From the third/ninth century, it became increasingly popular. Ibn Abī Ṭāhir's work on women's eloquence, which in pre- and early-Islamic time was primarily displayed in *sajʿ*, is a manifestation of this awakened interest.

## Women's desires and masculine ideals

The essence of Umm ʿAwf's criticism of her husband was his failure to match up with the tribal masculine ideal, the 'cardinal virtues', according to van Gelder: intelligence, courage, generosity and decency.[47] Similar expressions are used by other women in the chapter on conjugal disputes in *Balaghāt al-Nisāʾ*. Many women also blame their husbands for their unattractive appearance, unpleasant behaviour and old age, as well as for being impotent. Wives are obviously particularly knowledgeable about men's potency but allegations of impotence in poetry were not only expressed by women with direct experience of it, certain female poets are ascribed poetic accusations and lampoons of several men.

Women's censure of men for not living up to masculine norms is also a theme in anecdotes where women act as experts of men's attractiveness and sexual prowess. In one oft-quoted anecdote, the famous pre-Islamic poet Imru' al-Qays is thrown out by a woman who is disappointed at his performance in bed.

> Al-Haytham ibn ʿAdī related: Imru' al-Qays was detested by women. One day when he was with a woman, she said to him: 'Get up, you the best of young men, morning has come!' When he did not rise up, she went on urging him. Finally, he

> rose up and found that it was still night. He returned to her and said: 'Why did you do that?' She said: 'Because you have a heavy chest and a light backside, and are quick in coming.'[48]

The poet Imru' al-Qays boasts about his sexual affairs in his *mu'allaqa*, and it is not clear from where he got the reputation of being detested by women. In any case, the woman's remark is not flattering for him. The characteristics 'a heavy chest and light backside' is referred to occasionally as a quality women dislike in a male sex partner. However, potency and having a large number of sex partners were considered pre-Islamic masculine ideals, especially for the nobility, as in the following anecdote about a pre-Islamic personality who was recognized as a king.

> Al-Madā'inī narrated: 'Anaza captured al-Ḥārith ibn Ẓālim. A woman among them passed by him and saw a penis with a black head. She said: 'Be careful with your captive, for he is a king and the friend of kings.' They said: 'How do you know that?' (She said:) 'I saw a glans that was black from women's *furūm* (pl.).' *Farm* (s.) is what women use to contract their vulva, made of *rāmik*[49] or raisin pits or something else.[50]

In this anecdote, a tribal leader, al-Ḥārith ibn Ẓālim from Banū Murra, was taken as an anonymous captive, and then obviously stripped of his clothes when a woman passes by. As the scene takes place in *jahiliyya*, this is implicitly not a strange situation. Luckily, the woman, being familiar with men's private parts and women's sexual techniques, understands that the man is a king. Incidentally, the story includes an old recipe for tightening the vagina (see Chapter 1).

Women give their opinions about men and their attractiveness also in anecdotes clearly set in Islamic times. In the anecdote below three prominent early Muslim men are compared, of whom the third is found to be the superior.

> A woman saw Ibn al-Zubayr, and said: 'Who is this one who looks like a snake licking his lips?' She saw 'Alī and said: 'Who is this one who looks like he has been broken and then set again?' She saw Ṭalḥa and said: 'Who is this one who looks like Herakleios' dinār?'[51]

The woman is anonymous, while the men are some of the most famous early Muslim heroes and companions of Muhammad. She disparages the appearances of Ibn al-Zubayr and 'Alī ibn Abī Ṭālib, whereas she praises Ṭalḥa – he looks like Herakleios' golden dinar, which is often used for describing beautiful women. In an anecdote set in the Abbasid period a female slave evaluates her owner, who happens to be the linguist Abū 'Ubayda, but only after he asked her to do so.

> Abu 'Ubayda said to his slave-girl: 'Tell me sincerely what women dislike about me.' She said: 'They dislike that when you are sweating, you smell like a dog.' He said: 'You told me the truth. My family used to nurse me with milk from a dog.'[52]

As often is the case in Abbasid anecdotes, a *jāriya* is here put in the place of the honest and sharp-witted Arab woman.

Women's eloquence was not limited to blaming husbands, they also, occasionally, praised men. Among well-known early Arabic female poets, al-Khansāʾ did not only mourn her brothers, she praised them as well, and another famous poet, Layla al-Akhyaliyya, composed panegyrics for Umayyad caliphs and officials.[53] In the material collected by Ibn Abī Ṭāhir in *Balaghāt al-Nisāʾ*, there are several named and anonymous women who praise their husbands in poetry and rhymed prose. The praise is often in the form of descriptions (*waṣf*) of the husband's good qualities, in the same way as there are descriptions of a husband's bad qualities. The most famous of these descriptions is Umm Zarʿ's praising description of her husband and his family in a conversation with other pre-Islamic women, which was classified as a hadith as it was supposedly told by Muhammad to his wife ʿĀʾisha. Muhammad relates a conversation between eleven pre-Islamic women, who disclosed their feelings for their husbands. In the variant included in *Balaghāt al-Nisāʾ*, the first five women criticize their husbands while the last six praise theirs. The last woman, Umm Zarʿ, extolls her ex-husband and his family in extensive and difficult *sajʿ*, the text is interspersed with philological comments, and though he left her for what seems to be a sudden attraction, and she married a new, honourable man, she still cannot praise him enough.[54]

The hadith of Umm Zarʿ is only one of many examples of women's linguistic heritage which attracted the attention of linguists and philologists. What makes it exceptional is the attention it got from legal scholars. The hadith was considered reliable and was included in the canonical hadith collections. Scholars discussed how to interpret the women's descriptions, positive as well as negative, within an Islamic legal framework. They derived rules for gender relations and behaviour from it and continued to comment upon it for centuries; several monographs were written on the topic.[55] One of the issues that puzzled legal scholars was how women could be allowed to discuss their husbands with others, especially disclosing their flaws. In the ninth/fifteenth century, Ibn Ḥajar al-ʿAsqalānī wrote an extensive commentary, building on centuries of legal interpretations. He concluded that women are allowed to occasionally, not habitually, describe their husbands' bad and good qualities, and even exaggerate. It is permissible to disclose a husband's faults, but only if the intention is to persuade against errors.[56]

Women praise their husbands by mentioning masculine virtues such as providing for and protecting one's family, but a few women praised their husband's qualities in more sensual terms, for example for being a source of pleasure.[57] Ibn Abī Ṭāhir tells an anecdote about the daughters of the pre-Islamic poet Dhū al-Iṣbaʿ al-ʿAdawānī, who, to their regret, remained unmarried. One day, their father overheard them as they were discussing future husbands with each other and described their ideal men in poetry. Their convincing descriptions prompted Dhū al-Iṣbaʿ to marry them off, which must be considered a happy ending.[58] In another anecdote, the queen of Saba's female companion described the pleasure a wife can get from a husband so tellingly and convincingly that the queen, who had until then refused to get married, decided to marry a cousin. She did not regret her decision, and after the marriage she told her companions that he gave her 'uninterrupted pleasure'.[59] Women's words are overpowering in this anecdote, capable of igniting desire and passion, which was perfectly alright in this case, as the queen of Saba did not give herself over to fornication. Instead, she married a familiar individual and enjoyed licit pleasure.

The archetype Bedouin woman was eloquent and frank, but also chaste, according to most love stories in a Bedouin setting. When al-Aṣmaʿī conducted field work to collect tribal lore and sources for lexicography and poetry, one of his many informants was the poet Yazīd ibn Ḍabba, *mawlā* (client, adopted member) of the tribe of Thaqīf in al-Ta'if, where al-Aṣmaʿī met him.[60] Yazīd recited a poem for him by a Bedouin woman who described a young man in sensual terms. The woman once passed a group of men and saw a beautiful young man among them. She halted, exchanged some jokes with the men and approached the young man with the words:

> By the House of God, I witness that your teeth are pure and your waist is slender / You have broad forearms, a tall body, / and when alone with women, you are forceful. / You are the most excellent bedfellow / but when you look at women, you look at them chastely.

When her husband heard about the verse, he asked her who the attractive man she described was. She replied that it was him, her husband, but he did not believe her. 'My waist is not slender!' he answered, and implored her to tell him the truth. She agreed, on the condition that he did not tell anyone. The young man came from a powerful branch of Thaqīf, the banū Muʿattib, who were the guardians of the shrine of the Goddess al-Lāt, and she was apparently afraid of the young man's powerful relatives. After this incident, her husband divorced her, and broke his promise; he disclosed the origin of his ex-wife's poem. Apparently, the verse was not considered disgraceful for her as long as it was her husband she described as 'the most excellent bed-fellow'. Now, she expressed her disappointment over her treacherous ex-husband in a concluding verse: 'After having been sincere to each other you were treacherous and betrayed us/ the worst trusted lover is the one who betrays love.'[61]

The anecdote is interesting in many ways. The incident apparently took place before Thaqīf converted to Islam, with the more morally lax rules of *jahiliyya*. The woman severely broke the rules of female modesty when she first joked with a group of men and then recited an erotic poem about one of them. The woman was still chaste; however, she merely praised the masculinity of a worthy man and her attraction was understandable. The crux was that the praise could be interpreted as her own feelings; the young man became part of an erotic fantasy that her husband could not compete against. After certain pressure, she eventually shared her fantasy with him, believing that sincerity was a token of their love. Her husband fall short of the ideal sincere lover and divorced her, probably as a result of jealousy, as he later bitterly revealed her secret. The woman, apparently, did not believe she had done anything wrong; her husband was the wrongdoer since he betrayed their love by divorcing her and their sincere friendship by disclosing her secret. By getting the last word in this anecdote, which is built up around her two poems, she is the one who defines what is right and wrong. The themes in this anecdote are familiar. A woman describes and reviews a man's beauty, and in this case, his sexual prowess, which, in order to be a source for masculine pride, only women can describe. There is also a woman, who is so captivated by a worthy man's beauty and charisma that she, like Zulaikha in the story of Yūsuf, cannot but express her attraction. Zulaikha, who according to the popular story did all kinds of tricks to seduce Yūsuf, without success, had a favourable image in Abbasid *adab*.

Women also wrote love poetry in the form of *ghazal*. In the Abbasid era, this was the speciality of slave courtesans, but Abbasid philologists and historians preserved sporadic love poems attributed to early Islamic women. Altogether, there is a myriad of short love poems attributed to early Islamic and Abbasid women in classical anthologies and *adab* works, and several of them are collected in modern anthologies. It is perhaps pointless to attempt to find specific themes connected to the gender of the poet; female poets used the same tropes and imagery as male poets.[62]

## Anecdotal women

In an oft-cited book from 1991, Fedwa Malti-Douglas coined the term 'anecdotal woman' describing a certain witty character whose eloquence and wit arose from a wish to draw attention to her attractiveness, or, conversely, to distract from it.[63] Being a trickster she wins verbal battles, but not without using her body and her main stratagem, *kayd* (ruse). It is not a coincidence that this character is a woman, as these characteristics are inherited in the female gender according to male authors, as interpreted by Malti-Douglas. Moreover, she claims that this is the predominant representation of witty women in classical Arabic prose literature, where female witticisms 'revolve around female sexuality and women's bodies'.[64]

This claim is sweeping and can be criticized; Malti-Douglas quotes a few examples from literary works by authors living centuries apart, without taking into consideration genre and readers' expectations.[65] There are many more anecdotes about women that do not fit into this pattern. Reversely, probably many more witticisms revolve around male sexuality, even though the circumstances of jokes and witticisms about or emanating from an interest in female sexuality are different from those of men. Nevertheless, Malti-Douglas makes an important point and the term 'anecdotal woman' is especially useful when analysing anecdotes that do consider sexuality. In many cases, a female character in anecdotes finds herself in a situation in which her body or appearance is evaluated by a man, and succeeds in turning the situation to her favour.

The 'anecdotal woman' is successful in rebuffing unwanted attention in a public space, where her body is seen as common property, not the least if she is unveiled and walking alone. A typical setting is a meeting between a woman and an unrelated man on a road or another part of a journey. The man confronts the woman with a provocative expression but looses control over the verbal duel and the woman triumphs. The sympathy for such a woman lies in her ability to reverse a social subordinated role with the help of her witty words; she has the appeal of the underdog. The setting is the road in two anecdotes in *ʿUyūn al-Akhbār* by Ibn Qutayba that depict the superb dealing with this situation by an anecdotal woman. In both cases, her body is the target, but she takes control over the situation by using her verbal skill, wit and knowledge of poetry, the skills that constitute her street-smartness. In the first anecdote, a man called Abū al-Ghuṣn is on his way to Mecca to perform the pilgrimage when he notices a beautiful girl on the road. He joins a group of men who shout and stare at the girl, who does not wear a face veil.

> Abū al-Ghuṣn, the Bedouin, said, I went out to perform the pilgrimage. When I passed Qubā' the people there shouted to each other: 'The shiny one! The shiny one!' I looked, and I saw a girl with a face shining like a sword. When we hit her with our gazes, she dropped her veil over her face. We said, 'We are travellers and there is a reward for us, so let us enjoy your face!' She turned her heels, and I could discern the laugh on her face when she said: 'When you sent your glance as a seeker / for your heart, what you saw exhausted you / You saw something whose entirety you have no power / over and whose part you cannot withhold yourself from patiently'.[66]

The woman is called a *jāriya*, which in the Abbasid era and later mostly refers to a female slave, a 'slave-girl'. This would explain why she walked without a face veil, which slaves normally did not wear. In early Islamic and Bedouin settings, however, *jāriya* more often signifies a young woman or a girl. Regardless, walking without a face veil is taken as a permission for the men to stare at her and when the girl notices their interest, she quickly covers her face. Abū Ghuṣn does not know the other men, but he can easily join them and share their sense of entitlement. They have the right to see the girl's face as performing the pilgrimage will give them divine reward, and this is what they want as reward. They cannot accept that she covers her face. Nevertheless, she rejects them with a poem and gets the last word. She tells them that even if they could enjoy her face, which they likened to a sword, they would never be able to get more than that. She enjoys the situation, according to the narrator, apparently empowered by her superior wit and eloquence. What begins as unwanted attention ends in a verbal battle, as it turns out that her words are her sword, not her face.

The following anecdote begins in a similar way, with men taking the liberty of staring at an unknown woman who passes by them.

> A Bedouin woman passed a group of men from the Numayr clan, and they remained staring at her. She said: 'People from Numayr, by God, you have not adopted any of these two, neither God's saying: "Tell the believing men to lower their gazes" (Qur'an 24:30), nor Jarīr's poem: "Lower your eyes, you are from banū Numayr / You are not worth as much as members of the Ka'b or Kilāb tribes."' The people felt embarrassed by her words and bowed their heads in silence.[67]

The men in this anecdote stare at the woman but remain silent. She refers to two essential though different value systems, Islam and tribal pride, and demonstrates that she commands the discourse of both – the Qur'an and tribal poetry. She succeeds in criticizing their behaviour and tribal origin, as well as showing off her superior wit. By this, she does not only make them feel embarrassed, she also gives them an order; she tells them to lower their gazes and they do. In some cases, the anecdotal woman defends herself by admitting to an alleged shamelessness, and being proud about it, as in the following anecdote:

> Abū Ḥāzim al-Madanī said: When I was throwing stones[68] I saw an unveiled woman with the most beautiful face, throwing stones. I said: 'God's servant, do you not fear God! How can you unveil in this place and seduce the people!' She said: 'By God, old man, I am one of the women about whom the poet said: "One of those who do not make the pilgrimage seeking a reward in the world to come / but to kill the innocent and easily duped."'
>
> I said: Verily, I ask God not to punish this beautiful face with the fire![69]

The woman in this anecdote does not let the narrator define the situation. She is accused of an impudence to which she admits gladly.

## The purchase of a slave-girl

The motif of 'the anecdotal woman' might have been inspired by enslaved women's vulnerable situations, not the least when exposed on the slave market. The most striking examples given by Malti-Douglas are variations on the same theme: a female slave is presented for a high-ranking official, often the caliph himself, for a potential purchase. The potential buyer asks her something and she answers with a clever remark, showing off her wit and verbal skills, sometimes by alluding to her sexual skills, and thus convinces the man to buy her. The anecdotes are often short jokes with limited references to historical circumstances; Malti-Douglas gives examples of some common jokes. In one example, a slave-girl is asked if she can do something with her hands, whereupon she answers: 'No, but with my feet', meaning that she is a dancer.[70] In another, the buyer asks a slave-girl; 'Are you a virgin, or what?' and the woman answers: 'I am what, sir.' In a third example, the buyer asks the slave: 'Do you play the lute (*ʿūd*)?' and she answers: 'No, but I can sit on it'; *ʿūd* also signifies 'a stick'.[71] The sexual nature of the purchase is here explicit.

Malti-Douglas' examples are taken from later collections of anecdotes, but the theme has its origin in Abbasid literature. There are plenty of anecdotes about witty and eloquent slave women who are displayed before a caliph or another man, answering questions not only successfully, but also irresistibly.[72] The name of the buyer varies; the caliph al-Mutawakkil is one of the most commonly mentioned but sometimes the buyer is a famous character from earlier history, such as the Umayyad poet al-Farazdaq. In several of Malti-Douglas' examples, taken from Ibn al-Jawzī (d. 597/1201), it is instead the Abbasid intellectual al-Jāḥiẓ who initiates the dialogue, whereas he never figures in similar anecdotes in Abbasid literature.

The anecdotes are obviously fictional, but even so, the narrative setting reflects a reality in Abbasid society, where captives were still taken in the wars against the Byzantines and slaves were bought together with other goods from outside the caliphate, in addition to the slaves born to slave parents within. The international slave trade flourished and the caliphate was far from the only society with a high number of slaves among its population, but due to its wealth, slavery was widespread. Female slaves were primarily used as domestic workers and concubines.

Female slaves displayed at the slave markets for potential buyers were some of the most socially vulnerable individuals in Abbasid society. Islamic law regulated the trade in and treatment of slaves, giving them a minimum of protection, but it also allowed male owners to have sexual relations with their female slaves. They had no control over their own bodies as male owners had sexual access to them or could marry them off without their consent. The laws ensured that slaves' basic needs were catered for and that they were not mistreated, but there was probably a high level of abuse especially in the slave markets, even if there were rules that limited the exposure of female slaves' bodies.[73]

Nonetheless, slaves lived under very different conditions; while 'common' slaves were some of the most vulnerable in the society, elite slaves belonged to the elite of the society. The *jawārī* displayed for potential purchase in the anecdotes were clearly not ordinary slaves. The setting is often exclusive; several of the women are displayed for a caliph or high-ranking official, apparently in a private palace. Female elite slaves were normally not displayed in public. When they changed owners, they were usually presented for potential buyers in private or given away.[74] Apparently, the female elite slaves of Abbasid society, the educated slave courtesans, inspired the anecdotes about the purchase. They were beautiful and skilful girls who had been picked out and trained in schools managed by master musicians and singers: their job was to entertaine the elite. The courtesans participated in the cultural gatherings in the urban centres and contributed to the prosperous cultural milieu. Some of them became famous singers and poets, and, as royal concubines, mothers of princes and caliphs. They belonged to the cultural elite themselves and were also patrons of poets and culture.

Some anecdotes about the purchase of slave-girls involve named courtesans and are retold in history books which are apparently found reliable by historians.

The buyer was in these cases often one of the Abbasid caliphs, and al-Mutawakkil appears quite often in this context.[75] In general, the purchase plays a major role in the biographies of these women, not the least in *Kitāb al-Aghānī*, where Abū al-Faraj al-Iṣbahānī emphasizes the fantastic amounts of money the male elite were ready to pay for them. The price and the setting of the sale were indicators of the slaves' status. The women who attracted the most lavish buyers were often born in the caliphate, selected at a young age and taught reading and writing, together with skills such as composing poetry, dancing, singing or playing an instrument, as well as intellectual subject such as history and Islamic sciences. The stories about these women fascinated readers and continued to circulate for centuries. The purchase situation represents the entrance examination to the cultural elite for these women. Thoroughly trained and selected for this task, it was now up to them to prove their excellence.

Utilising sex appeal was a rational behaviour, not the least when displayed for sale. The purchase could be a resort for social mobility, and sex appeal could be a chance for the woman to get a better life. Even if their chances were considerable better if they had wit, eloquence and a particular skill, attractiveness could be enough. The purchase was a crucial occasion for slaves, not only for the educated slave courtesans who were presented in private, but also for the unfortunate women at the slave market. In just a few minutes they could make an impression that either attracted or put off potential buyers, which gave them a limited amount of agency, with the reservation that this 'agency' might have been forced upon them by the seller, in order to maximize profit. Nevertheless, it is not strange that this important moment in a slave's life became a literary topic. For a common female slave, becoming her master's concubine secured her standing and gave her better life conditions, at least if she was his favourite or gave birth to his child. In that case, she would became an *umm walad*, and her owner was forbidden to sell her and she would be freed upon his death.

## Women's verbal proficiency: concluding remarks

In the late second/eight century, philologists such as al-Aṣmaʿī and Abū ʿUbayda, the leading philologists from Basra, studied everything that was transmitted, orally or written, on the history and culture of the Arabs.[76] When the early philologists and historians searched for rare Arabic words and found explicit expressions attributed to women, they put down these words, often embedded in anecdotes, probably both for their linguistic and entertainment value. The corpus of linguistic examples from the early Arabs were important for later authors, but society had changed from Late Antiquity to the early medieval period. From the second/eight century onwards, free women's words and actions were strictly censored in literature. Explicit vocabulary was almost exclusively attributed to pre- and early Islamic women, slave courtesans or anonymous women, presumably from the lower classes.

Arab women's eloquence was a gold-mine for lexicographers and the stories collected by early Abbasid philologists emphasized this skill. The corpus of poems and oral communication attributed to women is clouded by uncertainty, however, and there have been no real attempts to detect traces of real women's literary production. Many scholars prefer to regard them as representations; the pre-Islam and early Islamic women in books written by Abbasid authors are representatives of a world gone by, imagined by Abbasid authors as a background against which the new society takes shape.[77] Umm ʿAwf's bold plea to the caliph, with nothing but her verbal skills to support her, became a symbol for a changing social reality, where it was possible for the apt and gifted intellectual to attain his goal, regardless of kinship and social background. Nevertheless, women's poetry in *Balaghāt al-Nisāʾ* is often expressive and seems to be an outlet for women's real emotions. The dominating emotions in poets by women complaining about their husbands are disappointment, aversion, hatred and disgust. In many cases, the poems are mocking and bawdy, but far from merry. Often, no reason or weak reasons are given as grounds for the woman's aversion; sometimes the reason is sexual and emotional dissatisfaction.

Whereas the poetry attributed to women seems to reflect genuine emotions, the anecdotes are fictional, even if they have a kernel of truth. Verbal proficiency is a main theme in many anecdotes, and used as a strategy by female protagonists in verbal duels against husbands to take some control over their lives. These verbal duels reflect a social reality in which marriage is the main factor that shapes a woman's adult life. In reality, without real power, women have to use subtle ways of manipulating to get what they want, but in early Arabic anecdotes eloquent argumentation could do the trick.

Verbal proficiency as a female strategy is a popular theme in anecdotes, embodied in the popular 'anecdotal woman', who, eloquently and cleverly, rebuffs unwanted advances or attracts the attention of benefactors. Eloquence is a strategy for equality in situations where the woman is socially subordinate, and, often, she wins the verbal battle due to her superior wit and eloquence. In the verbal battle, eloquence and wit challenge hierarchies between men and women, masters and slaves, superiors and subordinates.

# 5

# Sexual Comedy and Women's Bodies

Duqāq was one of the famous Abbasid courtesans and an accomplished singer, trained by the most prominent teachers in the caliphate. According to Abū al-Faraj al-Iṣbahānī, she was lady-in-waiting for caliph Hārūn al-Rashīd's daughter, princess Ḥamdūna, and then for Ḥamdūna's mother Ghaḍīḍ, one of the caliph's favourite concubines. She was a concubine herself, and belonged to a man called Yaḥyā ibn al-Rabīʿ. She gave birth to his son Aḥmad, which meant that she was freed when Yaḥyā died and after that, she married several times and inherited parts of her husbands' wealth, which made her a rich woman. For later generations, however, she became known for her alleged lewd behaviour. What we know about her comes from a few testimonies quoted by Abū al-Faraj al-Iṣbahānī in *Kitāb al-Aghānī*.[1] Aḥmad ibn Ḥamdūn, a companion and courtier of caliph al-Mutawakkil, claimed that Duqāq once challenged his father Ḥamdūn, a companion of al-Rashīd, in a verbal duel.[2] Duqāq sent Ḥamdūn a letter describing her own 'thing', supposedly in boastful terms; we do not know, as Abū al-Faraj did not quote this part. Ḥamdūn cannot have been unfamiliar with playful arguments, yet, apparently more prudish than the famous courtesan, he was incapable of answering and asked a friend for counsel. The friend advised him to let a *mukhannath* (transsexual) look at his 'equipment' and compose a poem about it, which he did with success; Duqāq was lost for an answer and Ḥamdūn won the challenge.[3]

The *mukhannath*'s prose poem is cited in *Kitāb al-Aghānī*; it depicts the genitals of Ibn Ḥamdūn's father in rhymed prose, with amusing and slightly blasphemous metaphors, such as 'a long, hideous trumpet, bald and plucked', and 'a minaret between two rocks'. Description of genitals, preferably in hyperbolic terms, was an established poetic motif long before Abū al-Faraj cited Ibn Ḥamdūn in *Kitāb al-Aghānī*. Yet, the implication of Ibn Ḥamdūn's account is that Duqāq's behaviour was unconventional, and that Ḥamdūn was too virtuous to lower himself to her level, but still won the duel. The fact that Duqāq's contribution is not cited in *Kitāb al-Aghānī* indicates that women describing their genitalia was too embarrassing for Abū al-Faraj and his sources. Abū al-Faraj usually defended the art of music and its practitioners, and was perhaps anxious about the reputation of the women in the field. He was not above retelling slander, however; he and earlier generations of scholars, poets and courtiers in Baghdad were less prudish about Duqāq's supposed lewd behaviour.

According to Abū al-Faraj and his sources, Duqāq was widowed several times, her husbands were all military commanders and high officials, who, the sources insinuate, died because of her. ʿĪsā ibn Zaynab, a poet at the time of al-Maʾmūn and al-Muʿtaṣim, accused her vagina for the death of three husbands:

> I said when I saw the house of Duqāq, / her beauty has harmed her lovers!
> Caution the miserable fourth against Duqāq / so that his star does not become invisible.
> Distract him from intercourse with Duqāq, as / the misfortune of her pussy has raised to the horizon.
> When she sleeps with a husband he does not arise undamaged. /No, he is wounded and his wound does not stop bleeding.[4]

The other accounts in Duqāq's biographical article in *Kitāb al-Aghānī* follow a similar pattern; men from the cultural and political elite in Baghdad and Samarra relate her unconventional or even debauched behaviour in different settings. ʿĪsā ibn Zaynab wrote another satirical poem about her alleging that she had sex with her two slave-boys. People said, he claimed, that once she commanded one of them to 'fuck her'; if he agreed, she would set him free. The slave refused and answered, defiantly: 'fuck me instead and sell me to the Bedouins'.[5] Normally, a slave would have to obey his owner, but her unfeminine behaviour deprived her of his respect; he preferred a much more uncomfortable life as a slave of nomads. The prince and musician Ibrāhīm ibn al-Mahdī (162–224/779–839) wrote a song about her promiscuity; it does not mention her name but Ibrāhīm's son claimed that it was about Duqāq: 'I am deprived of you, oh friend of everybody. / Are you in love with everyone? / How can you, when you mix the thin with / the flesh of the fat, not suffer from indigestion?'[6] Duqāq used to meet with a multitude of men, Ibrāhīm's son explained according to the musician and author Jaḥẓa (d. 324/936), whose books Abū al-Faraj relied on, and she made every one of them believe that she loved him.

One of the men who contributed to the rumours about Duqāq in *Kitāb al-Aghānī* is Ibn Abī Ṭāhir Ṭayfūr, the author of *Balaghāt al-Nisāʾ*. He had heard Abū Hiffān (d. between 255/869 and 257/871), a collector of anecdotes about poets, say that when Duqāq's owner Yaḥyā ibn al-Rabīʿ left the house, she did several extraordinary things, a rumour he complemented with a poem about Duqāq's alleged dissolute behaviour. The polymath Aḥmad ibn al-Ṭayyib al-Sarakhsī (286/899), who was a disciple of al-Kindī, is one of the main informants on the life of Duqāq.[7] He related that Duqāq was known for her *ẓarf* (stylishness), *mujūn*, and *futuwwa* (youthfulness).[8] These qualities were usually considered masculine; a *ẓarīf*, for example, was a man with refined taste, who nevertheless could appreciate *mujūn*, that is, burlesque and bawdy poetry, talk or behaviour. The term *mujūn* was first used as a generic description for the famous poet Abū Nuwās' (d. between 198 and 200/813–815) many poems about the sexual adventures of his poetic persona. Duqāq's behaviour apparently challenged gender norms, at least in the minds of those men who narrated her life story after her death.[9]

At least some could have been spreading rumours about Duqāq in order to disparage her son Aḥmad ibn Yaḥyā, who also was a singer and who was called Ibn Duqāq after her. Al-Sarakhsī relates that he once made fun of a Christian cloth merchant, Abū al-Jāmūs, at a social gathering. When Abū al-Jāmūs had enough, he turned to the others who were present and shared a memory from his childhood, intended to embarrass Ibn Duqāq. As a boy, he accompanied his master to the palace of Ḥamdūna with cloth for sale and there they met Duqāq. She received them with a fan in her hand with aphorisms written on both sides. On one side she had written, 'The cunt is in more need of two pricks than the prick of two cunts' and, on the other, 'the millstone is in more need of two mules than one mule of two millstones'. Abū al-Jāmūs' allegation effectively silenced Ibn Duqāq, according to al-Sarakhsī's informant.

How could a woman who was infamous for dissolute behaviour and promiscuity have access to the royal harem and serve a princess and a royal concubine? Or, to put it differently, how could an acclaimed singer, a companion to a princess and later a prosperous widow be remembered only for her sexual behaviour? The anecdote about the fan is humorous, even subversive in an environment where men could be legally promiscuous whereas women could not; it is also attributed to another singer, Danānīr, who supposedly wrote it on a wall on the pilgrim road to Mecca.[10] Nevertheless, the reason for attributing it to Duqāq here is apparently to humiliate her son. In fact, looking closer at her biographical article in *Aghānī*, most, if not all, anecdotes about her dissolute behaviour might have, at one point, been narrated with the aim of disgracing her son. Aḥmad ibn Duqāq was himself a mediocre singer, according to Abū al-Faraj, but he lived a long life and told many accounts about singers and the art that were written down by authors and musicians such as Jaḥẓa.

Many of the men who spread rumours about Duqāq lived one or more generations after her. We do not know when Duqāq was born or when she died, but as she worked first for Ḥamdūna and then for Ghaḍīḍ, we can get a clue. Ḥamdūna married her cousin Jaʿfar ibn Mūsā al-Hādī in 170/786, the year Hārūn became caliph, which was also the year Abū Nuwās came to Baghdad and started to become famous.[11] Ghaḍīḍ died during al-Rashīd's caliphate, according to Ibn al-Sāʿī.[12] Al-Rashīd died in 193/809 and it is possible that Duqāq became lady-in waiting at the royal palace before year 786 and that she left no later than 193/809. Ibrāhīm ibn al-Mahdī, who allegedly wrote a song about her promiscuity, must have met her as he was the uncle of princess Ḥamdūna. He was only seven years old in 170/786 when Ḥamdūna married, but Duqāq could of course have worked for the princess after that. ʿĪsā ibn Zaynab, who warned about Duqāq's vagina in a poem, composed poetry at the time of al-Maʿmūn and al-Muʿtaṣim, but he could have known Duqāq before that as his father was a high official for Hārūn al-Rashīd. Nevertheless, as much as the label *mujūn* is anachronic in regard to Duqāq, as the term was coined after Abū Nuwās, the allegations of sexual misconduct as they appear in *Kitāb al-Aghānī* are made after her death. Abū al-Faraj al-Iṣbahānī's readers and his audience at the salon of the Būyid *wazīr* al-Muhallabī, appreciated *mujūn* and for them Duqāq's alleged dissolution was merely entertaining. Bawdy talk and poetry thrived in the Būyid era; in the words of Zoltan Szombathy, 'it was arguably in this period that *mujūn* reached its apogee in terms of popularity and cultural impact as well as extravagance'.[13]

As we saw in Chapter 4, the presence of outspoken women in early Arabic literature is not astonishing; explicit language was appreciated and often considered humorous. In the case of al-Dahnāʾ, her outspoken desire for intercourse was countered by her husband's likening himself to a stallion. Explicit language was risky, however, at least for women, when it was taken out of context and spread to a wider audience not familiar with the situation in which it was articulated. It could definitely harm women's reputation when it was associated with promiscuity and extra-marital affairs. Duqāq was not only outspoken, she was also accused for breaking norms of female sexual behaviour, such as demanding sex from her male slaves (which was normal and licit behaviour for men). As a courtesan, her role was to provide elite men with an outlet for excitement and passion, which are suppressed in a highly segregated society where love and passion are separated from marriage.[14] However, Duqāq was not only a courtesan, she was also a mother, in addition to being the wife of several elite men. Even if her possible uninhibited behaviour was expected and appreciated by her peers, it broke the gender norms in the wider patriarchal society and could be used as a means to humiliate her son. This ambiguity is characteristic for women and sexual comedy; under certain conditions, female poets and artists could use sexual themes just as men did but their historic persona risked being exploited and ridiculed.

Duqāq was not the only woman who wrote a bawdy poem or even described her vagina in Abbasid literature. Women were not only targets of satire and objects of erotic descriptions; they also contributed to the fields of *mujūn* and sexual comedy, although they are not as visible as male *mujūn* poets are. In *Mujūn: Libertinism in Medieval Muslim Society and Literature*, Szombathy questions the existence of female libertines and the authenticity of *mujūn* attributed to women: 'Even though the sources do mention, if infrequently, female libertines, it is equally conceivable that male poets would amuse themselves and their friends by inventing such funny pieces – and the accompanying anecdotes – about the lax morals of women.'[15] Szombathy keeps the question about female authorship open, which is reasonable as he only refers to one source, *Kitāb al-Muwashshā* by Abū Ṭayyib al-Washshā᾽ (d. 325/937), and the licentious sayings attributed to the *mutaẓarrifāt* (sophisticated ladies) in Baghdad.[16] There are many more explicit poems and sayings attributed to female poets in other sources, most obvious in *Balaghāt al-Nisā᾽* by Ibn Abī Ṭāhir Ṭayfūr in the ninth century, which has a section on women's *mujūn*, and, in the tenth century, *Ash῾ār al-Nisā᾽* (*Poetry by Women*) by al-Marzūbānī (d. 384/994), and Abū al-Faraj al-Iṣbahānī's articles on female poets and singers.[17]

This chapter gives a survey of women's sexual comedy in early Arabic literature with a focus on poetic descriptions of female genitalia by male and female poets, the topic that was left out by Abū al-Faraj al-Iṣbahānī in his portray of Duqāq. I assume that women could be libertines and create explicit poetry, and that many of the poems attributed to women were also originally written by women, although possibly altered in transmission. Considering that we only have literary sources, this is impossible to prove, and I agree with Szombathy that some *mujūn* can have been falsely attributed to women, but there is no reason to believe that everything was. However, using images from their own bodies, especially the private parts, were especially risky for female poets, as the female body and sexuality were main targets of satire, even when the addressees were men. I will give examples of the misogynist trend in this chapter and also look into cases when women's historical persona have been used and abused with the intention of conveying entertaining and derogating images of women. Duqāq is not the only woman whose reputation was spoiled by accusations of promiscuity and non-conventional sexual behaviour. Eventually, women were much more often objects of sexualized jokes and satire than they were creators; they were targets of verbal assaults and female relatives were exploited for attacking male relatives, as in the case of Duqāq. Men's sexuality was of course also subject of verbal aggressions, but men could more easily turn the aggressions to their favour, as male promiscuity was not necessarily a negative quality.

## Battle of the sexes

Ḥamdūn was too prudish to write about his member, other men were not. The *mujūn* poet par excellence, Abū Nuwās, once wrote to the poet ʿInān, a slave courtesan, 'I have a nasty (*khabīth*) penis, its colour is reddish black. If it sees a cleft in the lowland, it mounts it until it dies.'[18] ʿInān answered him with an acid poem about Abū Nuwās' promiscuity, but she did not write anything similar about herself. The comparison between the male and female member is the theme of a verbal duel in *Jawāmiʿ al-Ladhdha*, staged as a *mufākhara* (boasting-match) between the vagina and the penis, attributed, probably falsely, to al-Jāḥiẓ. The story goes that a learned young man in Basra finally gets to meet his dream woman, an intelligent and quick-witted slave-girl called Badīʿ, who is a master of *mujūn*.[19] She initiates a debate on the merits of the genital organs: 'As far as I know, God did not create something more precious than the vagina.' Characteristically, she peppers her eulogy with blasphemy; God made the vagina superior, 'so that leaders, military commanders, and noble men submit to it; they profess their belief in it and rely upon it'. Badīʿs exposition turns eventually into a hyperbolic account of the vagina's dangerous power over men: it caused the downfall of pious men and prophets; it is more powerful than the greatest of rulers. Yet, it is also a source of comfort and joy, uniting people in love and happiness.

The attribution of this boasting-match is perhaps a confusion with al-Jāḥiẓ's *Boasting match between slavegirls and slaveboys* (*Mufākharat al-jawārī wa-l-ghilmān*), a well-known altercation between supporters of men and of women as sex partners. As a literary subject, it is related to the emergence of erotic poetry about boys (*mudhakkarāt*) as opposed to erotic poetry about women (*muʾannathāt*).[20] The literary form, 'boasting-matches' or altercation between supporters of two objects or concepts, or between the objects themselves, was popular during the Abbasid era. The arguments in these debates were presented in the form of anecdotes and poetry, sometimes also with references to religious authorities, tradition and wisdom, in the spirit of *adab* literature. An adaption of the al-Jāḥiẓ boasting-match is included in *Jawāmiʿ al-Ladhdha* but attributed to Aḥmad ibn al-Ṭayyib al-Sarakhsī, who heard it from Ibn Abī Ṭāhir Ṭayfūr. In both these debates the disputants are men; women do not play an active role. That is to say, the opponents are not the 'slave-girls' and 'slave-boys' themselves, but men defending their sexual preferences: 'fornicators', who prefer sex with women, and active male homosexuals, who prefer sex with boys. The perspective is exclusively male; the only justification for the existence of *jawārī* and *ghilmān* in this text is the pleasure of privileged men. The arguments focus on the degree of pleasure men can derive from women versus boys, and their relative beauty and pleasantness are compared and discussed from this perspective. The differences between these two 'groups' are not the main point of these debates, however. The debates are pure entertainment in *mujūn* style addressed to a mainly male audience, expecting entertainment. Neither the homosexual debaters nor their heterosexual opponents are above engaging in illicit sex, as indicated by calling them 'fornicators', and the reader can expect some spicy stories. As Rosenthal notes, this literature is 'often aimed at provoking laughter rather than proving some point of sexual preference'.[21]

Another literary contest in *Jawāmiʿ al-Ladhdha*, between a slave-girl and a slave-boy, is more interesting, as it is not merely a humorous comparison of the genital organs; it brings up more arguments for the advantages of women and not only for being the preferred sex partner. The slave-girl initiates the altercation, claiming that women are more loving, beautiful and loyal than men are. The slave-boy counters with arguments taken from the androcentric religious and medical traditions. According to the Qurʾan, men are in charge of women because they have been given an advantage from God (Q 4:34) and women are less reliable witnesses (Q 2:282). Hadiths and proverbs depict women as more prone to deceit, sin and falseness than men are. Also according to hadiths, women were created from men's ribs. Moreover, women are a tilth for men (Q 2:223), which the slave-boy points to as evidence that women were created for the benefit of men, not the other way around. Another proof for men's advantages is that they do not have to cover themselves with the veil, whereas women's bodies are *ʿawra* (private and shameful). Another evidence is the saying about women's *shahwa* (sexual appetite) being nine times bigger than that of men, which means that women need men more than men need women. He also brings up the medical theory that female genital organs are inverted and imperfect copies of male organs. Moreover, Muhammad warned against female rulers according to hadiths and it is evident in history that prophets, kings, caliphs and judges have been male.

These are only a few examples of the slave-boy's arguments – his evidence, taken from several androcentric traditions, is overwhelming. Yet, the girl does not despair. She refutes several of the boy's arguments one after another and adds new arguments for the advantages of women. There have been several female rulers in history and they were better rulers than any king was. There were for example Bilqis, princess ʿĀbida, a powerful ruler according to the slave-girl, and Queen Helena, who fought for Christianity. She argues that women are more loyal than men and as a proof she mentions several famous female lovers who suffered from unfulfilled love. The best example, she says, is Hind bint al-Nuʿmān, who loved another woman, al-Zarqāʾ. After the premature death of her beloved, Hind renounced the pleasures of life and became a nun in a convent she funded herself. The slave-girl also refutes the claim that women have a greater libido than men have, although she leaves the question open. If women really are more desiring, their ability to abstain from sex after childbirth is indeed further proof of their moral superiority.

These arguments are followed by beautiful descriptions of vaginas. She cites parts of an ode by the pre-Islamic poet al-Nābigha al-Dhubyānī (flourished end of sixth century), which describes a woman's genitalia and a sexual union:

> When you touch it, you touch something solid (*ʾajtham*) that remains in its place (*jāthim*), protruding so that it fills the hand.
> When you stab, you stab into something elevated (*mustahdif*), swelling when you touch it (*rābī al-majassa)*, daubed in perfume.
> When you pull out, you pull out from something tight (*mustaḥṣif*), like a strong young man pulling a tightly twisted rope (with a bucket from the well).
> He who comes to drink from it will not go back to the place of return, and he who returns after drinking from her, will not go back to the place of coming.[22]

Al-Nābigha's ode paints the picture of a gorgeous woman with the help of images from nature and animal life. Her speech is so beautiful that it attracts 'the mountain goats of the smooth hill'. Her hair is intensely black, wavy and abundant, growing 'like grape vine inclining against a trellis'. The slave-girl only quotes four verses, but they are preceded by an unknown verse, which serves as an introduction to al-Nābigha's verses: 'When you look, you see a moon, luminous and well-composed, daubed with fragrance, like a round stone.'[23] A new poem is created, relevant and understandable in the new context. In distinct *mujūn* style it borrows a motif from love-poetry, the likening of the beloved's face with the moon, but instead it is the vagina that is the moon. Yet, there is nothing ridiculous in this image; the only hyperbole is the exaggeration of its beauty. The word for fragrance is *zarnab*, perfume derived from sweet-smelling yew, which was one of the ingredients in a fumigation that ensures the love of the husband, which the physician al-Ṭabarī took from the Indian woman's book (see p. 37). It is also mentioned in the hadith of Umm Zarʿ (see p. 105) when the eighth woman said:

'My husband has a touch like a hare (*arnab*), and he smells like *zarnab*.'[24] The commentators, as Rosenthal points out, do not give these words a sexual meaning, but the fact is that both are used as metaphors for the vulva in later literature. Some say, according to Ibn Manẓūr, that the *zarnab* is a name for the female genitals if they are large (*farjuhā idhā ʿaẓuma*).[25] In all, this paraphrase of al-Nābigha's poem emphasizes the beauty of the female organ, indicated by the exclusion of a verse in his ode likening the vagina to a toothless old man ('When it bites, it squeezes it like an old, toothless man bites'). The debate ends with a burlesque scene with the male audience kneeling down and swearing their faithfulness to the vagina. The debate is playful, but still demonstrates that religious, medical and intellectual traditions that gave women a subordinate role were perceived and used as evidence for women's inferiority outside these traditions. Nonetheless, the contesting woman could also find evidence from the cultural heritage that proved the opposite.

Elsewhere, Ibn Naṣr maintains, with the help of medical and religious traditions, that the penis is the best part of the body.[26] He argues that as the Qurʾan gives men an advantage (*faḍl*) over women and, as the penis is the organ that sets men apart from women, this organ must be the reason for men's advantage and dominance over women. He illustrates this claim with a poem attributed to Ibn al-Rūmī: 'The penis (*zubb*) is a lord (*rabb*) for women, whom they love and fear / They find it so sweet and enjoyable / that if they could, they would eat it out of desire and drink it.'[27] Its witticism lies in the similarities between *rabb* (lord) and *zubb* (penis); they are only separated with a dot in Arabic. Nevertheless, this notion gives women a crucial role, as without them, the superiority of the penis would not have been acknowledged. In line with this poem, an important part of the advantage of the male genitalia is the pleasure it gives to women and the fact that women love it. According to ʿAlī ibn Naṣr, 'the predecessors in the science of coitus' (*ʿulamāʾ fī ʿilm al-bāh*) maintained that the penis is the best and most noble body member and stressed specifically the joy and comfort it gives to women.[28] These learned men, or perhaps ʿAlī ibn Naṣr himself, elaborate on women's adoration of the penis into accounts of veritable madness. The effect of the penis on women is formidable; they adore its appearance so much that they cannot take their eyes from it, and they love the sensation of holding it in their hands so much that they cannot let go of it, and so on. Whereas men are aroused by a combination of several attractive features, such as firm breasts and belly, an ample bottom, white thighs and small feet, women need only to see an erect penis to become aroused.[29] This supposed obsession is undeniable owing to male authorship and the expectations of the readers, a female author would probably have put it differently.

## The vagina as a poetic motif

Al-Nābigha's poem inspired many later poets, and descriptions of the vagina became an established poetic motif. Towards the end of the third/ninth century, the interest in poetry incited critics to classify rhetorical figures and poetic motives, exemplified with samples from poetry, whose imagery they found novel and original. Some critics found the topic sensitive; Abū Bakr al-Ṣūlī (d. 335/947) remarks almost apologetically in his work on Abū Tammām and modern poetry that this theme is a 'description of a topic rarely broached'.[30] He quotes two verses of al-Nābigha's poem followed by a poem by Ibn al-Rūmī (283/896), with motifs of tightness and immense heat: 'She has a pussy that borrows its fire / from a lover's passionate heart and a chest full of hatred. / When you feel its heat / it's as if your own innards were on fire / It gets tighter in the grip of love / like the noose of a rope.'[31] Al-Sūlī also quotes two poems by Abū al-Najm al-ʿIjlī, a late Umayyad poet, and Bashshār ibn Burd (d. 168/784–785) on the motif of size; both are mocking, and, according to al-Sūlī, very popular. Al-ʿIjlī's poem is a parody, a woman lifts 'her torn shift', and exposes something that looks like 'a half of a camel's hump with the other half thrown on top'. Her pubic hair is like 'the goatee on the face of a Yemeni sheikh'.[32]

Al-Sūlī's selection of vagina poems was apparently well-received and quoted in later motif catalogues, such as *Dīwān al-Maʿānī* by Abū Hilāl al-ʿAskarī (d. *c.* 400/1010), from Khuzestan, which is a thematically arranged poetry anthology directed towards aspiring scholars and officials.[33] Abū Hilāl includes al-Sūlī's selection of vagina poems in the section on love poetry and descriptions of beautiful women, but instead of stating that this topic is 'rarely broached', he explores a variety of motifs: tightness, heat, size, looseness, and rare images and adds several examples. Tightness is the most common motif, but he also gives an example of the opposite in Ibn al-Rūmī's mocking description of a grossly wide vagina.[34] A rare image was used by the poet al-Nājim, a contemporary of Ibn al-Rūmī, who likened the backside of a young woman to 'a baker's dough', and the front to 'cheese'. Another curious image is evoked by Abū al-Qāsim ibn al-Muʿadhdhal (d. 240/853), a satirical poet from Basra, likening a vulva with 'the egg of an ostrich', and its pubic hair with 'black cumin on a cake of bread'. The Umayyad poet al-Farazdaq (d. 114/732), uses curious images in a slightly blasphemous poem: 'She guards herself against me with a frowning face with no weapons', which looks like 'the nose of a bull'.[35] The vagina looks 'as if a pomegranate had been opened and poured out inside it', and it is so hot that it 'almost ignites a fire at the Night of Power (*Laylat al-Qadr*)'. While hot is a good quality, and probably the pomegranate too, *jahm* (frowning face) signifies an ugly, course face, but also a lion; an unflattering image, especially when combined with the bull's nose.

ʿAlī ibn Naṣr, the author of *Jawāmiʿ al-Ladhdha*, shares the interest in rare, innovative and beautiful images of the vagina and he quotes the same poems as al-Sūlī and Abū Hilāl, in addition to numerous others about male as well as female genitalia in a chapter called *Manāqib al-Dhakr wa-l-Farj* (*The Virtues of the Penis and the Vagina*).[36] The title is slightly blasphemous; the word *manāqib* was usually a term for the virtues of different tribes or for prominent Muslims, such as the Prophet's companions. In line with the elevation of sexual pleasure in this book, the verses describing genitalia are there to make us see their beauty, to laugh at them in a convivial manner and to feel enlightened. The verses and epigrams are attributed to well-known male poets, as well as anonymous male and female poets and a few named women. In addition to the poets mentioned above, Ibn Naṣr cites the early Islamic poet Suḥaym ʿAbd banī al-Ḥasḥās, the Umayyad poets Muḥammad ibn Duʾayb al-Fuqaymī (al-ʿUmānī al-Rājiz) and Muṭīʿ ibn Iyās (who lived through the Abbasid takeover), as well as the Abbasid philologists Mubarrad (d. 285/899 or 286/ 900) and al-Aṣmaʿī. The recurrent motifs are the same as in *Dīwān al-Maʿānī*; heat, looseness, tightness, and occasionally size.

In a poem attributed to al-Mubarrad, a vagina is likened to a drinking bowl of gold (*qaʿb niḍār*) and cheese from Baalbek. The bowl is also evoked by al-ʿUmānī al-Rājiz. Some twenty epigrams are attributed to anonymous men, sometimes specified as Bedouins, who replicate and elaborate upon the similes from al-Nābigha's poem: *mustahdif* (elevated) *jāthim* (remaining in its place), *akhtham* (solid) and *rābī al-majassa* (swelling when touched). Moreover, some sixteen epigrams are attributed to female poets, a few of them named, which will be discussed below.

In contrast to al-Nābighas' poem, in which penetration is likened to a stab (a thrust with the spear into a target) violence is not common in the poems cited in *Jawāmiʿ al-Ladhdha*. There are a few exceptions. In one poem al-Farazdaq describes a rape when the poetic persona deflowers virgins after having wrestled them down on the ground. The vagina is instead potentially violent in a verse in which it is likened to the jawbone or the forehead of a hungry lion with a large nose, not satisfied even if it eats a horn.[37] The image of the lion is used in another poem where the female member is likened to a hungry, biting lion followed by the more conventional 'like a bowl', and then by the unconventional 'and the udder of a she camel abounding with milk'. This vagina is *ajtham* (solid), a word taken from al-Nābigha's poem, and hot 'like blazing fire', and then, unexpectedly, 'it looks as if it has been treated with cupping glasses'.

As we will see below, at least some of al-Farazdaq's images implied sexual violence against women from a poetic opponent's family or tribe, and his language is arguablly sometimes misogynistic. However, mocking and unflattering images like al-Farazdaq's 'frowning face' and 'nose of a bull' lose their satirizing effect when taken out of context, in the poetry anthologies they are merely innovative and humorous.

## Sexual comedy and female authorship

My vagina, a noble vagina, suffices me
Like a horseman standing at the top of the hill
If I lie face down, it raises me up
If I walk uphill, it throws me down
Through it, I have given birth to eight children,
yet its opening has remained as it was[38]

Anonymous poet, cited in *Encyclopaedia of Pleasure*

When Duqāq sent a description of her own vagina to Ḥamdūn, she was not the first woman to write on this particular topic. Women boasting about their genitalia appear here and there in the Arabic literary tradition. In Ibn Qutayba's *adab* compilation *ʿUyūn al-Akhbār*, an anonymous Bedouin blames her husband for being impotent and at the same time she boasts about her smooth vulva: 'We have clefts (*ṣudūʿ*) in smooth stones (*ṣafan*); an impotent man has no luck with us!'[39] Ibn Qutayba's compilation intended to be a digest for aspiring officials, providing them with conversation topics and quotes for all kinds of situations. This particular report was perhaps intended as a *mujūn* topic, but it is also an example of Bedouin womens' command of poetic description (*waṣf*) in prose. Boasting about the vagina and comparing it to a cleft in a rock is probably intended to be humorous, yet it stands out as a proud declaration, perhaps referring to tribal pride; 'we' are the women in her clan, or perhaps women in general. The image is not necessarily a hyperbole; *ṣafan* can signify smooth, hard rocks, but they can also be smooth stones the size of a vulva.[40] Smoothness and solidity were considered attractive descriptions: *ṣudūʿ* (plural of *ṣadʿ*) signifies clefts, splits, or cracks, 'in a hard thing ... such as a glass vessel, and a wall'.[41] The implication is that these vaginas are tight, solid and not easy for a slack penis to penetrate.

There are also named women in the literary tradition. Laylā and ʿAmra, daughters of al-Ḥumāris of Banū Taghlib, were known for their humorous and explicit poetry. It is possible that they are the same woman, but given different names by later authors. An anecdote about them in *Ashʿār al-Nisāʾ* by al-Marzubānī is attributed to the philologist Abū ʿUbayda, who also wrote about al-Dahnāʾ in Chapter 4. According to him, their father al-Ḥumāris was very jealous and for this reason he did not want to marry off his daughters. The abstinence made them desire sex so eagerly that they could not stop themselves from reciting erotic poetry in the presence of their father; one of them described her own vagina. Their father was shocked and married them off the same day.[42] The same plot, an overprotective father who has to give in to languishing daughters when they express their desire, seems to have been quite popular as it occurs elsewhere (see p. 106).

Both Laylā and ʿAmra are attributed poems in which they describe and boast about their genitalia. The historian al-Madāʾinī (d. 228/843), cited in *Ashʿār al-Nisāʾ*, attributes the following verse to Laylā bint al-Ḥumāris al-Taghlibī: 'Who will lead a bachelor, putting the animals out to pasture,[43] / to the daughter of al-Ḥumāris, the hairy old man? / With plump and solid thighs and a bulky vulva / which moves and groans when being penetrated / like the cry of a workhorse lagging behind the caravan.'[44] A similar poem is attributed to Laylā's sister, ʿAmra bint al-Ḥumāris, by another historian, Muṣʿab al-Zubayrī (d. 236/851):

> I am al-Ḥumāris' daughter, the hairy old man. / I have rounded buttocks and a bulky vulva.
> It guides the creeper to something wonderful / which moves and groans when being penetrated,
> like the cry of a workhorse lagging behind the caravan. / Inside its sheath, when it turns over,
> it looks like a pomegranate has been split open and the grains pouring out.[45]

The pomegranate was, as we have seen, used as an image of the female genitalia by ʿAmra's contemporary al-Farazdaq. In the hadith of Umm Zarʿ, Umm Zarʿ lost her beloved husband Abū Zarʿ when he met a woman with two children who were 'like panthers' playing with two pomegranates underneath her waist. This scene made him divorce Umm Zarʿ and marry the other woman. The pomegranate is normally an image for breasts, as Rosenthal points out, but here it appears below the waist of Umm Zarʿs rival. Abū ʿUbayda explained the meaning as follows: 'Her posterior was so big that when she was lying on her back, it raised her body above the ground and formed a gap large enough for a pomegranate to pass through.'[46] The same image is used in the poem in the beginning of this section, but without the pomegranate.

The licentious themes of their poetry notwithstanding, the sisters seem to have had some standing in Umayyad society. Supposedly, ʿAmra bint Ḥumayris al-Taghlibiyya visited the Umayyad prince ʿAbd al-ʿAzīz ibn Marwān (d. 85/705), governor of Egypt, and composed a poem about his slave-girl.[47] According to Ibn Abī Ṭāhir, she visited another Umayyad prince, the successful military commander Maslama ibn ʿAbd al-Malik (d. 121/738), and, for unknown reasons, recited a rather ugly poem about her vagina: 'Between us is a shouter with crispy hair, / like the nostrils of a bull, stung by flies. / In the top it is swelling when touched and in the bottom narrow[48] . . . In its centre a fire is burning / as if masonry ovens are in flames.'[49] Maslama asked ʿAmra to marry him, Ibn Abī Ṭāhir's informants continues, without telling us if it happened before or after her recitation of the poem. She declined due to his low ancestry; his mother was a slave concubine, which meant that he was not a pure Arab. This incident may seem bizarre, but, regardless of its veracity, the Taghlib tribe to which the sisters belonged was powerful and maintained good relations with the Umayyads, who were also known for enjoying light entertainment.

ʿAmra had a poetic exchange on an explicit theme with another famous Umayyad poet, al-Akhṭal (d. 92/710), also a Christian from the banū Taghlib, according to al-Marzūbānī, who also cites a bawdy poem she made in the month of Ramadan.[50] Laylā, in turn, is attributed an entirely decent poem by al-Balādhurī, on the occasion of a tribal skirmish with the Qays tribe. Nevertheless, it was the indecent poems that survived and a daughter of al-Ḥumāris appears occasionally in later literature as the creator of erotic poetic images. In *Lisān al-ʿArab* and other classical lexicons, Bint al-Ḥumāris is cited as having used an obscure word for sexual intercourse, *ʾarr*. ʿAmra composed a poem about an erect penis, which earned some fame and was cited both by al-Marzūbānī and ʿAlī ibn Naṣr in *Jawāmiʿ al-Ladhdha*.[51] The ninth-century author and poetry critic Ibn Abī ʿAwn fuses the poems attributed to ʿAmra and Laylā in his book on similes, *Kitāb al-Tashbīhāt*: 'Who will lead a bachelor, putting the animals out to pasture, / to the daughter of al-Ḥumāris, the hairy old man? / With a smooth back and a bulky vulva / as if the flesh inside when turned over / is a pomegranate split open with the grains pouring out.'[52]

Textual variants are common and the confusion between ʿAmra and Laylā is not a proof that this (or these) poet(s) ever existed. Still, later critics did not find it unbelievable that Umayyad women composed explicit poems and bragged about their vaginas. ʿAmra bint al-Ḥumāris is also cited in *Jawāmiʿ al-Ladhdha*, although she is here referred to as ʿUmayra and four epigrams are attributed to her.[53] Altogether, there are at least sixteen vagina poems attributed to female poets in the chapter on the virtues of the genital organs, all are short epigrams consisting of two to five verses.[54] Two other female poets are named in this chapter: an otherwise unknown woman named Lubāba bint Jaḥwān and Dubāʿa bint ʿĀmir ibn Qurṭ. Dubāʿa bint ʿĀmir is a pre-Islamic woman who allegedly walked around the Kaaba naked because of a pledge that she broke.[55] Her poem in *Jawāmiʿ al-Ladhdha* is not part of the main story about her.

The poems in this section build on stock images for vagina poems, also used in poems attributed to male poets, which we recognize from Bint al-Ḥumāris' poems: the ideal vagina is hot, bulky and narrow. There are also some innovative images, seemingly derived from female experience. One poem, attributed to an anonymous Bedouin woman, borrows images from the domestic sphere, the preparation of bread and heating with burning coal: 'My vagina (*hanī*) is leavened and kneaded dough (*khamīra maʿjūna*) / hot as if burning coal inside / for the one who wishes for it / a modicum is enough to be satisfied.'[56] Another poem, quoted above, expresses a woman's pride that her vagina 'has remained as it was', although she has given birth to eight children. Like male penis poems, the genitals are hyperbolically large and bulking, like a hill.

Several poems follow the same formula, beginning with 'my vagina is', mostly using the word *ḥirī*. This is followed by the description, which is often flattering. An anonymous poet declared, for example: 'My vagina (*ḥirī*), its beauty goes beyond the desires of the desiring/ My vagina, God embellished it from top to bottom / My vagina, if your penis could see it, may God prolong its life.'[57] Instead of commending its beauty, another poet praises its taste: 'My vagina is like sugar from Ahwāz.' Another epigram begins with deriding images known from Abū Nuwās and Ibn Hajjāj but then suddenly the vagina turns into something appealing: 'My vagina is solid and coarse, like the udder of a pregnant camel / My vagina, if you fuck it one day, you will swim in it for a year / My vagina is honey mixed with wine from Babel.' Many of these verses seem to have been put together by an editor rather than a poet; it could also be that the poets used a set of stock motifs as the realm of erotic images was wide and rich.

## Women's bodies in satire and *mujūn*

Umayyad satire contains extremely offensive images of women; the target was often not the women themselves, however, but a male relative. Poets who lampooned men could do so by accusing the women of their opponents' clans and their female relatives of promiscuity and other non-normative behaviour.

For men, promiscuity was not a problem; the Umayyad poet al-Farazdaq for example, who excelled in misogynistic language, was known to be promiscuous.[58] Al-Farazdaq is famous for his poetic duel with Jarīr, called *naqā ʾid*, performed at the Umayyad court and other prestigious arenas for about forty years.[59] The poetic duels were appreciated entertainment for the male audience, although fuelled by tribal rivalry, and degradation of women was part of its humour.[60] Cory Jorgensen argues that the 'hyperbolically misogynistic lampoon' was part of the poets' strategy to attract and keep the audience's attention; it was part of the performance.[61] The humorous satire against women includes gross language, depictions of women as promiscuous and as prostitutes, as well as descriptions of rape and other cruel and violent abuse. These verbal abuses would not have been appreciated, however, in a less androcentric culture; Jorgensen suggests that the misogynistic discourse encouraged male bonding in a homosocial society.[62]

According to a definition brought up by van Gelder, even though women and their bodies can be exploited for lampooning their male kin, they cannot themselves be targets of satire.[63] The Abbasid literary critic Qudāma ibn Jaʿfar (d. after 320/932) maintained that women could not be objects of true *hijā ʾ* (neither could they be objects of *madīḥ* or *rithā ʾ*), because *hijā ʾ* can only attack the cardinal virtues, namely intelligence, courage, justice and chastity, which women do not possess. Blaming someone for his or her appearance or low origin is improper *ḥijā ʾ*.[64] Qudāma's opinion is only one among many, however, later critics objected that according to this model, most invective poems would not be classified as true *ḥijā ʾ*. Nevertheless, it had a certain impact, as Qudāma's book *Naqd al-Shi ʿr* is considered 'the first true Arabic poetics.'[65] Criticising women, a theme called *madhammat al-nisā ʾ*, is such a common poetic theme that a whole section is devoted to it in Abū Tamām's *Ḥamāsa*. Women, who are often the poets' wives in this section, are described in grotesque and bawdy terms; yet this is not satire, but part of the light-hearted theme of pleasantries (*mulaḥ*), according to van Gelder.

In Abbasid society, tribal identity did not play the same role, and verbal duels on tribal ground were no longer part of elite culture. New poetic themes and genres emerged and became popular in poetic circles. As mentioned above, Abū Nuwās was the first poet who composed the kind of poetry that was classified as *mujūn* by later Arab critics. These poems corresponded to *naqā ʾiḍ* and Umayyad satire in their often grotesque images and profane language, but the context is different.[66] They describe the poetic persona's predatory behaviour in urban settings, often in taverns, and the victims are both women and boys. Female sexuality was a target for verbal abuse, also in *mujūn* poetry.

Julie Scott Meisami defines *mujūn* as 'a type of social (or anti-social) behaviour, and a type of writing which reflects, or purports to reflect, that behaviour'. She identifies two major themes in *mujūn* poems: Bacchic and erotic, which often coexisted in the same poem.[67] Everett Rowson defines *mujūn* in a similar fashion; it is 'applied both to behaviour, and particularly sexual behaviour, which flouted societal and religious norms, and to the literary expression of such behaviour'.[68] Poems belonging to the genre of *mujūn* bring up illicit acts in a humorous way, adulterous sex in particular, but also drinking wine and revelling at the taverns. However, Rowson states that 'it is less the illicitness of the subject than the presence of explicit vocabulary and graphic descriptions' that characterizes the genre.[69] It is this explicit vocabulary I refer to as 'sexual comedy', a term that allows us to include explicit motifs that are not defined as *mujūn*, such as the provocative humour in *hijāʾ* and *naqāʾiḍ* that was created before the term *mujūn* was coined. However, it is not always easy to differentiate between what is meant to be humorous and what is not: scathing satire, for example, or beautiful and titillating erotic descriptions. I therefore use a broad definition of comedy, presuming that satire is partly humorous and that even the most beautiful erotic description is to some extent indecent, and therefore humorous, when produced in a society in which sexual relations are strictly regulated.

As in the *naqāʾiḍ*, the degradation of women and female bodies in *mujūn* was intended to be comical. In Abū Nuwās' poetry, the male body most often stands out as attractive whereas the female body generates disgust. Women's bodies are portrayed as abnormal and grotesque, especially the private parts. While possibly beautiful on the outside, their vaginas prove to be a trap, or rather a deep sea in which the poet risks drowning. The vagina as a sea is one of Abū Nuwās' recurrent motives, and so is the vagina as a mouth or jaw, often with teeth – the *vagina dentata*, which in his case is more humorous than frightening.[70] Hyperboles are also used for describing the poetic persona's own genitals, but in this case, the exaggerated size is a reason for pride, such as when the gigantic phallus reaches the stars.[71] The genitals were a source of pride but also of disappointment. The poet Abū Hukayma (d. 240/854) composed parodic elegies over his member, the *ayriyyāt* (penis poems), in which he complained over its dysfunction. He puts at least some of the blame on the female partner, who is old or has 'a grotesquely loose vagina'.[72] In the late fourth/tenth century, the poet Ibn al-Ḥajjāj (d. 391/1001), continued the tradition of *mujūn*, and called his poetry *sukhf*. Like his predecessors, he peppered his poems with grotesque female images, such as hyperbolically giant vaginas and repulsive nude female bodies. Sometimes the vagina is likened to a sea, occasionally the vagina has teeth; in both cases, the vagina poses a danger to the poetic persona who risks drowning or being smashed.[73] Ibn al-Ḥajjāj's *sukhf* does not only denigrate women's genitalia, but also their bodies and characters. Women are hypersexual, demanding and promiscuous, and often old and ugly. Sexual intercourse is a further humiliation for women, emphasized by Ibn al-Ḥajjāj's referring to a female partner as a 'bound horse or mount'.[74]

Sinan Antoon argues that *sukhf*, parodying the bodies of common people, was one way for the elite, to which Ibn al-Ḥajjāj belonged, to distinguish themselves from the lower strata of society: 'The grotesque and inferior bodies of the lower strata of society were exposed and ridiculed, and their imperfections were catalogued and displayed.'[75] Antoon admits that most grotesque bodies in *sukhf* are female, but seems to downplay this point; the depictions of deformed female bodies merely parody the idealized women in traditional *nasab*. Yet, the feminization of the grotesque is too striking to be ignored. What is it, exactly, that the male elite distinguish themselves from when Ibn al-Ḥajjāj exposes and ridicules the 'inferior bodies' of women, and catalogues 'their imperfections'?

## Defaming women: Ḥubbā al-Madīniyya

As we saw in the beginning of this chapter, later authors were fascinated by dissolute female characters and helped to spread rumours about historical women. One of these women was Ḥubbā al-Madīniyya, who appears as a wise woman and erotic expert in *Jawāmiʿ al-Ladhdha* (see Chapter 2). There are also entirely decent aphorisms attributed to Ḥubbā; she was apparently considered a wise woman.[76] She was a historical person, according to the historians al-Balādhurī and al-Ṭabarī. From their accounts, we know that Ḥubbā was respected by the elite in Medina and had a salon where the *fityān* (young men) of Quraysh gathered. She lived in Medina when ʿAbdullāh ibn al-Zubayr proclaimed himself caliph in 683, supported by the Hijāzī aristocracy and later prosecuted by the Umayyads. The Umayyad caliph ʿAbd al-Malik was interested in Ḥubbā's opinion, according to al-Balādhurī and al-Ṭabarī. When the caliph travelled from Damascus to Mecca for the pilgrimage in 689 or shortly thereafter, he stopped by her house and informed himself about her and her guests' health.[77] When he left, he gave her five hundred dinar and he kissed her farewell. ʿAbd al-Malik met with Ḥubbā again when he was on his way to Mecca in 691, after ʿAbdullāh's brother Musʿab was killed. According to al-Ṭabarī, Ḥubbā asked

ʿAbd al-Malik about the killing, whereupon the caliph felt the need to justify himself.[78]

Ḥubbā is also mentioned in connection with the poet Hudba ibn Khashram al-ʿUdhrī, who was famous in Hijaz in the early Umayyad era.[79] He was one of the *fityān* who visited her house, and when he killed his relative in a dispute and was sentenced to death, she criticized him for abandoning his wife. This annoyed Hudba and according to al-Mubarrad and Abū al-Faraj al-Iṣbahānī, he retaliated with a biting poem that he recited when he walked towards the site of his execution, insinuating that Ḥubbā was attracted to the youth and appearance of her husband, but did not love him truly:[80]

> No mother has loved the way I love her
> [My love is] not like Ḥubbā's love for Ibn Umm Kilāb
> She saw him with long, beautiful forearms
> Perhaps she was revived by strength and youth.[81]

Ḥubbā was brave and eloquent, the epitome of an Umayyad woman as represented in Abbasid anecdotes, and was well respected by the caliph. Yet, in later literature, she is most of all known for being outspoken and dissolute. For unknown reasons, Ḥubbā's historical persona was used for creating a *mujūn* character for the amusement of Abbasid readers. The character, Ḥubbā al-Madīniyya, was the protagonist of anecdotes told by the early Abbasid historian al-Haytham ibn ʿAdī (d. 207/822).[82] His written works are all lost; but from references and citations in later sources, it is evident that he wrote narrative reports about female personalities, as well as anecdotes and humorous stories about named and unnamed women. In *Mufākharat al-jawārī wa-l-ghilmān*, Jāḥiẓ relates that Ḥubbā was one of the *mughtalimāt* (lustful women) who gave the women in Medina sexual education. She taught them *qabʿ* (sighing) and *gharbala* (motion) during sex and told them stories from her own life. Once she accompanied the caravan of the caliph ʿUthmān ibn ʿAffān with her husband and when they sneaked away to have sex during a break, she sighed so loudly that the caliph's camels were scared and fled.[83] What is more, al-Jāḥiẓ continues, she also gave advice to her own son how to please a woman.[84] The anecdotes about Ḥubbā are retold by Ibn Abī Ṭāhir Ṭayfūr in *Balaghāt al-Nisāʾ*; here, her audience is not the women in Medina, but her own daughters and, with her son as an intermediary, 'the young men from Quraysh'.[85] Moreover, Ḥubbā allegedly encouraged her daughters to tell her their most exciting experiences. She also told the young women in Medina how she had sex with her grandson's dog and they responded that she should not be ashamed, as it was 'a noble deed'.

Later, Ḥubbā appeared in *al-Maḥāsin wa-l-Aḍdād*, a book that contains quasi-historical tales by an anonymous writer;[86] here, she is called Ḥawwā' (Eve) and she is a matchmaker in Medina. She socialized with the important men in Quraysh, who provided her with a generous stipend. All families in Medina let their boys suckle her or her daughters' breast, which allowed them to visit her. She gave sexual education to the women in Medina and taught them *al-naq'*, *al-gharbala* and *al-rahz*.[87] Ḥubbā's licentiousness grew with each generation of scholars who used her for spicing their writings. She gave name to the saying 'hornier than Ḥubbā' (*ashbaqu min Ḥubbā*), used for people with a strong libido.[88] Her libido made her marry a younger man, and when her son complained, she answered him: 'You son of the donkey saddle, have you seen that tall young man? By God, let him throw down your mother right in the doorway, so that he may cure her ardent desire and may her soul go forth below him. I wish that he was a lizard and that I was his little friend, then we would have found a vacant place.'[89]

From where came the rumours about Ḥubbā's libidinous behaviour? Perhaps Hudba's poem gives a clue; accusing Ḥubbā for loving Ibn Umm Kilāb for 'his long, beautiful forearms' and 'strength and youth'. At least for later authors, this means that her husband was much younger than she was. Al-Jāḥiẓ claims that Ḥubbā married Ibn Umm Kilāb when she was almost fifty, and that her son was upset by that.[90] Judging from profanities directed against opponents' mothers, this situation was a male nightmare. The humorous stories about Ḥubbā sanction a posthumous shaming of a strong, female personality. We could read them as the prejudices of the exclusively male readership at this time.[91] It is also possible to read them as part of a type of literature that we could label 'shameful ancestry', which seems to have been entertaining in a sensational way and at the same time derided certain people for the low origin of their ancestors. Among titles with this content, we find al-Haytham's *The names of the prostitutes of Quraysh before Islam and the names of their children*.[92] Abbasid historians like al-Haytham were looking for the spicy parts of the pasts, and shameful incidents of the ancestry of people – and the easiest objects for this were women.

## Defaming women: the Abbasid courtesans

Slave courtesans were often accused of loose morals and falseness, most famously in al-Jāḥiẓ' epistle on the female singers, *Risālat al-Qiyān*. The slave singer became the archtype of the immoral woman: she associated freely with men and did not shun fornication. Although the slave courtesans' role was to provide elite men with an outlet for love and passion, their reputation was vulnerable, as we have seen in the example of Duqāq. ʿInān was one of the earliest courtesans in the Abbasid empire and the most quoted slave-poet; Abū al-Faraj al-Iṣbahānī asserts that she in fact was the first famous slave poet in the Abbasid era.[93] Al-Iṣbahānī praises her in his books on slave singers, *al-Imāʾ al-Shawāʿir* and in *Kitāb al-Aghānī*. Other scholars also recognized her as a fine poet, including Ibn al-Nadīm, who mentions her poetic oeuvre in *Fihrist*. Yet we know very little about her life, except that a man called al-Nāṭifī bought her and brought her to Baghdad. He received guests, some of them famous poets such as Abū Nuwās, and let them exchange poetry with ʿInān. Her contributions were appreciated and her interactions with Abū Nuwās became famous.[94]

ʿInān is one of the few women whose poem is cited in the prestigious anthology *Ṭabaqāt al-Shuʿarāʾ al-Muḥdathīn* by ʿAbdullāh ibn al-Muʿtazz (247–295/861–908), the prince who became caliph in 296/908 but was killed shortly after. The poem quoted there is a eulogy to the *wazīr* Yaḥyā ibn Khālid al-Barmakī.[95] She asks the powerful *wazīr* for a favour; apparently she hoped that he could persuade the caliph Hārūn al-Rashīd to buy her, a motif we recognize from the humorous anecdotes about female slaves in Chapter 4. If she was purchased by the caliph, she would move up from her position in a relatively modest house to the imperial court, that is, the centre of Abbasid culture. She would also have company with a large number of other talented courtesans, several of them singers, poets and educated women. Her dream was stopped, according to narrators of her biography, when she fell out with Abū Nuwās, and he wrote a derogative poem about her. He accused her of promiscuity, and stigmatized prospective buyers: ʿInān al-Nuṭṭāf is a slave-girl / whose pussy has become a playground for fucking / Nobody would buy her except for the son of a whore / or a pimp, whoever he may be.'[96] Hārūn al-Rashīd had heard about ʿInān's talent and was on the point of buying her. After this verse by the famous poet, however, it was impossible; he did not want to risk being likened to 'a son of a whore'. Abū Nuwās' allegation was an effective way to humiliate and defame ʿInān, but she was not short of an answer. In a bitter tone, she attacks his habit of destroying reputations:

> Nuwāsī, you garbage of God's creation, through me, you have attained
> reputation and glory.
> You can die when you want; I have praised you in poetry,
> so let your garment drag on the ground out of pride.
> Many had their clothes stained by the dung from your mouth, you are full of
> scorn and evil.[97]

Her poem is biting, but did not help her regain her reputation, and her further whereabouts are obscure. If it is true that ʿInān attempted to be transferred to the imperial court but that Abū Nuwās' words put an end to her ambition, this is an example of the power of poetry; in this case only two verses, a major theme in narratives about disputes and discord before and after Islam. The story is touching; a talented and ambitious young woman, confined by her gender and bondage, has her dreams crushed by a few verses from the famous but controversial poet who befriended her for a while but then got tired of her. A woman's reputation could be destroyed by a few words questioning her virtue, which was not difficult for an opponent to do.

As we saw in the case of Duqāq, Abū al-Faraj al-Iṣbahānī, who normally portrays the famous singers in positive terms, was not above citing some defaming rumours about some of the female musicians and courtesans. ʿUbayda was another female musician whose historical persona was defamed by later authors. She was one of the best tanbur players of her age, praised by Isḥāq al-Mawṣilī (235/850), the most influential musician at the time of Hārūn al-Rashīd and his sons. The tanbur player Abū Ḥashīsha (d. *c.* 250/865) acknowledged her as a master and teacher. The author Jaḥẓa, who was a tanbur player himself, wrote that she was the best female player in history, and that her compositions are marvellous. Yet, the main topic in the portrait of the musician ʿUbayda is her supposed promiscuity.[98]

Abū al-Faraj devotes a major part of the biographical article about ʿUbayda to rumour spread by Aḥmad ibn Ṭayyib al-Sarakhsī. According to Jaḥẓa's book on tanbur players, cited by Abū al-Faraj, al-Sarakhsī wrote to a man called ʿAlī ibn Aḥmad al-Marwazī and asked him about ʿUbayda. ʿAlī had been courting her as a young man, he reported, and 'spent a fortune on her'. ʿUbayda's father, ʿAlī said, was the *mawlā* of a boon companion to ʿAbdullāh ibn Ṭāhir (d. 230/844), governor of Khurasān, and one of his friends taught her how to play the tanbur when she was a child. When her father died she had to play for her living. She was talented and soon became sought after as a musician and a woman. According to al-Sarakhsī's informant, 'she loosened her trousers' for anyone, a habit she could not stop even when she was married. When she gave birth to a daughter, her husband secluded her, but this did not stop her promiscuity. Using pretexts such as visiting the bath, she left his house and 'had sex with anyone she liked, and who liked her'. Her daughter died and her husband divorced her, but she continued to see new lovers. She was 'extremely lustful' and 'did not say no to or dislike anyone, old or young'. Finally, she had a slave-boy who she exploited whenever she was horny and did not have anyone else behaving somewhat like Duqāq, according to the rumours. How could Abū al-Faraj give so much space to one single, derogative, account about ʿUbayda? The negative account might be coloured by the fact that she was a free woman, not a slave courtesan. Being a musician and having to play for one's living was apparently not considered a proper occupation for a free woman; which is perhaps the reason why her legacy was dominated by rumours of her depravity.

## A woman's response: ʿArīb

The singer and courtesan ʿArīb is one of the Abbasid women who talked about her sexual practice, at least according to anecdotes quoted in *Kitāb al-Aghānī*, where she refuses to let male companions ridicule or shame her. ʿArīb was, according to Abū al-Faraj al-Iṣbahānī, the most accomplished and famous of the Abbasid slave singers.[99] Born in 181/797, she became a royal courtesan after the death of Hārūn al-Rashīd and was freed by the caliph al-Muʿtaṣim. She continued to be close to the court until she died at an advanced age in 277/890. For later authors, she was primarily associated with al-Maʾmūn, and many of the anecdotes in her biography take place in his court. According to Abū al-Faraj's sources, she composed one thousand songs. ʿAbdullāh ibn al-Muʿtazz, who wrote a book about her, cites one of her poems put to music, a love poem she wrote to the military commander Muhammad ibn Ḥāmid al-Khaqānī, known as the brute, the most well-known of her lovers. The form of the poem is the typical *ghazal* where a male poet describes the body and appearance of an exchangeable female beloved. This time, the exchangeable beloved is a man and the lover is a woman: 'How dear to me is every blue-eyed / blond and fair-skinned man / whom my heart has been infatuated by. / My infatuation cannot be condemned.'

Ibn al-Muʿtazz tells about an incident that supposedly occurred in 830, during al-Maʾmūn's first campaign against the Byzantines. His source is Ibrāhīm ibn al-Mudabbir (d. 278/892–893), who would later become a high official and a boon companion of al-Mutawakkil. ʿArīb was a famous singer at al-Maʾmūn's court and already legendary. The poem referred to in the anecdote was written by ʿĪsā ibn Zaynab, who also wrote a satire about Duqāq. ʿĪsā ibn Zaynab was the son of ʿArīb's first owner, al-Marākibī, and in the poem he ridiculed his father for having allowed ʿArīb to escape from his house to her lover.

> I went out with al-Maʿmūn to the land of the Byzantines, searching for wealth as young men do. We travelled with a military unit. When we had departed from

> Raqqa, we saw a group of women in covered litters on camels. We were a troop of companions; one of them said to me: 'In one of those litters is ʿArīb.' I answered: 'Who bets with me that I can pass alongside those litters and recite ʿĪsā ibn Zaynab's poem: ʿDamn, she is good, ʿArīb! / She did a wonderful thing?' One of them bet with me and we settled an amount. I went alongside the women's litters and recited the poem with a loud voice, until I had finished. Then a woman looked out from a litter and said: 'Young man, have you forgotten the best and most delightful verse? Have you forgotten that he recited: "ʿArīb has a moist vagina / She has fucked in many ways." Go and collect what you have agreed upon!' She pulled the curtain aside, and I saw that she was ʿArīb. I hurried to my companions afraid that the servants would do me harm.

Reciting a mocking poem about ʿArīb, this man apparently behaves 'like young men do'. He intrudes into her private sphere, moving freely on his horse, while she, stuck in a covered litter cannot avoid listening to his verbal attack. ʿArīb on her part does not behave like women are supposed to do. Ignoring the insult, she takes the control of the situation and outwits him by provokingly describing the vulgar description of her genitalia as 'the best and most delightful verse'. Ibn al-Mudabbir's attempt to embarrass her fails, and he is the one who is pushed away.

Another story from al-Maʾmūn's military campaign is told by Aḥmad ibn Ḥamdūn on the authority of his father Ḥamdūn, who supposedly exchanged letters with Duqāq. One night in al-Maʾmūn's camp, Ḥamdūn encountered ʿArīb riding in the dark. He asked her where she had been, and she answered that she had visited Muhammad ibn Ḥāmid, the military commander who was known as her lover. When the narrator asked her what she had been doing at Ibn Ḥāmid's, she answered: 'Idiot! ʿArīb comes from Muhammad ibn Ḥāmid at this time, she leaves the caliph's camp and when she returns to it you say to her: "What have you done at his place?" Do you think I have prayed the *tarāwīh* prayer with him? Or recited from the Qur'an to him? Or studied *fiqh* together with him? Fool, we have argued, discussed, reunited, sung, had sex with each other, and then we departed!' When Aḥmad returned to al-Maʾmūn, he wanted to tell him about ʿArīb, but was afraid of the caliph's reaction. He decided to hint at it with a poem about a promiscuous woman:

> Salute the ruins of the camping-site of the hospitable woman,
> a sociable woman, who makes the best man of a people equal to the worst.
> If they, who spend the night at the highland by Ṭayy's two mountains and the
> lowland of al-Ḥabl, remain sitting with her until the shadow becomes short,
> so, when they depart, all of them would have had a reunion with her.[100]

The comical ending of the anecdote lies in al-Maʾmūn's answer, which illustrates the power ʿArīb supposedly had over him. He urges Aḥmad to keep quiet so that ʿArīb does not hear him, in case she would think that they were talking about her. The great Abbasid caliph is portrayed here as a laughable cuckold, something that probably amused Abū al-Faraj's audience.

The hospitable woman by Ṭayy's two mountains is supposed to be comparable with ʿArīb, who rides out in the night of Anatolia to meet with her friend and lover. Still, the differences are significant. The hospitable woman is immobile, passive and indiscriminate, she is sitting and waiting for the men to come to her. She does not discriminate among men, she accepts anyone. ʿArīb, on the other hand, is bold and takes great risks to meet with one particular man, while she obviously offends others, such as the narrator. The activities she performs with her lover are all on equal terms or with her as the active party. She is mobile, it is she who visits her lover, not the reverse, and she does it on horseback under quite severe weather conditions. She also insists on formulating her own version of her actions; the question 'What have you done at his place?' does not necessarily demand such a detailed answer.

Several of the anecdotes about ʿArīb depict the social life in Samarra, which was the imperial capital between 221/836 and 279/892. The following incident supposedly took place when ʿArīb was old and the narrator is ʿAlī ibn Muḥammad ibn al-Furāt.[101]

> One day I was at my brother Abū al-ʿAbbās' house, and ʿArīb was there, sitting separately on the seat of honour. Her *jawārī* were singing for us and behind a curtain. When the caliphs were mentioned, I told my brother that ʿArīb had said to me: 'Eight of them have fucked me, but the only one of them I desired was al-Muʿtazz, because he looked like Abū ʿĪsā ibn al-Rashīd.' Ibn al-Furāt continued: I turned to one of my nephews and asked him: 'What do you think about her sexual appetite today?' He laughed; she noticed that, and asked: 'What are you talking about?' I refused to answer, so she told her *jawārī* to stop singing, which they did. She continued: 'They are free to go away, all of them, if you do not tell me what you were talking about! They are free if I become annoyed about anything that has happened, even if it is despicable!' I told her the truth, and she said: 'So what? Regarding the appetite, it is as it should be, but the instrument is not working. Return to whatever you were doing!'

The conversation can be read as an attempt to ridicule the old woman, a typical strategy of power. The male company speaks about ʿArīb and laughs at her while she is sitting on the periphery, unable to hear them clearly. She is segregated as a mark of honour, but the segregation rather enhances her alienation due to sex and age. They laugh at the thought of an old woman's desire, but she keeps her dignity and refuses to be shamed. Instead she outwits them by confirming her former statement – or boast – about her sexual experience with caliphs, and, on top of it, using vulgar language, as if societal values did not differentiate between men's and women's experience. Her provocation, in *mujūn* style, works on several levels. She uses a metaphor for her genitalia which was commonly used for men's, since the male organ is seen as the active one.[102] Her relations with the earlier caliphs were well-known, but the supposed love-affair with al-Muʿtazz was unexpected. She was sixty-nine years old when al-Muʿtazz was appointed caliph in 252/866 and he was nineteen. Moreover, he was the son of her friend, caliph al-Mutawakkil's favourite concubine Qabīḥa and ʿArīb performed at the occasion of his circumcision.[103]

In one anecdote, a narrator called Abū al-ʿAnbas, who probably is the same Abū al-ʿAnbas who wrote erotic books at the court of al-Mutawakkil, relates about ʿArīb's outspokenness. He claims that he visited her one day and when she asked him to stay longer, he said yes on the condition that she answered an embarrassing question. She responded that she already knew what he wanted to ask her, 'You want to ask me about which criteria I have,' implicitly in choosing a lover. Of course, that was what Abū al-ʿAnbas wanted to know, and ʿArīb continued: 'My requirements are a hard penis and a fresh breath. If he, in addition, is admirably beautiful and handsome, I will appreciate him even more, but the first two are necessary.' The anecdote is typical in that ʿArīb does not let the narrator put the question, she formulates the question as well as the answer, with a complete disrespect for the gendered norm of modesty.

When the character ʿArīb speaks openly about her sexual appetite and lives out her desire, she lives up to the readers' expectations. If a free woman did the same she could expect to be shamed. In one anecdote, ʿArīb is in the company of Jaʿfar, son of the caliph al-Maʾmūn, when she reveals a secret about one of the caliph's female relatives, Umm Muhammad, daughter of Ṣāliḥ al-Miskīn, granddaughter of caliph al-Manṣūr and married for a while to caliph Hārūn al-Rashīd, her cousin. Umm Muhammad had a love affair with the poet Abū Muḥallim and used to spend the nights with him and ʿArīb.

> One day we were drinking at Jaʿfar ibn al-Maʾmūn's home, and ʿArīb was there, when someone sang the following song:
>
> Oh full moon, you have been dressed so that you resemble
> the face of this shining and bright beauty.
> I see you passing away and waning
> while her beauty lasts for days, it does not depart

> ʿArīb laughed and clapped her hands. She said: 'I am the only one on this earth who knows the truth about the song!' Nobody among us dared to ask her about it except me. I asked her and she answered: 'I will tell you the story about it as the main character is dead, or else I would not have told it. Abū Muḥallim came to Baghdad and stayed at an inn close to Ṣāliḥ al-Miskīn's palace. One day Umm Muḥammad, Ṣāliḥ's daughter, looked down and saw him urinating. She liked his equipment and wanted to get together with him. She made herself a pretext to achieve this, by sending him a request to lend her money. She let him know that she had got into straits and that she would return the money to him in one week. He sent her ten thousand dirham and swore that if he had more in his possession, he would have sent it to her. She appreciated this and initiated a relation with him and made the loan a reason for meeting him. She let him in at night and I used to sing for them. One night, we drank in the moonlight. Abū Muḥallim looked at the moon, and then he asked for an inkhorn and a piece of paper. He wrote his poem on it: "Oh full moon, you have been dressed so that you resemble / the face of Umm Muḥammad, Ṣāliḥ's daughter" and the other verse. He asked me to compose a melody to it. I did so; we liked the song and drank to it. At the end of the sitting, Umm Muḥammad said to me: "My sister, you have done something brilliant with this poem, but it will remain a disgrace for me for ever!" Abū Muḥallim said that he would change it and instead of Umm Muḥammad, Ṣāliḥ's daughter, he wrote "this shining and bright beauty". I sang it the way he changed it and people learnt it from me. If Umm Muḥammad were alive, I would never have told you this!'[104]

This rumour about a close female relative to the caliph was utterly shameful for her and her male relatives, especially as ʿArīb is careful to point out that she chose her lover based on the size of his 'equipment'. This is evidently in line with the notion of the hypersexual woman in erotic literature, as we have seen in Chapter 2, but we should also understand stories like this in the context of Abū al-Faraj' audience, for whom the early Abbasid caliphs were acceptable laughingstock.

## Concluding remarks

Poetry and verbal exchanges in early Arabic literature often contain explicit sexual expressions and images. In poetry, depictions of genitalia, for example, occurred in love poetry as well as satire. A few sexually explicit poems were attributed to female poets, and although their provenance is uncertain, it is possible that women could be libertines and create explicit poetry, and that many of the poems attributed to women were also originally written by women, although possibly altered in transmission. However, sexually explicit themes were especially risky for women, as both social norms and legal rulings restricted female sexual behaviour and expression much more than those of men.

In this chapter, we have seen examples of famous women who were supposedly sexually outspoken, and therefore shamed after their death, when rumours about their supposedly lewd behaviour were written down and transmitted as humorous anecdotes. 'Shaming' and women's responses to it were also suitable motives in anecdotes, in line with the favourite structure of anecdotes that we saw in Chapter 4.

All the while, unmistakeable misogynistic motifs flourished, especially in poetry. In Umayyad *naqāʾiḍ* and satire, women's bodies were depicted in grotesque images and female relatives to the male poetic opponent were attacked for supposedly lewd behaviour. In Abbasid poetry, *mujūn* poetry denigrated women and female bodies, and in the late fourth/tenth century, the misogynistic motifs culminated in *sukhf*, which, according to Antoon, was a means for the male elite to distinguish themselves from 'the lower strata of society'. Perhaps this wide-ranging degradation of the female body and of women emerged from the changes of women's roles in society that had been implemented gradually for a long period and reached a critical point in the late tenth-century society of Ibn al-Ḥajjāj. Yet, the author of *Jawāmiʿ al-Ladhdha* does not cite Ibn al-Ḥajjāj, and the occasionally grotesque images in poetry cited by him are, taken out of context, entirely comical and creative.

The 'boasting-match' between the slave-girl and the slave-boy in *Jawāmiʿ al-Ladhdha* indicates that although Abbasid society and literature was androcentric, individuals could, and did, question the norms of male dominance and female subordination. Theories that position men as superior by nature and favoured by God were presented as unquestionable truth in medical and religious discourse, but the fact that the author of *Jawāmiʿ al-Ladhdha* has to argue for this, for example about the superiority of the penis, shows that he expected objections and had to convince his audience. At the same time, he let his female characters object, and the slave-girl argues convincingly for the advantages of women.

# 6

# Sisters and Lovers

The court poet Abū al-ʿAtāhiya (d. 210/825 or 211/826), known for his ascetic poems, was in love with a professional mourner in his youth, according to an anecdote in *Kitāb al-Aghānī*.[1] Her name was Suʿdā; she was an Arab woman from al-Hira, close to Kufa in Iraq, where Abū al-ʿAtāhiya lived when he was young. The anecdote tells us that Abū al-ʿAtāhiya was not alone in courting Suʿdā, one of his rivals was ʿAbdullāh ibn Maʿn, the son of a military commander and governor.[2] Abū al-ʿAtāhiya was poor, he worked as a pot seller and Suʿdā was probably out of reach of him. She belonged to the family who protected his family when they converted to Islam and hence she was his superior. At that time, converts to Islam had to affiliate themselves with an Arab tribe, and become their 'clients', a subordinate position. In any case, something went wrong in Abū al-ʿAtāhiya's relationship with Suʿdā – perhaps she rejected him – and he wrote a poem accusing her for practicing *saḥq*, apparently intending that she engaged in lesbian sex:[3]

> You lesbians (*dhawāt al-saḥq*) in west and east,
> recover, for fucking (*nayk*[4]) is a better remedy than rubbing (*saḥq*).
> Recover, for bread with spread is more desired,
> while the throat does not swallow bread with bread easily
> I see you patching holes with the same kind,
> but which intelligent person patches a hole with a hole?
> Is a mortar usable without its pestle,
> the day it is needed for pounding?

At this time, Abū al-ʿAtāhiya socialized with the libertine poets in Kufa, which may explain his rude language to a former beloved. For a while he belonged to the circle of Wāliba ibn al-Ḥubāb, who was the teacher of Abū Nuwās and known as a pederast.[5] When he, on this occasion, endorses 'fucking' instead of 'rubbing', he apparently defends heterosexual sex against lesbian sex, even though he was associated with the *mukhannathūn* ('effeminate transvestites'), who, in the Abbasid era, were known for ambiguous gender identity.[6] Considering the explicit vocabulary, the poem belongs to the genre of *mujūn*; it alludes to illicit sex, whether in the form of *nayk* or *saḥq*. Yet, it is more descent than many *mujūn* poems composed by Abu al-ʿAtāhiya's contemporary Abū Nuwās, for example, who frequented the same libertine circles in his youth in Kufa. The words *nayk* and *saḥq* may seem vulgar, but were used as commonplace terms for penetrative sex and tribadism.

Abū al-ʿAtāhiya's poem is quite unique in that it addresses women's sexual preferences. Usually, it is men's preferences that were discussed by poets and scholars in early Arabic literature and sometimes debated. Pederasty was a quite popular theme, not the least in poetry. The master of early *mujūn* poetry, Abū Nuwās, excelled in licentious descriptions of the seduction of young boys. The pros and cons of pederasty versus heterosexuality for men were explored in the 'boasting matches' between men who preferred women as sex partners and those who preferred boys, as we have seen in Chapter 5. Nevertheless, the poem attributed to Abū al-ʿAtāhiya in *Kitāb al-Aghānī* suggests that there was an ongoing poetic debate about the merits of heterosexuality, represented by *nayk*, versus homosexuality, represented by *saḥq*, of women, just as there were literary debates on men's preferences. In this chapter, I present the topic of female homosexuality in early Arabic medical and legal discourses. Most importantly, however, I examine instances in literature when women speak up and defend their sexual orientation, most of them from a chapter on female same-sex desire in *Jawāmiʿ al-Ladhdha* which contains a corpus of letters and poems attributed to women. The women are anonymous and it is not possible to determine the authorship of the poetry, yet at least a few of them give a realistic picture of women's concerns at this time.

In addition to Abū al-ʿAtāhiya's poem, there are occasional allusions to lesbianism in *Kitāb al-Aghānī*. *Saḥq* is associated with the *qiyān*, the highly skilled and educated slave artists in the caliphal court and Abbasid elite society. One of the most skilful singers was Badhl, who knew thirty thousand songs; she was also rich and had many admirers and friends. Once when she sang for the caliph al-Maʾmūn, she changed the phrase 'Oh, I do not know anything more pleasurable than a promise' to 'Oh, I do not know anything more pleasurable that *saḥq*'.[7] The caliph put down his drinking cup and turned to her; 'No Badhl', he said, '*nayk* is more pleasurable than *saḥq*.' Badhl, who was the slave of al-Maʾmūn's brother and enemy al-Amīn before he was killed in the civil war, feared his reaction, but al-Maʾmūn closed the topic without getting angry. Nothing more is said about Badhl being lesbian, but according to Abū al-Faraj she turned down marriage offers from several military commanders, high officials and Abbasid princes. She preferred to live alone with her slave-girls, and did so until she died.[8]

According to another anecdote about a situation that took place decades later, when al-Mutawakkil was caliph, the equally famous singer ʿArīb, who was freed at the time, had a relationship with a palace eunuch. When the caliph's slave courtesans (*jawārī*) laughed at her because of that, she hit back by accusing them of being lesbians. She said: 'You lesbians (*saḥḥāqāt*), what I do is better than what you are up to.'[9] Accusing the *jawārī* for being lesbians was meant as an invective, yet, it indicates that it was not astonishing to find lesbians among the slave courtesans and the female singers.

## Female homosexuality and *saḥq*

The word *saḥq*, which means rubbing or grinding, is the term for a sexual act performed by two women, and in this sense, tribadism is perhaps the most correct English translation. Other words from the same root are used as well, namely *siḥāq* and *musāḥaqa*, but *saḥq* is the most used in sources from the ninth and tenth centuries. The woman who prefers this activity is referred to as a *saḥḥāqa*.[10]

Several historians have highlighted the inconsistences between the harsh attitudes towards homosexual acts in Islamic law and the fact that homoerotic desire has been a common motif in literature in the Islamic world, not the least in Arabic, Persian and Turkish poetry. Many have suggested that homosexuality was more or less tolerated in certain contexts and time periods. This supposition has been criticized by Khaled El-Rouayheb, who argues in *Before Homosexuality in the Arab-Islamic World, 1500–1800* that we have to distinguish between homosexual acts and (what we today would call) homosexual behaviour.[11] El-Rouayheb claims that Arab-Islamic culture lacked the concept of homosexuality as it is understood today. Scholars who adopt a constructionist view call attention to the fact that there are different terms for being active and passive in regard to male sexual intercourse and that active/passive should be seen as an act, not an orientation. People were classified accordingly, not as 'homosexuals' but as either active or passive in sexual relations, although according to El-Rouayheb, the distinction of active or passive was only one of the lenses through which male homosexual behaviour and feelings were understood in the Arab Ottoman world.

The distinction between the active and passive party is used interchangeably with the distinction between the penetrator and the one who is penetrated, which is not necessarily applicable on female same-sex relationships. In analogy with this distinction, though, *saḥq* can be understood as an act, not an orientation. Rowson defines *saḥq* as the act of rubbing, regardless of the sex of the partner, as it can also denote female masturbation.[12] Hence, he chooses to translate *saḥḥāqa* as tribade rather than lesbian, implying that the woman who is called a *saḥḥāqa* is not necessarily attracted to women, but to the act of rubbing. The act of rubbing should be understood as clitoris stimulation without penetration. The ninth century author al-Jāḥiẓ's discussion of *saḥq* seems to confirm the definition of the term as an act of rubbing. He links *saḥq* to genital cutting and explains that 'one of the main reasons why women are attracted to *saḥq* is the fact that when they rub the places where they are clitoridectomised together they find this wonderfully pleasurable', indicating that only part of the clitoris has been removed (in accordance with the hadith, see p. 81–2). Therefore, 'skilful men' know how to 'put the glans of their penises on the place of clitorectomy, for that is the seat of *shahwa*'.[13]

A statement in *Jawāmiʿ al-Ladhdha* also confirms this definition, namely that some women prefer *musāḥaqa* with eunuchs. As evidence, Jaʿfar, son of the caliph al-Muktafī (r. 902–908), relates a shocking story about a palace courtesan, an esteemed woman called Laylā, who stopped at nothing to satisfy her desire to rub.[14] She used to single out beautiful, young slave boys and rape them with a knife in her hand and a eunuch with a drawn sword standing on guard at the door. In these cases, however, the third form of the verb is used: *tusāḥiq* ('she rubs') and *musāhaqa* (the act of rubbing), whereas all other instances in *Jawāmiʿ al-Ladhdha* (as well as *Kitāb al-Aghāni*) – which all involve only women – use the first form of the verb, and the act is called *saḥq*. Perhaps ʿAlī ibn Naṣr wanted to separate between two forms of tribadism, one that only involves the act, and another that involves the act and attraction to the female sex. However, Laylā is presented as exceptional and in all other examples in *Jawāmiʿ al-Ladhdha* it is taken for granted that *saḥq* is performed between two women. Likewise, the women – fictional or real – whose words about *saḥq* he quotes, tend to equate their desire for *saḥq* with desiring women. Therefore, I have chosen to translate *saḥq* as tribadism but *saḥḥāqa* as lesbian. Nonetheless, in this chapter, I will let the sources speak for themselves; as we will see below, contemporary medical scholars gave both biological and social explanations to homosexual desire and attraction and some of their explanations support the definition of *saḥq* as the attraction to 'rubbing', the sex of the partner notwithstanding.

Religious scholars had in general a very negative attitude towards homosexual acts between men, but had less to say about women.[15] Most of the (few) religious scholars who mention tribadism regard it as a sin, liable to punishment. The oldest reference to tribadism is attributed to Mujāhid ibn Jabr (d. 100–104/718–722), one of the most prolific early Qur'an interpreters, who maintained that 'lewdness' (*fāḥisha*) in Q4:15[16] is *musāḥaqa*, not, as is commonly believed, *zinā* (illicit intercourse).[17] As for the subsequent verse, 4:16[18] he agreed with the majority interpretation that it referred to a heterosexual couple, who will be forgiven if they repent.

Jurists disagreed on whether or not tribadism is *zinā* and indictable with *ḥadd* punishment after four male free Muslims witnesses have testified, or *ta'zīr* (judicial discretion) and up to the individual judge to decide. The *ḥadd* punishment for *zinā* was fixed: flogging for a person who is categorized as a non-*muḥsan* (a slave and a free Muslim who has not been married), and stoning to death for someone who is a *muḥsan* (a free Muslim who is or has been married). The schools of law agreed that homosexual acts between men are *zinā*, but they had different opinions about the punishment for tribadism (mostly called *siḥāq*). The Shafi'is were in favour of *ḥadd* punishment (flogging for a non-*muḥsan* and stoning for a *muḥsan*), whereas the Malikis and Hanbalis argued for an even harsher punishment, namely stoning for both the *muḥsan* and the non-*muḥsan*. The Hanafis and the Ẓāhirīs, instead, advocated for *ta'zīr*, which was up to the judge to decide but always lighter than *ḥadd*.[19]

Jurists were generally more lenient when it came to homosexual acts between women, if they mentioned it at all, probably because there is no penetration.[20] A few pre-canonical hadiths state that *siḥāq* is indeed *zinā*.[21] According to one hadith, quoted by 'Abd al-Razzāq al-Ṣan'ānī, the Prophet cursed both the active and the passive committer of *saḥq*. The terms used are *al-rākiba* and *al-markūba*, meaning 'she who rides' and 'she who is ridden', perhaps in analogy with passive and active male homosexuality, for which there are specific terms. 'Abd al-Razzāq also quotes religious scholars who maintain that the punishment for both the active and the passive partner (*al-fā'ila wa-l-maf'ūla bi-hā*) should be one hundred lashes.

Camilla Adang summarizes different opinions specified by Ibn Ḥazm (d. 1064/456), who was the leading jurist of the Ẓāhirī School, besides being the author of the well-known literary work *The Ring of the Dove*. According to him, some jurists maintained that female offenders should be punished by flogging with a hundred lashes, which is the punishment for a non-*muḥsan* involved in *zinā*.[22] This view was hold by Shi'i jurists, who limited the punishment for sexual relations between women to one hundred lashes.[23] Another group regarded *siḥaq* permissible as long as it was performed in order to avoid *zinā*. Several early jurists argued, as Juynboll points out, that *siḥāq* was a *ta'zīr* crime when it was practiced in order to avoid pregnancy or fornication; in the latter case it meant masturbation.[24] This was also Ibn Ḥazm's own opinion, and, according to him, the punishment should not exceed ten lashes.[25]

Some scholars warn women from putting themselves in a situation in which they may feel desire for another woman and not to imitate men by way of dressing. One hadith states that women should not be naked or half-naked before each other and another states that a woman should not touch another woman.[26]

## Lesbians speaking out

In the chapter on female same-sex desire in *Jawāmiʿ al-Ladhdha*, which is the oldest extant substantial treatment of female homosexual attraction and behaviour in Arabic, lesbian women express their desires and explain their orientation. In a number of poems and verbal exchanges women defend *saḥq* and explain why they have chosen to engage in it or argue against it. The poetry is bawdy and seems to be motivated by the simple dichotomy between penetrative sex and tribadism put to verse by Abū al-ʿAtāhiya. In response to his poem, they turn his argument around, and simply claim that *saḥq* is better than *nayk*, as in the following poem:

> Praise the lord of the creation, my beloved, *saḥq* has made our life agreeable
> but *nayk* makes its pursuers ugly, so may that which we love last forever[27]

At first, it resembles an ordinary love poem addressing a beloved, but then, almost immediately, comes the twist: Rather than expressing love, the poetic persona defends the mutual practice of tribadism as being better than penetrative sex. The poem is part of a series of short love letters between women, remotely similar to the love letters in the etiquette manual *Kitāb al-Muwashshā* by Abū Ṭayyib al-Washshāʾ. It is perhaps the carnivalesque humour of *mujūn* that is at play here, but there are, in fact, similarities between the group of *saḥḥāqāt* in *Jawāmiʿ al-Ladhdha* and the *mutaẓarrifāt* (ladies) in *al-Muwashshā*. They are represented as a separate social group in Abbasid high society, admired for their elegance on the one hand, and standing outside because they are slaves or rejected men on the other.[28]

The author of *Jawāmiʿ al-Ladhdha* opens the chapter with a sociological explanation of tribadism. Some women, he claims, choose tribadism for fear of loosing their virginity and good reputation or for fear of pregnancy. This claim is then demonstrated by a few anecdotes and three poems attributed to women. The first poem is directed to a female beloved, called 'sister':

> How much we have practiced tribadism (*saḥaqnā*), my sister! For ninety years[29]
> and it is more enjoyable and concealed than the inserting of penises and pregnancy,
> the knowledge of which would please the enemy and, worse than that, the censure of the blamers.
> We are not imposed *ḥadd* punishment for tribadism, as for fornication (*zinā*),
> even though it is more desirable for women who take the active role (*fawāʿil*).[30]

This poet makes a strong argument for lesbian intercourse; it does not lead to unintended pregnancy, which in turn provokes gossips and censure. Pregnancy is also the ultimate proof of fornication, for which there is a harsh penalty in Islamic law. The assertion here, that tribadism is not imposed *ḥadd* punishment, was in fact disputed at the time when the poem was written as there were divided opinions among Islamic scholars, as we saw above. Notably, the poetic persona has not chosen tribadism only because it is safer, she also claims that it is more pleasurable, especially for a certain category of women – those who like to take the active role. This is the only instance in the poetic corpus where a lesbian sexual encounter is described in terms of active/passive dichotomy, whereas hadiths seem to take for granted that there is an active and a passive partner.

Avoidance of pregnancy is the excuse for engaging in tribadism in the next poem, which accentuates the dire consequences for girls of losing their virginity.

> I was content with my beloved woman and refused something[31] the consequences of which make a noble woman condemned,
> when they say, 'She is pregnant!' May bastards, making me unhappy, be far off!
> What would be my excuse to my parents if fornication had cut the ropes of my virginity?

In another poem the poetic persona admits that she began practicing tribadism to avoid pregnancy but found it satisfying and therefore continued to practice it. It also hints at the understanding of lesbianism as being more than a practice. It is a lifestyle that makes her part of a female community.

> I drank wine for love of romance and embarked on tribadism for fear of pregnancy
> I slept with my beloved in private and surpassed men in performing well.
> If tribadism satisfies me, I am content with it and reject men.

Other poets in the chapter on female same-sex desire defend tribadism for the sole reason that it is more pleasurable, regardless of if it is safer or not. Tribadism is compared favourably to heterosexual sex, as if the poets participated in the debate initiated by Abū al-ʿAtāhiya. They exclude men, not only as objects of desire, but also as active participants. The happiness promised by tribadism is out of reach for men, who are excluded from participating. But according to the following verse, beardless men – boys and eunuchs – are likely to desire this type of sexual encounter:

> May the pleasure of life be granted those who practice tribadism until the Day of Judgment.
> If men tasted it, they would not refrain, but the one who desires tribadism has never had a beard.[32]

To practices tribadism, according to the following poem, means belonging to a sisterhood:

> By God, *saḥq* is what we yearn for, my sister; *nayk* is nothing but futility.
> *saḥq* is preferred for us white, eloquent and laughing women,
> So renounce *nayk* and similar things, for *nayk* is falseness.

Who were the 'white, eloquent and laughing women', a group to which the poetic persona belongs? The epithet 'white' can naturally mean light skinned, but it can also denote free from faults and noble.[33] The indication made by the poet here is that she belongs to a group of women who do not have to go out in daylight, to work like women from the lower classes or do errands like an ordinary slave girl. They are eloquent and laughing, meaning they are skilled in improvising poetry and mastering the language, while at the same time enjoying *mujūn* and other amusements. Their male equivalents wrote about their drinking sessions, not the least at the taverns, and the women in their company are generally supposed to be courtesans and prostitutes; women who depend on men for their incomes. When the poetic persona instead, albeit humorously, calls on her sociable female friends to renounce sexual relationships with men, she also evokes the world of the tavern and *qiyān* houses, where men and women seemingly associate freely, but where women, depending on the men for their livelihood, have to adjust their feelings and preferences.[34]

The final part of the chapter on lesbians in *Jawāmiʿ al-Ladhdha* includes some sayings by former lesbians who have renounced tribadism and engaged in relationships with men. In later treatises on tribadism this is the dominant theme, but in *Jawāmiʿ al-Ladhdha* there are only a few examples.[35] In two examples, the women who renounce tribadism are named: ʿĀʾisha bint Abī Hārūn al-Tammār and Bint Bulbul al-ʿAṭṭār. ʿĀʾisha, who was the daughter of a date-seller (*tammār*), was 'one of their grand ladies' and Bint Bulbul, whose father was a seller of perfume (*ʿaṭṭār*), was infamous for her bawdy jokes (*mujūn*).[36] They regretted their former decision to engage in tribadism, and inscribed their experience on their rings: 'I have never seen anything good until I got to know the penis,' ʿĀʾisha wrote, with *khayr* and *ayr* as the rhyming words, whereas Bint Bulbul's verse is without rhyme: I got tired of lies and returned to the truth.

Verses inscribed on rings seem to have been popular among the refined society in the late third/ninth century, at least according to *al-Muwashshā* by al-Washshāʾ. He describes verses inscribed on rings and other items worn by the elegant men and women in Baghdad, *al-ẓurafāʾ* and *al-mutaẓarrifāt*.[37] According to *Jawāmiʿ al-Ladhdha*, some women wore rings with witty sayings announcing their sexual orientation in simple rhymed prose. The sayings are always indecent and sometimes irreverent. A woman named Wuhayba, for example, engraved on her ring, 'I seek protection by God from the penis and from the monk entering the monastery'; the rhyming words are *ayr* and *dayr*.[38] A woman who had given up tribadism inscribed on a ring that she gave to her former girlfriend, 'If you had tasted his penis (*ayrahi*), you would not enjoy anything else (*ghayrahi*).'[39]

Some of the sayings can probably be read as satire against lesbians, but the examples in *Jawāmiʿ al-Ladhdha* do not convey sharp criticism against tribadism, as later anecdotes do. The point is rather the indecent witticism of the verses. The indecency is often irreverent, as we have seen above. The following letter from a lady to her former lover is written in elegant *sajʿ*:

> A cultured woman (*ẓarīfa*) wrote to her beloved who had befriended[40] a man and after that stayed constantly in his house, 'If the muezzin does not step down from the minaret, people cannot start the congregational prayer (*jamāʿa*). How can you admire a leather bucket that has been dipped in a thousand wells? It came to you after its handles were broken, its rope threadbare and the two cords that hold it up weakened. If you return to the truth you will find that walking in pleasure gardens is easier than on mountain roads.' Her beloved wrote to her as an answer, 'I used to eat a pregnant camel, without knowing the taste of the stallion.[41] After having tasted it, I have sworn that I will never eat anything else and I will never break my oath. Remove your love for me from your heart! I have replaced it with a love that will never be removed from my heart, without my soul removed along with it.[42]

In order to convince her beloved, the cultured woman presents two main arguments: tribadism is more equal and male genitals are more unpleasant, especially when they are old. The religious imagery may seem shocking and is certainly innovative. The likening of the penis to a minaret is not new, we saw it in Ḥamdūn's prose poem to Duqāq in Chapter 5, but the role of the muezzin is exceptional and so is the image of congregational prayer, ensuring heavenly bliss to its practitioners.[43] The image of the muezzin alone up in the minaret alludes to haughtiness and isolation, whereas the congregational prayer is a communal act, alluding to a more equal practice. The beloved's male friend is ridiculed and his genitals likened to a leather bucket with imagery alluding to his old age and promiscuity. It is common to insinuate that women's gentials are 'worn out', as we saw in an anecdote about the courtesan ʿArīb in Chapter 5, but men are less often satirized for being promiscuous. The contrast between loneliness and haughtiness on the one hand and community and bliss on the other is paralleled by the images of the mountain roads and the pleasure gardens. One could perhaps understand the irreverence of the first woman as a result of her licentious lifestyle, whereas the second woman, who has chosen the right path, uses a more (but not totally) chaste vocabulary.

One long poem quoted in *Jawāmiʿ al-Ladhdha* depicts a debate between a lesbian and a married woman; they argue about who of them has the best life. The lesbian tries to convince the heterosexual woman with rational arguments giving a quite realistic picture of women's living conditions. In spite of this, the heterosexual woman wins the debate, and she does so by describing a sexual scene with a man that arouses the lesbian's desire and makes her denounce tribadism. The message is that female nature, with its excessive sexual appetite, will eventually make a women choose men.

A lesbian said to a woman who preferred men (*ṣāḥibat al-faḥl*[44]):

You have been degraded, what you do is worse than what I do.
You left a way that God made safe from difficulties,
Like a sandal easily covers another.
You are eager for relations with men though others are more devoted and more worthy of love and relationships.
Do you not know that with tribadism we steer clear of your crying the night of giving birth?
Midwives do not expose us to dishonour when they examine something guarded, which is not easily discovered.
We are not like sheep breastfeeding a long necked lamb and are not distressed by raising children.
When one of us meets a sister, we are free from the trouble of the ritual cleansing.
And if we wish to go out to a park and enjoy ourselves, we are not afraid of being divorced by the husband.

We are happy women, created for wellbeing, while you are unfortunate, created for humiliation.

The other woman said to her:

By the truth of Muhammad, I see a scabbard taking the place of a sword.
You have made your tribadism like measuring a sandal with a sandal,
But can a man take on one sandal on both feet?
You stupid woman, what is the beauty of a ring if the finger of an intelligent man does not penetrate it?
Which millstone revolves if there is no fixed pole in the centre, let us know your excuse!
And without dipping the eyeliner in the eye, the eyes of beautiful women would not be refreshed by kohl.
You are like a hungry person rolling the morsel between the lips, while he is occupied by hunger.
You are like a diseased treating his back with medicine, while the disease is boiling in his interior.
Stop telling lies, my sister, and repent! There is no better counsellor for you than I.
I swear, you should have seen me the day my friend visited me, like a fresh branch of the ben oil tree,
When he wrapped me, naked, inside his garment (*izār*), I found a penis (*jildan*) that had been hard since yesterday.
The thorn of his hair enticed me and touched my vulva like a path of ants.
When the thing that I cannot tell happened to me, I lose my mind with pleasure.
And he did other things after that, which if I told you what, you would climax immediately.

The lesbian told her, stop! I will repent from my sin and turn away from my ignorance.
I am so madly longing for that which you described for me that I do not fear becoming a disgrace for my family.
God bless you for it! Now, after what you have said, I regard tribadism as an act of ignorance.[45]

In line with the dialogical style of classical Arabic poetic debate, both participants have a voice and defend their own positions. The lesbian's arguments are reasonable and she points to the obvious fact that women who stay away from heterosexual intercourse are safeguarded from the dangers of childbirth and the troubles of parenting, as well as the restricted life under a man's control.

All jurists would not agree that lesbians are exempted from full-body ritual cleansing (*ghusl*), which is obligatory after penetrative intercourse, as some argue that women have to perform it even if penetration does not occur, as long as they ejaculate. Eventually the heterosexual woman, who has a moral advantage, wins the lesbian over to her side. She does not use moral arguments, however. Instead, she argues that heterosexuality is natural and that women and men complement each other, using different metaphors with the same meaning: Everything round needs something straight. This argument is not what wins the lesbian over, however, but the explicit description of her sexual encounter with a man and his hard member. That this is the best argument is in line with the representation of women as being governed by their sexual appetite. In the end, the lesbian is a woman, and as a woman, her lust is stronger than her reason.

## Lesbian love and comedy

Tragic love stories and love with unhappy, even disastrous, endings were a favourite theme in the early medieval Islamic world. The names of loving couples were familiar to everyone, Majnūn and Layla, Jamīl and Buthayna, ʿUrwa and ʿAfrāʾ, Qays and Lubnā, Kuthayyir and ʿAzza, and others. Chastity is a main component in these stories, and even when the lovers wished to engage in physical love, the obstacles were insurmountable. Not all love couples were heterosexual, however, at least a few involved two women. Especially famous was the story about Hind bint al-Nuʿmān, daughter of the last Lakhmid king of al-Ḥīra, al-Nuʿmān III ibn al-Mundhir (r. 580–602). She was the first Arab woman who fall in love with another woman, according to Ibn al-Kalbī, who relates that her beloved was the legendary Zarqāʾ al-Yamāma.[46] Her name, *zarqāʾ* means 'blue-eyed', but her eyes were more than that; miraculously, she could see from a very far distance.[47] One day, she spotted an enemy tribe advancing towards the place in al-Yamāma where she lived and warned the others. Nobody believed her, and her people was massacred. She herself was taken captive by the raiders, according to this version. They tore out one of her eyes and found that its veins were black. She died a few days after this violent treatment, and when Hind got the news, she withdrew to a convent and stayed there until she died. In addition to the miraculous eyesight, the story includes incredible and very violent events that are undoubtedly fictitious.[48]

According to the another version of Hind's life-story, she married the poet ʿAdī ibn Zayd, who was affiliated to the court in al-Hira; perhaps because this poet mentions a woman named Hind – a very common name – in some of his poems quoted in *Kitāb al-Aghānī*.[49] According to Abū al-Faraj al-Iṣbahānī, they met when the princess was only eleven years old, but already 'one of the most beautiful women of her time', endowed with a tall and perfectly built body. ʿAdī fall in love with her and conspired with one of the princess' ladies-in-waiting, a slave called Māriya, who herself was in love with the handsome poet, to meet with Hind.[50] In return, the story goes, ʿAdī took Māriya to a wine shop in al-Hira and slept with her, a detail that perhaps added eroticism to the story and proved ʿAdī's pre-Islamic manly charisma. Māriya, who was supposedly content with that, went to the king and managed to make him marry his daughter to the poet. Eventually, the story goes, the king fell out with ʿAdī and killed him. Now, there are different versions of what happened. One says that Hind became a nun after the death of her husband and isolated herself in a convent outside of al-Hira that was named Dayr Hind after her.

The story of Hind's love for another woman was perhaps more appealing and is retold in history books. In *Jawāmiʿ al-Ladhdha*, the narration is attributed to Diʿbil (d. 246/860), who maintained that Hind bint Nuʿmān's partner was another legendary pre-Islamic woman, Bint al-Khuss, famous for her eloquence. Bint al-Khuss is commonly known as Hind, but here she is referred to as al-Zarqāʾ.[51] The two women are mentioned again in *al-Fihrist* by Ibn al-Nadīm, now as Hind – perhaps Hind bint al-Khuss – and Bint al-Nuʿmān, in a short section with the title *Asmāʾ al-ḥabāʾib al-mutaẓarrifāṭ* ('Names of Elegant Female Loved Ones'). Ibn al-Nadīm enumerates eleven female couples, probably love couples, whose stories apparently were told by people in tenth-century Baghdad. There are Ruqayya and Khadīja, Sukayna and al-Rabbāb, Salmā and Suʿād, and eight other female couples whose stories are extinct today.[52]

Another tragic tale about a woman who loved another woman is quoted by al-Washshāʾ in *al-Muwashshā*. It is a story about unfulfilled love and suffering leading to death, some favourite topics of al-Washshāʾ. Unusually, however, this particular story is a love triangle: a young woman loves a young man but the young man loves a female singer (*qayna*), who in turn loves the young woman.[53] It was supposedly narrated by the young woman's father in *majlis* of al-ʿUtbī (probably the poet from Basra, d. 228/842–843). He had, at another *majlis*, heard the singer performing a song about love's inevitable suffering, which caused the young man's immediate death. Upon hearing about the death of the young man, his daughter perished, which, in turn, caused the death of the singer. The love triangle, thus, had an utterly tragic ending – three people died from love suffering.[54]

Less tragic is a quotation in *Jawāmiʿ al-Ladhdha* attributed to Abū al-ʿAnbas al-Saymarī, who, according to Ibn al-Nadīm, also wrote a book on lesbians and passive sodomites (*Kitāb al-saḥḥāqāt wa-l-baghghāʾīn*).[55] This book is not extant, but judging by the citations in *Jawāmiʿ al-Ladhdha*, it contained a mixture of serious or quasi-serious attempts to describe and explain lesbianism, as well as humorous anecdotes in *mujūn* style. The *saḥḥāqāt* describe themselves in rhymed prose and figurative language. 'We, the company of lesbians', it begins, and continues with descriptions of the perfect lesbian beloved. These women are clearly not primarily attracted to the act of rubbing, they appreciate many aspects of female beauty. Initially, the beloved's beauty is described in fairly conventional terms. Her cheeks are like apples from Lebanon and her breasts like pomegranates, for example. Then the figurative language turns burlesque, with imaginative and slightly indecent descriptions of the intimate parts. Her vagina is hot like an oven; it looks like a golden cup, a citron, and a cake of sweet bread with black caraway. The beloved's vagina looks like a crouching hare (*arnab jāthim*), a duck from Kaskar rising as if it were the full moon and, oddly, Salomon's altar in Jerusalem.

The text is full of references and we recognize images from the vagina poems in Chapter 5: *jāthim* is an attribute to the vagina in al-Nābigha al-Dhubyānī's poem and the hare occurs for example in the hadith of Umm Zarʿ. Now, the genre is clearly *mujūn*, and the description turns irreverent with allusions to sacred history and prophets. Her labia are thicker than the heifer of Israel. Her vulva is protruding like the hump of the she-camel of Thamūd, an allusion to sura 7:37 in the Qurʾān about the she-camel sent by God to the prophet Sāliḥ of Thamūd. It is pressed down like the buttocks of Abraham's ram. It has the colour of ivory, the smoothness of brocade and is perfumed with musk and saffron, as if it was Khosrow Anushiruwān sitting cheerfully in the middle of his palace. Finally, among her many beautiful qualities is her way of walking; she walks proudly like Abū Dujāna – a companion to Muḥammad and a famous fighter – on his way to war with God's Messenger. Then Abū al-ʿAnbas describes a lesbian intercourse in a passionate manner but without irreverent allusions. The bodies of the two lovers match each other; their likeness makes them compatible, the chest with the chest, the breast with the breast and the vulva with the vulva. The friction of the two bodies generates heat that rises to the head, the breaths of the lovers become louder, until they snore and sights and move in excitement.

Abū al-ʿAnbas's expressive description of the encounter between two female lovers is certainly humorous, but it is still a tribute to female lust, although slightly satirical, and acknowledges that passionate devotion between two women can be beautiful. For certain poets, allusions to a woman's homosexual desire are more explicitly used as invectives and especially connected to ugliness and meanness. Abū Tammām (d. 231/846), for example, quotes a poem in a chapter called *madhammat al-nisāʾ* ('blaming women') in his *Ḥamāsa*, which describes a woman as extremely ugly, and, on top of that, 'she loves women and refuses men'.[56]

Other humorous stories and poems about lesbian women use the same or similar metaphors as those in Abū al-ʿAtāhiya's poem, two items of the same type do or do not join together. Several of them are collected in the *adab* collection *Nathr al-Durr* (*Scattering of Pearls*) by al-Ābī (d. 421/1030), who was vizier at the Buyid court in Rayy. Tribadism, one woman said jokingly, is like performing ablution with sand (*tayammum*) when no water is available.[57] The assumption behind this and similar jokes is that women need an outlet for their sex drive. There was an impotent man, one story goes, who took his wife by surprise one day as she was with another woman. He said, 'Woe to you, what good is a hole on a hole?' 'It is good enough,' she answered, 'until God grants me with a patch.'[58] The point of both these stories is that if there is no man available, or when the man is impotent, women are good enough for satisfying women's desire.

In another anecdote, a woman criticizes her former girlfriend, who has given up tribadism and married: 'My sister, how ugly a *ṣād* is with a *lām* (Arabic letters), and how beautiful a *ṣād* is with a *ṣād*!' The joke relies on the by now familiar association of sameness with tribadism and difference with heterosexual sex, strenghtened by the fact that a *lām* consists of a line protruding straight upwards, whereas a *ṣād* has a circle. A woman who had renounced tribadism tried to convince her former friends with the following metaphor, 'My sisters, have you ever seen a lock unlocked by a lock?' They said no, and she continued, 'I have found a key for my lock that is greater than a thousand locks.'[59] Finally, another of the common themes for discussions on tribadism, the fear of pregnancy, is taken up in al-Ābī's collection of humorous stories as well, completed with explanations of the puns so that no one will miss their meaning.

> A lesbian said to another, 'there is nothing more delicious than bananas' – she meant sexual intercourse. The other lesbian answered, 'You are right, but it gives you a bloated stomach' – she meant pregnancy.

Female homosexuality is one of many themes in al-Ābī's collection of jokes, and lesbians are not necessarily represented more negatively than other groups.

Other literary works are more negative towards tribadism and take the opportunity to condemn the practice.[60] The above examples show that female desire could be a topic of jokes without being seen in a negative light. Yet, even if these jokes somehow reflect societal attitudes, they say nothing about real women's concerns and possibilities. Moreover, even if the existence of female homosexuality was acknowledged, it was not necessarily accepted.

## Why *saḥq*? Medical and social explanations

Medical theory, with its holistic understanding of the body and psyche, could potentially explain deviations from what was regarded as normal sexuality. Some physicians describe the causes of *ubna*, passive male homosexuality, which was regarded as a serious defect.[61] Fewer mention tribadism, but judging from citations in *Jawāmiʿ al-Ladhdha* and a few other instances, there were attempts to explain female homosexuality as well. According to ʿAlī ibn Naṣr, Galen investigated the causes of tribadism; a claim that is perhaps not astonishing considering Galen's reputation among Islamic physicians as the foremost authority. Galen had a daughter who was a lesbian, ʿAlī ibn Naṣr explains, and taking the opportunity to find out more about this condition, the famous physician examined the veins of her pudendum. He could not find anything unusual, however, and concluded that tribadism must be a type of itching occurring between two halves of the labia.[62]

This sensational statement is followed by a report attributed to the physician Ibn Māsawayh (777–857), who had read in 'old books', that tribadism is caused by certain vegetables and herbs eaten by the mother or wet-nurse while breast-feeding. He mentions especially celery and arugula.[63] ʿAlī ibn Naṣr also refers to the philosopher and scientist al-Kindī, who gives a somewhat curious explanation, in a quotation attributed to Abū al-ʿAnbas.[64] The extant text is sometimes difficult to follow, but, roughly, al-Kindī claims that tribadism is a natural desire emanating from an ulcer-like condition inside the labia, which generates vapours that in turn generate heat and an itching sensation. The only way to recover from this condition, to soften the ulcer and cool the heat, is by scratching and ejaculation. The female sperm that is generated from tribadism is very cold, in contrast to the sperm that is generated from heterosexual intercourse, which is hot, as it is produced by converted blood.[65] Therefore, it is only tribadism that can recover this condition, as only a cold sperm can cool down the heat. In al-Kindī's explanation, tribadism is a necessary action for a specific condition. The afflicted woman, the *saḥḥāqa*, is not necessarily a lesbian in terms of preferring women, she needs clitoris stimulation by means of rubbing, which could also be performed in a heterosexual relation. When the *saḥḥāqa* has intercourse with her husband, al-Kindī continues, she cannot feel pleasure unless she grabs his penis and rubs it against her labia.

Al-Kindī's student Qusṭā ibn Lūqā put forward a theory for the origin of homosexual desire, primarily male but indirectly applicable to women, in his treatise *Causes of Difference in People's Characters, Ways of Life, Appetite, and Choices* (*Kitāb fī ʿIlal Ikhtilāf al-Nās fī Akhlāqihim wa-Siyarihim wa-Shahwātihim wa-Ikhtiyārihim*). The theory is based on a typology of personality variations in men and their origins in the physiological constitutions of four vital organs, the brain, heart, liver and testicles.[66] According to him, same-sex desire is a natural characteristic that has to do with variations in human temperament (*mizāj*). There are six types of appetites, according to Qusṭā ibn Lūqā – appetites for food, drink, sound, sex, property and reputation – and the distribution of these appetites differ in accordance with men's constitutions.[67] As for sexual appetite, men can be inclined towards women, boys (*ghilmān*) or both. Within each group, they have different preferences for sex partners, as to body size, race and colour. Qusṭā ibn Lūqā does not explicitly mention female personality variations, but he probably assumed that women possess the same kind of variations as men do. The outcome would be somewhat different, however, as women's physical constitution in general was believed to differ from that of men (they are colder and moister as we have seen in Chapter 1).

Homosexual attraction is innate in some people, according to Qusṭā ibn Lūqā's theory, although it can be adjusted somewhat, as we will see below. Yet, he concludes that only heterosexual love is universally natural, as it is decreed by God, although he acknowledges that there are religious men who claim that homosexual relations are not forbidden, as neither the Gospels nor the Qur'an explicitly forbid them.[68] This kind of justification of homosexuality is due to a casual attitude to religion, he continues, instead of careful study. How people deal with their homosexual attraction depends on accidental properties, such as strong or weak discernment, attitude to religion, good or bad judgement, and customs and habits. People with bad judgement believe in occasional foolish physicians who claim, falsely, that homosexual intercourse with boys is better for the body. This is wrong, Qusṭā ibn Lūqā objects, as women's sexual organs were created for intercourse with men and have the right humidity for the male organ, whereas intercourse with men exhausts the organ and the body; an idea both he and al-Rāzī attribute to the Greek physician Rufus.[69] Qusṭā ibn Lūqā attributes the first opinion to al-Kindī, who apparently theorized about homosexuality and is quoted in *Jawāmiʿ al-Ladhdha*, as we have seen. According to him, al-Kindī claimed that homosexuality is a natural desire, proved by its existence among certain species of animals, something that Ibn Lūqā argues against, pointing to the differences between animals and humans.

Quṣṭā ibn Lūqā argues that strict segregation between men and women can be a contributing factor for developing homosexual attraction. He is entirely interested in men's perspective, contrary to the twelfth century physician al-Samawʾal who is discussed below, but his theory is valid for women in analogy. Men are accustomed to seeing other men's slave-boys everywhere, whereas slave-girls are confined to the houses and only visible for their owners. A man's desire may be aroused at times when he is outside his house and have no access to slave-girls, Qusṭā ibn Lūqā continues, whereas slave-boys are easily available.[70] Hence, starting out as an alternative solution, sexual relations with boys become a habit and men get used to it. They start to frequent private places and baths for their meetings, places which women are ashamed to visit. Men's free wives are not even mentioned as sources of attraction, probably out of modesty.

Qusṭā ibn Lūqā concludes that although homosexual desire is caused by a man's constitution, which he cannot change entirely, he can choose not to fulfil his desire. There is, individual temperaments notwithstanding, a universal nature decreed by God, and that is heterosexuality. A man with good discernment and a balanced constitution never chooses anything that goes against God's decree, regardless of his own bodily craving. Qusṭā ibn Lūqā relates that he has himself met men who inclined towards homosexual desire but succeeded in subduing their passion, as they were honourable and keep to what is right.

Al-Rāzī traces the cause of passive homosexuality to the properties of the male and female sperm at conception, and in analogy his theory relates to both male and female homosexual attraction.[71] As we have seen, Islamic physicians believed that both women and men have semen, which have to mix in order for conception to take place. There were different theories about how the foetus becomes male or female, but according to al-Rāzī it depends on whether the female or the male sperm prevails at the moment of conception and transforms the other. If the female sperm prevails, it transforms the male sperm and the foetus becomes a female child and vice versa. In rare cases when none of the sperm prevails and transforms the other, a foetus is produced by two independent sperm. In this case, the child will be born intersexed (*khunthā*), having both female and male genitalia.

Each of the sperm also provides the child with a certain degree of femininity or masculinity – that is characteristics associated with females and males –

depending on its strength and forcefulness. The male sperm provides masculinity and the female provides femininity. Its force is moderate most of the time, but it happens that the sperm is extremely strong and forceful or extremely weak. In the first case, it conveys an extremely high degree of femininity to the female child, if it is a female sperm, and an extremely high degree of masculinity to the male child, if it is a male sperm. In the second case, the sperm instead conveys an extremely low degree of femininity or masculinity, which means that the person, when she or he grows up, tends to possess characteristics associated with the other sex. Masculine women sometimes menstruate very little or have no menstruation at all; and more striking, they sometimes have facial hair. Al-Rāzī had seen a bearded woman with his own eyes, he tells us, who had been taken to be displayed at the court of al-Muʿtaḍid.

For men, a low degree of masculinity is a constituent to becoming a passive homosexual. Although it is already caused before the child is born, it is possible to cure if it is not fully developed and the patient has a strong will to do so. He has to avoid all temptations, such as places were this kind of fornication ordinarily takes place. Notably, al-Rāzī recommends the use of beautiful slave women to put the man's desire right. This can be done as slave women and their bodies are nothing but vehicles for men's desire. Al-Rāzī does not discuss the sexual orientation of women with weak femininity, and whether they tend to be attracted to women, perhaps he did not regard lesbianism as a problem. In real life, most women would not be in a position to reject men, as they would be married off regardless of their orientation.

Later Ibn Sīnā criticized physicians such as al-Rāzī, who believe that passive male homosexuality is caused by a man's constitution (*ṭabʿī*), and therefore a natural condition.[72] According to him, passive male homosexuality is an imaginary (*wahmī*) condition and caused by a depraved life-style rather than having natural causes. The only cure is to keep back thoughts of boys and if this is difficult, Ibn Sīnā suggests drastic methods, such as starvation, distress, beating, withholding of sleep, and arrest.

Contrary to al-Rāzī, Ibn Sīnā mentions women's desire for other women, but he concludes that the reason is quite simple. It is caused by lack of satisfaction from the heterosexual intercourse and can be cured by orgasm, helped by sexual technique:

> Female orgasm is most often tardy, and therefore they remain unable to satisfy their desire, which means there will be no offspring. Instead, she remains excited by lust, and if she is not guarded, she will, in this condition, let whoever she finds

> fall upon her. For this reason, they engage in lesbianism, so that they together find satisfaction for their desire.[73]

For this reason, Ibn Sīnā stresses the importance of considering women's needs, and gives some advice about tools to stimulate it (see Chapter 1).

Alī ibn Naṣr gives another explanation for tribadism in *Jawāmiʿ al-Ladhdha*; namely that lack of sexual satisfaction in some women is caused by an anatomical variation, namely the length of 'the neck of the vagina', which connects the vagina to the womb. If the neck is longer than normal, but the penis is of normal size, the woman cannot feel pleasure from the intercourse, as she feels pleasure only when the penis reaches the bottom.[74] In this case, she risks becoming lesbian. His understanding of tribadism is similar to that of Ibn Sīnā: if women do not feel pleasure from penetrative intercourse, they will turn to other women. Compared with Ibn Sīnā's explanation, in this case, the condition is difficult to treat. Women with this condition either have to marry well equipped men, or their husbands have to use one of the remedies for penis extension recommended by physicians (see Chapter 1). If not, one wonders what kind of pleasure women get from tribadism if their pleasure is derived from stimulation of the bottom of the vagina. Women do not get pleasure from stimulating the external parts of the vagina, the author emphasizes, obviously arguing against what he perceives as a common misbelief. Pleasure is derived from stimulating the internal part as the penis has to reach and stimulate the womb.[75] This curious statement indicates that the author lacked the basic knowledge of women's experience of pleasure that one would expect from a self-proclaimed expert on women and an author of a sex manual. Women's source of pleasure cannot be stimulation of the external parts, he claims, as in that case, all women would become lesbians, which does not only mean practicing tribadism, but also rejecting men all together. This 'logical' explanation follows the topos that women would do precisely anything to satisfy their desire, and therefore are always potentially dangerous for the societal order, and in this case, for the survival of the human race. Nevertheless, the author of *Jawāmiʿ al-Ladhdha* never allows this topos to be his sole explanation of women's behaviour as the basic principle behind his reasoning is that people are different. Elsewhere, he admits that women can get pleasure from stimulation of the external parts and still be heterosexual, when he advise men to rub their genitals against the labia, which is pleasurable for both partners.

## Al-Samawʾal on *saḥq*

In the twelfth century, the physician and mathematician al-Samawʾal al-Maghribī summed up opinions about the causes of tribadism in his sex manual *Nuzhat al-Aṣḥāb fī Muʿāsharat al-Aḥbāb*.[76] Some of the ideas are recognizable from the extant body of literature surveyed here, but others are not. Some of the observations may be his own. There are, according to him, several causes behind women taking to tribadism, some inherent to the woman's physiology or depending on her anatomy, others sociological or a matter of taste.

The first cause, which should be easily correctable after studying the sex manual, is the disagreement between the woman's and the man's rhythm. If the man reaches climax before the woman, he will leave her with the fire still burning, which will make her go out of her mind. The motif of the unsatisfied woman as crazy and dangerous, which occurred in ninth and tenth century literature, was still effective in the twelfth. An unsatisfied woman, al-Samawʾal claims, would, if not protected, satisfy herself with a horse if that is the only thing that is offered. She could also resort to tribadism with a woman or a eunuch, who is entrusted to her. Tribadism is thus only one of several ways to get satisfaction, and this kind of woman would renounce it if she found a man who reaches his climax as slowly as she does.

The other way around, a woman who is quicker than her partner, is not good either. When she ejaculates, her semen cools off the penis, and causes the man to be even slower. Meanwhile, as the man takes his time, she will get a second orgasm, which exhausts her if she has a weak constitution, which is often the case. She will lie quiet and calm while the man is active, and as he is approaching his climax, she only wants to rest. This may cause her losing interest in men and taking up tribadism. As in the first example, she will recover if she finds a man who is as quick as she is.

Anatomical disagreement can also cause tribadism, as also ʿAlī ibn Naṣr maintained in *Jawāmiʿ al-Ladhdha*. Whereas he attributed it to a 'long' vagina, however, al-Samaw'al attributes it to the opposite condition. If the neck of the womb is short and the penis long, the woman feels pain from intercourse and may prefer tribadism as long as she does not find a suitable man. Some women can experience pain during intercourse for other reasons, such as disease or deformities in their vaginas. These women avoid penetration and prefer tribadism.

Perhaps inspired by a poetic theme, women's preference for young beardless men rather than mature men with beards, al-Samaw'al then asserts that some women hate to kiss a bearded mouth or feel a bearded cheek against theirs. If they cannot find a young beardless man, these women will look for beautiful girls. This explanation seems to be a matter of taste, but women's aversion for beards is perhaps thought to have physiological or other reasons. Finally, al-Samaw᾽al also provides a sociological explanation for women choosing sexual relations with other women, namely seclusion. Women who are confined to strict seclusion may not have another option.

The examples above point to an understanding of tribadism as a practice that is interchangeable with penetration, depending on the circumstances. Al-Samaw᾽al also provides a possible physiological explanation, in line with his predecessors. According to al-Samaw᾽al, this cause is an imbalance in the temperature of the womb, which is temporarily restored by tribadism, as the friction of rubbing generates more heat than penetration. This means also that women who suffer from excessive coldness feel more pleasure from tribadism, and choose it when they can.

Female partners in the examples above are substitutes for males in circumstances when women are forced to take up tribadism to satisfy their natural desire. They could as well satisfy themselves with available men, for example eunuchs or, in some cases, beardless or impotent men. There are also cases of women who always prefer women, rather than choosing the act of tribadism regardless of the partner's sex. These women possess masculine characteristics and resemble men in their way of moving and talking. Their sexual behaviour is also similar to that of men, they want to take the active role and be a *fā῾ila* (doer) and cannot accomplish intercourse if their desire is not strong enough. Moreover, they have difficulties conforming to men's sexual wishes, which urges them to engage in tribadism instead. To this group belonged learned women, female scribes and Qur᾽an reciters, a rare affirmation of women working in these professions.[77] Samaw᾽al does not suggest treatment for this category of women who engaged in tribadism and, unlike al-Rāzī, does not try to explain their behaviour in terms of physiology or the characteristics of the semen.

## Concluding remarks

In the chapter on female same-sex desire in *Jawāmi῾ al-Ladhdha*, lesbian women express their desires and explain their sexual orientation. The poetry is occasionally bawdy, belonging to the genre of *mujūn*, but some poetic personas picture a realistic background when they describe their sexual orientation. It is possible that the poems were written by female poets, but even if the poetic voices are fictional, several of them take women's concerns seriously and express women's potential fears and preferences. Some women explain their choice to engage in tribadism as being more pleasurable, others have chosen it due to social constraints. Most notably, they want to avoid pregnancy; they state several times that they do not want to be a disgrace to their family. They also hint at tribadism being a more equal practice, as unmarried women they do not have to fear their husbands, and are free to go out and enjoy themselves in the park, for example. In their explanations, *saḥq* is often more than a choice of method for stimulation. Rather, it involves a female partner and a sisterhood that sometimes explicitly rejects men.

Male scholars were not that positive and regarded homosexual attraction as something that had to be cured. Physicians often explained female homosexual desire as being caused by their lack of satisfaction from heterosexual intercourse and Ibn Sīnā advices men how to confront this problem (by means of sexual technique). Others explained lesbianism as a result of strict segregation between the sexes. Qusṭā ibn Lūqā maintained that segregation could be a reason why men engage in homosexual activities and al-Samaw'al adds that women who are confined to strict segregation may not have another option. This is only one of several reasons for homosexual behaviour, according to them, but it is a plausible explanation. As we saw in the beginning of this chapter, the elite *jawārī* of the third/ninth century were sometimes 'accused' of lesbianism, and in their case, although they were sometimes concubines, they were surrounded by women most of the time. It is, in any case, interesting that the sources give different reasons for homosexual behaviour: social, biological or an active choice. It is equally interesting, that though the sources are few, they point to *saḥq* as being an established practice in the Abbasid period that was accepted in at least some circles.

# Conclusion

Considering the weight put on women's sexual appetite and female desire in other fields of learning in the early medieval Islamic world, it is remarkable that the early juristic discourses consistently prioritized men's sexual needs and preferences over those of women. Wives' sexual availability was part of men's marital rights, as defined by the jurists, and they also had the right to pleasure, as the legal term for a husband's sexual claim on his wife was *istimtāʿ*, 'enjoyment' or 'pleasure'. This meant, according to some, that wives should not only be available, they should be beautiful and pleasant in order to arouse and please their husbands. The jurists did not grant the same rights to wives. The gender system produced by early jurisprudence is remarkable, considering that other male-dominated discourses could handle women's need for sexual satisfaction without challenging gender hierarchy.

Early medieval Islamic physicians relied on androcentric Greek theories of sex differentiations, which explained sex differences as caused by different body temperature as men are hot and women are cold; some added other causes, such as moistness and dryness and if the foetus is produced on the left of right side of the uterus. Whatever the cause, all agreed that the outcome is that women are biologically inferior and men superior. As explained by al-Majūsī, the causality is remarkably simple. The male body is more perfect because it is hotter; some outer signs of their heat are their broader chests, bigger heads and more body hair, which, in turn, make men more intelligent and courageous. Female bodies have less body hair because their constitution is colder; hence, women are less intelligent and less courageous, etc. The notion of balance is essential for the natural law of male perfectness and female inferiority as the male and female bodies complement each other: female coolness complements male hotness. Al-Majūsī gives a concrete example when he describes how the cold and thin female sperm tempers the hotness and thickness of the male sperm, which otherwise risks spoiling the foetus. The consequence is that the male body cannot be superior without the inferior female body.

Nevertheless, the gendered understanding of natural law and the notion of male perfectness did not reduce physicians' concern for women's health. Even though women were largely excluded from the medical discourse, sex was considered a health issue for women as well as for men. There is a significant number of pleasure enhancing therapies in medical compendia in Arabic, many of them are directed to men or are not gender-specific, but some are specifically directed to women. In the beginning of the eleventh century, the highly regarded physician Ibn Sīnā recommended 'penis enlargement' when women cannot reach orgasm because the genitals do not 'match' each other. Women's satisfaction is not only necessary for reproduction, he explained, but also for avoiding adultery. Admittedly, many remedies addressed to women are intended to help them manipulate their sexual assets in order to gain men's love, attention and attraction, for women, sexual agency could be a strategy for gaining advantages. Nevertheless, the underlying conviction in medical discourse is that women's pleasure and satisfaction are desired by their male partners and essential for their own wellbeing and for the future of humanity.

All Islamic physicians at this time embraced the two-seed theory, and the notion of female seed made them emphasise the importance of female orgasm and they encouraged men to see to their wives pleasure. Islamic physicians even maintained that women feel more pleasure than men do as they have more sources for pleasure than men have. Traditions about female emission of semen indicate that the jurists accepted the two-seed theory and the notion of female semen had impact on purity laws. Yet, early jurists did not give explicit consideration to the significance of female sexual satisfaction that follows from the notion of female semen. The importance of 'mingling' of semen was not considered by them, or, at best, seen as non-problematic.

Ideas in favour of female satisfaction circulated in medical literature from the middle of the ninth century onwards. They coincided with the interest in erotology, which emphasised the importance of mutual pleasure on the one hand, and conveyed the notion of the hypersexual women on the other hand. Erotology was also a male-dominated pursuit as it accepted the notion of the defective female nature and women's subordination; it was, after all, a hegemonic notion in intellectual discourses. Representations of the hypersexual woman are connected to the notion of female defectiveness that was conveyed by medical theory. Women are not endowed with self-reflection, as portrayed in erotic literature, or able to make rational choices about their own future; they reject wealth in favour of sex, for example, and it is men's duty to help and guide them. The solution proposed by the author of the earliest erotic compendia,

*Jawāmiʿ al-Ladhdha*, is not to oblige women to obey their husbands and seclude them in their houses, as the jurists would suggest, but to learn how to 'understand' them and 'be in harmony' with them, in order to make them sexually satisfied and, consequently, content and happy.

Nevertheless, the author of *Jawāmiʿ al-Ladhdha* occasionally contests this representation. He refutes this idea himself, claiming, on empirical grounds, that women are different, just as men are, and some have more appetite, others less. Given the diverse traditions of its sources, it is difficult to distinguish a single worldview or a single notion of female sexuality. However, an 'empirical track' runs through the book, and this track is always pragmatic. Eventually the theories have no practical bearing in the erotic compendium. They are conflicting and often obscure and seem to display sophisticated knowledge as a way for the refined readers to distinguish themselves from the commoners.

Admittedly, men are also represented as driven by physical desire in the erotic genre, but at least they are supposed to be able to digest the sometimes obscure theoretical explanations in *Jawāmiʿ al-Ladhdha*. The construction of the hypersexual woman is sometimes straightforward misogynistic, most notable in invective poetry. Umayyad as well as Abbasid poetry contain disturbing images of grotesque female bodies, and abound with sexual violence. The degradation of the female body peaked with the obscene poetry of Ibn al-Ḥajjāj in the late tenth century, which might be an indication of changes in society and women's diminishing societal roles. However, the misogynist motif is hardly noticeable in *Jawāmiʿ al-Ladhdha*, from the same time-period. In erotic literature, the hypersexual woman is a male erotic fantasy, yet it actually promotes female sexual agency. In erotic literature, women are experts and advisers; they articulate their wishes and realize their desires. Women have a voice and describe their own experience.

In her influential book *Women and Gender in Islam*, Leila Ahmed blamed the 'ideology of gender' in Abbasid society in Iraq for enabling an androcentric definition of Islam, as its legal authorities 'interpreted the religion as intending to institute androcentric laws and an androcentric vision in all Muslim societies through time'.[1] According to Ahmed, the ideology of gender in Abbasid society, especially among its dominant urban classes, was the product of an unfortunate combination of misogynist attitudes and practices that existed in the area before the Islamic conquests and the enormous wealth and slaves that were brought in by the conquests. This enabled rich men to keep large harems with numerous slave concubines, in line with earlier practice among the Persian elite.

As we have seen in this book, early Abbasid society also contained attitudes and practices that were less misogynist, as far as they at least considered women's wishes and desires, and its literature gave room for women's own voices. The mores of the dominant classes, which Ahmed blamed for reproducing this particular gender ideology, were in actual fact multifaceted and shared by women. Take for example the judge and astrologer Abū al-ʿAnbas, companion to caliph al-Mutawakkil, who wrote about lesbian love in a book quoted in *Jawāmiʿ al-Ladhdha*. He was friends with the elderly (probably) singer ʿArīb, who was famous for her many love affairs. The narrative about lesbians attributed to him is crammed with blasphemous references to religious and political discourses.

In offering a sexual ethics for the elite, *Jawāmiʿ al-Ladhdha* gives another picture of the mores of the elite. According to this ethics, cultured men should strive to be beloved by women and satisfy their desire; the ultimate goal is mutual pleasure in the form of simultaneous orgasm. ʿAlī ibn Naṣr uses both medical and religious discourses to support this theory. The cultured men that he addresses in his book, could, if the dating of the encyclopaedia is correct, be secretaries in the Buyid administration.

Although the early jurists hesitated to grant women sexual rights, there were traditions that promoted female sexual expressions. Female lustfulness was desirable, according to some, as long as it was directed to the husband, and one of the requirements of marital obedience (*ḥusn al-tabaʿʿul*), which was obligatory for women, according to early jurists. The houris, as described by Qurʾan interpreters, resembled the female ideal in erotic literature and the same epithets about lustfulness are used to describe them, with the difference that the houris are obedient. Hadiths about female nature being more libidinous than male, and that God therefore made women bashful, circulated in the early medieval Islamic world, taken from Greek mythology and, possibly, Persian stories.

Jurists envisioned female sexuality as being controlled by men, but there are many examples in literature of women's sexual agency and sexual attractiveness as a resource for women. We have seen both freeborn Arab women, such as al-Dahnāʾ, and slaves put up for sale using their sexuality in order to change the course of events to their advantage. Remedies for enhancing sexual pleasure and gaining men's attraction were addressed to women and were supposed to be administered by them. Books such as *Asrār al-nisāʾ* (*Women's Secrets*) presuppose female readers, and there are also indications of a 'courtesan's handbook' in Bunyāndukht's advice to women on how to seduce men. The hypersexual women portrayed in *Jawāmiʿ al-Ladhdha* have more to do with male fantasies than social reality, and its potential readers were men from the elite who wanted to distinguish themselves by their knowledge of everything new and cosmopolitan. There are nonetheless instances when women's real concerns are dealt with in this rich book, such as when lesbian women express that their fear for pregnancy and social exclusion are reasons behind their choice to have sex with women, and there are also generally favourable portraits of elderly women (which is not always the case in the later tradition). Moreover, in the stories, women are given the leading role; they are experts and educate men and women. The citations from available literary traditions give the encyclopaedia a distinct female voice, although much of it seems to originate in a masculine fantasy of excessive female sexuality.

Abbasid literature is notorious for not having any female authors. Toorawa suggests that the absence of female authors has to do with the transmission from a primarily oral culture to a literary culture in the third/ninth century, which led to a marginalization of women. The use of classical Arabic was linked to gender, Toorawa suggests, which explains the absence of female authors. Before this shift from a primarily oral culture to a literary culture, free women seem to have contributed to the literary achievements, shown by the many female oral narrators quoted in the sources, as well as many female poets and other verbally eloquent women. By the Abbasid era, classical Arabic was primarily used by educated men and learned outside the home, primarily in male environments.[2] As women did not have the same opportunities to learn classical Arabic, they did not write and speak Arabic as frequently as men did. Educated slave courtesans (called *jawārī* and *qiyān*), who were singers and poets, participated in cultural salons and some of them became famous for their poetry and command of the language. The educated slave courtesans were, in Toorawa's words, 'women prepared for and inducted into the male environment of the classical language'.[3] Their role in the cultural salons was perhaps to add flavour to the all-male gatherings. However, women's exclusion from classical Arabic should not be exaggerated. Although they did not leave many traces in literature, free elite women held cultural salons and enjoyed the company of the most accomplished female slave singers, poets and courtesans.[4] Women took part in cultured conversations and produced poetry and other cultural media, decent or indecent.

There are many indications that women's oral culture continued in classical Arabic, although it was not written down. Female poets are mentioned in the sources, although most are anonymous and perhaps fictional. It is not unlikely that the poems were written by female poets, but even if the poetic voices are fictional, several of them take women's concerns seriously and express women's potential fears and preferences.

There is also a corpus of anecdotes with female protagonists from the early Islamic period, depicting women, real or fictitious, who cope with the realities of a patriarchal society in different ways, sometimes angrily, but often proudly and with a good portion of humour. It is possible to read them as female strategies for living in a patriarchal society, which is perhaps part of their success. Al-Dahnāʾ who litigated against her husband in order to get a divorce, used one of the few options she had as a woman – accusing him of impotence. She seems to have been disappointed when the governor gave her husband a deadline of one year to prove his potency, which was to become the standard. Yet she was resigned to the governor's authority, but not without declaring that she did so proudly and by her own will. She could have run away from her old husband like an 'uncompliant young camel' but she chose to follow the rule of law.

For later female readers, al-Dahnāʾ's words might have been reassuring, for if they chose to concede to an unfavourable decision, they always had the option, at least theoretically, to do so proudly, knowing that they followed the rules and satisfactorily performed their role as women. Moreover, in the daily life of women and men, notions and concepts are sometimes far apart, and theoretical hierarchies are often overturned. In the body of anecdotes with female characters in, for example, *Balaghāt al-Nisāʾ* by Ibn Abī Ṭāhir Ṭayfūr, the socially subordinate individual often wins the verbal battle, by means of her skill and inner strength. The intellectual classes had reason to be impressed by and admire the woman who walks up to the caliph, alone, with no family to support her, and asks him to rule in her favour against her husband, who sits with the caliph together with other noble men. She knows she is right, and succeeds in convincing the caliph with her eloquence and wit as her only assistance. This situation was similar to that of the ambitious learned man who came to Baghdad to make himself a living as an author and intellectual, with his eloquence and knowledge as his only capital. Both chastity – a theme in women's poetry and a word that has not been dealt with in this book – and sexual comedy can be interpreted as female strategies to express their individuality. Women used the same motifs as men did in their poetry, even sexual comedy, and apparently felt they were free to do so. Others deliberately chose homosexual relations as a more equal alternative to the hierarchical relations with men.

# Notes

## Introduction

1 For an overview of Western research on women in early Islamic societies up to 2000 see Roded, 'Mainstreaming Middle East Research'. See also Bray, 'Men, Women, and Slaves', pp. 122–3. For women in premodern Islamic and Arabic sources, see Roded (ed.), *Women in Islam and the Middle East: A Reader*, and Marin and Deguilhem (eds), *Writing the Feminine*; Hambly (ed.), *Women in the Medieval Islamic World.*

2 See for example Cortese and Calderini, *Women and the Fatimids*; Rapaport, *Marriage, Money and Divorce in Medieval Islamic Society*; Peirce, *Imperial Harem* Ali, *Marriage and Slavery in Early Islam.*

3 For research reviews and reflections, see Marin, 'Women, Gender and Sexuality'; Peirce, 'Writing Histories of Sexuality in the Middle East'; and Semerdjian, 'Rewriting the History of Sexuality in the Islamic World'.

4 Ali, *Marriage and Slavery*. The seminal work *Sex and Society in Islam* by Basil Musallam, which is based on an imposing number of primary sources, discusses ideas about contraception and the rights of women as if these ideas had no history. He claims that no jurist denied free women the 'right to sexual fulfilment' and that all jurists granted them a 'basic right to sexual pleasure' (Musallam, *Sex and Society*, p. 31). What the early jurists generally granted them, as we will see in Chapter 3, was the right to conceive, not to pleasure.

5 *Fitna* is often referred to as a misogynist term, e.g. Mernissi, *Beyond the veil*. This meaning is refuted by Meisami, 'Writing medieval women', pp. 66–7.

6 Peirce, 'Writing Histories of Sexuality', p. 1329. There are a few articles that (more or less) consider female sexuality in medical discourses: Ahmad Dallal, 'Sexualities', Sherry Gadelrab, 'Sex Differences'; (for later time periods) Emily Selove and Rosalind Batten, 'Making Men and Women'; and Nahyan Fancy, 'Womb Heat'. There are also a few monographs that consider aspects of female sexuality, Albert Gewargis, *Gynäkologisches*, from 1980 (on al-Majūsī); Ursula Weisser, *Zeugung*, from 1983 (on theories of conceptions and embryology); Monica Green, 'Transmission', from 1985 (on gynaecology); and Kathryn Kueny, *Conceiving Identities*, from 2013.

7 I will give both the Hijri and Gregorian dates most of the time, in this order (third/ninth century); occasionally, I give only the Gregorian date.

8 Gacek, *Arabic Manuscripts*, Chart 2. The chart is based on and used for the fields of Islamic manuscript studies and Islamic art.

9 Aerts, 'Canon and Canonization of Ḥadīth'; Rippin, 'Tafsīr'.

10 Hallaq, *Origins and Evolution*, p. 79.

11 For the translation movement, see Gutas, *Greek Thought*, and the excellent article by D'Ancona, 'Greek into Arabic'.

12 In spite of the huge interest in Islamic medicine, there is, in fact, relatively little written on the subject of sexuality in medical discourse; Musallam's seminal work on birth control is one of few exceptions (*Sex and Society*, 1983). Except for the works mentioned in note 6, see Gerrit Bos' introduction to Ibn al-Jazzār, *Ibn al-Jazzār on Sexual Diseases*, as well as his articles on the same physician, and Pormann, 'Al-Rāzī'.

13 Temkin, *Galenism*, pp. 69–71; Pormann and Savage Smith, *Medieval Islamic Medicine*, pp. 12–15.

14 'Galen was present in the minds of the whole erudite class of Muslim society as a natural scientist of paradigmatic stature. Thus we may expect to find quotations from his works anywhere in the vast scholarly Arabic literature of the Middle Ages', Strohmaier, 'Uses of Galen', p. 114.

15 Much has been written on Islamic medicine, and there is a substantial secondary literature on the general medical ideas, the transmission from Greek medicine, and individual medical authors. Excellent introductions for the modern reader are *Medieval Islamic Medicine* by Peter Pormann and Emilie Savage-Smith, Savage-Smith et al., 'Ṭibb' and Savage-Smith, 'Medicine in Medieval Islam'. See also the classical works by Manfred Ullmann, the shorter *Islamic Medicine* and the comprehensive *Die Medizin im Islam*. Ullmann defends the use of the term 'Islamic medicine', even though many physicians were not Muslims, along these lines: 'All these scholars lived within the sphere of Islamic culture and have helped in a most enduring way to shape this culture and to give it its particular stamp. So when we talk of "Islamic medicine", we are thinking of Islam as a cultural force; we are looking at a culture which has absorbed many different currents within itself and integrated and developed them' (*Islamic Medicine*, p. xi).

16 For the various traditions that shaped Islamic medicine; see Pormann, 'Islamic Medicine Crosspollinated'.

17 E.g. Cheikh-Moussa, 'L'Historien et la littérature arab médiévale'; El Cheikh, 'In Search for the Ideal Spouse'.

18 The *majlis* signifies, literally, a place for sitting, and its meaning depends on the participants; it can be a literary salon, learned circle, musical session or a court.

19 Toorawa, *Ibn Abī Ṭāhir Ṭayfūr*, p. 121.

20 Eg. Dimitri Gutas, *Greek Thought*.

21 Pellat, 'Abū ʾl-ʿAnbas'.

22 Ibn Abī Ṭāhir wrote praise poetry to ʿAlī ibn Yaḥya al-Munajjim, a courtier of al-Mutawakkil, and was probably supported by him; Toorawa, *Ibn Abī Ṭāhir Ṭayfūr*, pp. 120–2.

23 Günther, 'Abū l-Faraj al-Iṣfahānī'.
24 Cf. Kraemer, *Humanism in the Renaissance of Islam.*
25 Gutas, 'Greek Thought', p. 151.
26 Ibn al-Nadīm, *Kitāb al-Fihrist*, vol. 1, p. 406. This is suggested by Franz Rosenthal in 'From Arabic Books and Manuscripts VI' and 'Fiction and Reality'. He suggests a later date elsewhere, though; see 'Male and Female: Described and Compared'. Rowson assumes that the book was written in the late tenth century; see Rowson, 'Arabic', p. 48.
27 Ḥajji Khalīfa (Kâtip Çelebi), *Kashf al-Ẓunūn*, vol. 1, p. 571. The author given here is probably the Samanid scientist with the same name, a colleague of al-Birūnī, famous for his mathematic and astronomical writings.
28 I rely on four manuscripts for this study: MS Aya Sofya 3836 (533/1139), MS Aya Sofya 3837 (634/1236), MS Fatih 3729 (582/1186) and Chester Beatty ar4635 (724/1323). There are a few modern editions of *Jawāmiʿ al-Ladhdha*, all transcriptions of a Cairo manuscript, which only covers the second half of the book and is attributed to the wrong author. There is also a translation, which is useful but not entirely reliable; it often abridges or excludes difficult paragraphs; Abū al-Ḥasan 'Alī b. Naṣr al-Kātib, *Encyclopedia of Pleasure.* I owe this information to Everett Rowson and I am very grateful to him for sharing some of his knowledge with me.
29 The encyclopaedia is quoted by al-Shayzarī (fl. sixth/twelfth century), both in his *Rawḍat al-Qulūb* and *al-Īḍāḥ fī Asrār al-Nikāḥ*; Mughulṭāy (d. 1361), *al-Wāḍiḥ al-mubīn*; al-Samawʾal, *Kitāb Nuzhat al-Aṣḥāb*. The unknown author of the popular *Akhbār al-Nisāʾ* (often attributed to Ibn al-Jawzī, d. 597/1201 or Ibn Qayyim al-Jawziyya, d. 751/1350) cities it extensively. Al-Suyūṭī (d. 911/1505) relies on it to a great extent in both *al-Wishāḥ* and the popular *Nawāḍir al-Ayk fī Maʿrifat al-Nayk.*
30 Al-Jāḥiẓ, *al-Ḥayawān*, vol. 2, p. 280.

## Chapter 1

1 Ibn al-Nadīm, *Fihrist*, vol. 1, p. 469. Ibn al-Nadīm spells the names Bardān and Ḥabāḥib (the editor Fuʾād Sayyid's vocalization). The 'book' on the two women is rather a story. In the manuscript copies of *Jawāmiʿ al-Ladhdha*, which contain the oldest citations from this story, the names are spelled *Burjān/Barjān/Barḥān* and *Ḥabāḥib/Ḥubāḥib* (cf Rowson, 'Arabic', pp. 47–8).
2 ʿAlī ibn Naṣr al-Kātib, *Jawāmiʿ al-Ladhdha*, MS Aya Sofya 3836, fol. 103a.
3 The manuscript has 'the female appetite comes from the brain whereas the male appetite comes from the back', but I have interpreted appetite (*shahwa*) as denoting semen, in line with the king's question.
4 D'Ancona, 'Greek to Arabic'.
5 Marlow, *Counsel for Kings*, vol. 2, pp. 45–6.

6 Strohmaier, 'Ḥunayn b. Isḥāq'.
7 This treatise is not extant; Ullmann, *Medizin*, pp. 75, 194.
8 There are two extant treatises on sexuality attributed to Qusṭā ibn Lūqā, both available in single manuscript copies.
9 D'Ancona, 'Greek into Arabic'.
10 Ibn al-Nadīm, *Fihrist*, vol. 2, pp. 182–94.
11 For ʿAlī ibn Sahl Ṭabarī's biography, I follow Thomas, 'al-Ṭabarī'. See also Ullmann, *Medizin*, pp. 119–22; Browne, *Arabian Medicine*, pp. 37–44; Meyerhof, 'Paradise of Wisdom'; Ibn al-Nadīm, *Fihrist*, vol. 2, pp. 296–7; al-Qifṭī, *Ḥukamāʾ*, p. 231.
12 Al-Qifṭī, *Ḥukamāʾ*, p. 187.
13 Weisser, *Zeugung*, pp. 16–17.
14 Meyerhof, 'Paradise of Wisdom', pp. 12–14, 16.
15 Goodman, 'al-Rāzī'.
16 D'Ancona, 'Greek into Arabic'.
17 Goodman, 'al-Rāzī'.
18 Cristina Alvarez Millan, 'Case Histories', p. 294.
19 Dols, 'Origins', p. 370.
20 Pormann and Savage-Smith, *Medicine*, p. 95.
21 Bowen, 'Aḍud al-Dawla'; Richter-Bernburg, 'ʿAlī b. ʿAbbās Majūst'; Micheau, 'ʿAlī b. al-ʿAbbās al-Majūsī'.
22 Bos, *Ibn al-Jazzār on Sexual Diseases*, p. 5.
23 According to Pormann and Savage-Smith, there is no evidence in his medical writings that he ever practiced as a physician (*Medicine*, pp. 117–18).
24 Cadden, *Sex Difference*, pp. 16–17.
25 Dean-Jones, *Women's Bodies*, pp. 44–6; King, *Hippocrates' Woman*, pp. 32–3.
26 Dean-Jones, *Women's Bodies*, p. 44; see also Green, *Transmission*, p. 14. This is not true for the Hippocratic writers, however, who, as Cadden points out, were not uniform in their application of the right–left dichotomy (*Meanings of Sex Differences*, p. 17).
27 May, 'Introduction' to *Galen*, p. 57. Galen, *Usefulness*, pp. 626, 634–6.
28 This is the so-called 'one-sex model', which, according to Laqueur, dominated European biological thought until as late as the eighteenth century (*Making Sex*, 1990). Laqueur's thesis has been convincingly refuted by King (*The One-Sex Body on Trial*), Cadden (*Meanings of Sex Difference*, 3) and others, who have shown that the explanatory models and the transmission of them are much more complex. For the Islamic medical tradition, see Gadelrab, 'Sex Differences'.
29 ʿAlī ibn Naṣr, the author of *Jawāmiʿ al-Ladhdha* and arguable a layman, instead claimed that women are dry; *Jawāmiʿ al-Ladhdha*, MS Aya Sofya 3836, fols 39b–40a.

30 Al-Ṭabarī, *Firdaws*, pp. 34, 35–6.
31 Al-Majūsī, *Kāmil*, vol. 1, p. 116.
32 Al-Ṭabarī, *Firdaws*, p. 31.
33 Al-Majūsī, *Kāmil*, vol. 1, p. 116.
34 Ibn Sīnā, *Qānūn*, vol. 2, p. 556.
35 May, 'Introduction' to *Galen*, p. 56; Galen, *Usefulness*, pp. 627–31; Green, 'Transmission', pp. 40–1; Dean-Jones, *Women's Bodies*, see esp. pp. 56, 58, 85–6.
36 Qusṭā ibn Lūqā, Kitāb *fī al-Bāh*, p. 15 (Arabic text).
37 Man's hair as evidence for their body temperature as the opposite of women's was used by Greek philosophers as the far back as the pre-Socratic thinkers. They have different opinions, however, whether men's generally hairier bodies depends on their temperature being hotter or cooler than that of women; Dean-Jones, *Women's Bodies*, pp. 44, 83–5.
38 Al-Majūsī, *Kāmil*, vol. 1, p. 38. For these ideas in Ibn Sīnā's *Shifā* and *Qānūn*; see Gadelrab, 'Sex Differences', p. 65.
39 Dean-Jones, *Women's Bodies*, pp. 149, 151.
40 Ibid., pp. 155–7.
41 At least he appears to put forward a one-seed model. Sophia Connell (*Aristotle*, p. 101) argues that the female contribution through menstrual blood and milk that is suggested by Aristotle is similar to that of the male semen, and that Aristotle could as well be labelled a 'two-seed theorist'.
42 May, 'Introduction' to *Galen*, pp. 57–8.
43 Weisser, *Zeugung*, pp. 118–19. Not until Ibn Rushd a prominent Islamic physician in the twelth century, fully accepted the one-seed theory. For various ideas among medical and religious scholars on seed, conception and sex differences, see Kueny, *Conceiving Identities*, pp. 53ff.
44 Weisser, *Zeugung*, p. 123. For Ibn Sīnā's discussions about female semen, see ibid., pp. 122–38.
45 Connell, *Aristotle*, pp. 97–8; *Hippocratic Treatises*, pp. 1, 2, 4. In the Arabic version of *On Generation*, (English) pp. 1, 3.
46 Hippocrates, *Kitāb al-Ajinna*, pp. 1, 3; (Arabic) pp. 31, 33. These sentences correspond to 'the sperm of the human male comes from all the humour in the body' (1.1) and 'the greater part of the sperm travels from the head past the ears' (2.2) in Lonie's translation of *The Hippocratic Treatises*, pp. 1 and 2.
47 Lyons' and Mattock's 'Introduction' to Hippocrates, *Kitāb al-Ajinna*, pp. ii–iii; Ullmann, *Medizin*, p. 27, who also mentions ʿArīb (who relied on al-Ṭabarī, see below) and Ibn Sīnā.
48 Al-Ṭabarī, *Firdaws*, p. 31. Al-Ṭabarī's view is followed by the Andalusian courtier and scholar ʿArīb ibn Saʿīd, who wrote a book on embryology, and maintains that

female and male pleasure is the same. It is felt in the whole body, and is therefore an evidence for the pangenetic notion of procreation, that the seed is produced in the whole body; in Weisser, *Zeugung*, p. 119. See also Forcada, '`Arīb', for `Arīb's reliance on al-Ṭabarī and the Arabic version of Hippocrates' *On Generation*.

49 Weisser, *Zeugung*, pp. 100–17.

50 Al-Kindī, *Kitāb al-Bāh*, p. 21.

51 Ibn al-Jazzār, *Sexual Diseases*, Arabic text (p. 75), English translation (p. 241).

52 Al-Majūsī, *Kāmil*, vol. 1, p. 212.

53 Ibid., p. 117.

54 Ibid., p. 118.

55 Gadelrab, 'Sex Differences', p. 66. For the contradicting ideas of Ibn Sīnā, see Weisser *Zeugung*, pp. 122–38. See also Dallal, 'Scientific Discourses', on Ibn Sīnā's reliance on Aristotle vs Galen.

56 WHO, *Defining Sexual Health*, p. 5.

57 Al-Ṭabarī, *Firdaws*, p. 275.

58 Al-Rāzī, *Ḥāwī*, vol. 10, pp. 280ff.

59 For Rufus' lost book on coitus in Arabic, see Ullmann, *Medizin*, p. 75. For the genre, see ibid., pp. 193–8, and Bos, *Ibn al-Jazzār on Sexual Diseases*, pp. 250–3. Ullmann treats this genre together with later erotic handbooks and compendia, however, they are not the same (although ideas from the genre of *`ilm al-bāh* normally were included in erotic handbooks).

60 Ḥunayn's book is not extant. For `Isā ibn Māssa, see Ullmann, *Medizin*, pp. 122–3; al-Kindī, p. 123; Qusṭā, p. 194. `Isā ibn Māssa's book should perhaps not be classified as belonging to this genre. It follows the question-answer-model of the Problemata, although all questions deal with sex. For Problemata as a source for Islamic medicine, see Ullmann, *Medizin*, pp. 93–6.

61 Sezgin, *Geschichte*, vol. 3, p. 223 (Jābir), pp. 226–7 (Jibrīl).

62 The section on benefits is translated into English by Pormann; 'Al-Rāzī', pp. 135–7.

63 Al-Kindī's treatise, which is very short, does not have any subsections with titles.

64 Al-Rāzī, al-*Manṣūrī*, pp. 220ff.

65 Al-Rāzī, *Ḥāwī*, vol. 10, pp. 280–337.

66 E.g. al-Majūsī, *Kāmil*, vol. 1, pp. 212–15; vol. 2, pp. 17–18.

67 For instance, ibid., vol. 2, p. 419, where, while writing in general terms about sexual appetite, it is evident that the addressee is a man.

68 Ibn Sīnā, *Qānūn*, vol. 2, pp. 535–7. This part, chapter 20, briefly addresses women, in connection to a pleasure-enhancing method; ibid., p. 550.

69 Ibid., vol. 2, pp. 556ff.

70 Qusṭā ibn Lūqā, *Kitāb fi al-Bāh* (1973), pp. 39–49 (in the Arabic edition). The shorter version is *Kitāb fi al-Bāh* (1974); Sezgin, *Geschichte*, vol. 3, p. 272. On Qusṭā ibn Lūqā's focus on women's sexual health, see Pormann, 'Al-Rāzī', p. 141.

71 Hippocrates, *On Generation*; the Arabic version in *Kitāb al-Ajinna*, p. 4 (English), p. 38 (Arabic). The Greek version in *Hippocratic Treatises*, p. 3.
72 Green, 'Transmission', pp. 17–18.
73 Ibid., pp. 19–22; King, *Hippocrates' Woman*, pp. 36–7, 214–22, and see pp. 205–46 for diagnosis of hysteria after the Hippocratics.
74 Green, 'Transmission', pp. 47–51.
75 Galen, *On the Affected Parts*, 6.5; King, *Hippocrates' Woman*, p. 233; Green, 'Transmission', p. 51.
76 King, *Hippocrates' Woman*, pp. 234–5.
77 As pointed out by Green, the Islamic medical writers did generally not rely on the works of Soranus, the foremost Greek gynaecologist, who criticized the idea of a wandering womb and remedies such as scent therapy. Instead, they relied on Galen, who did not write extensively on gynaecology; Green, 'Transmission,' p. 71–2
78 Al-Ṭabarī, *Firdaws*, p. 275.
79 Ibid., p. 274.
80 Ibid.
81 Ibid., pp. 278–9.
82 Ibid., pp. 40, 274.
83 Al-Rāzī, *Ḥāwī*, vol. 9, p. 129.
84 Qusṭā ibn Lūqā, *Fī al-Bāh* (1973), pp. 40–1.
85 Ibid. (1974), pp. 25–6; see Ullmann, *Medizin*, p. 75.
86 Pseudo-Ibn Qurra, *Dakhīra*, pp. 116–17. This book is considered an important early Arabic medical contribution. Ullmann (*Medizin*, p. 136) suggests it was written in the first half of the tenth century, after al-Rāzī's death in 925, which means that the attribution to Ibn Qurra is wrong. If it was written earlier, al-Rāzī would have mentioned it in *Ḥāwī*.
87 Al-Rāzī, *Ḥāwī*, vol. 9, pp. 56–75.
88 Al-Rāzī, '*Kitāb al-Bāh*' (ed. 1999), p. 161. The attribution to Galen may be a scribal error, however. Both printed editions have 'it is also said about it (coitus) on his (Galen's) authority', but they rely on one unidentified manuscript each, although this book is represented in numerous manuscripts all over the world.
89 Al-Rāzī, *Ḥāwī*, vol. 9, pp. 56–7 (quoting *On Diseases and Symptoms*).
90 Yoḥannān bar Serāpyōn was Christian medical writer who wrote a medical handbook in Syriac 873, which was translated to Arabic. Sābūr ibn Sahl was a Christian physician and pharmacologist who died 255/869 and was for a period one of several court physicians of the caliph al-Mutawakkil. Ullmann, *Medizin*, pp. 102–3; al-Rāzī, *Ḥāwī*, vol. 9, p. 65. Kahl, 'Sābūr'; al-Rāzī, *Ḥāwī*, vol. 9, p. 68.
91 Ibid., p. 61; Ullmann, *Medizin*, pp. 87–9.
92 Dietrich, 'Māsardjawayh'; al-Rāzī refers to him as al-Yahūdī, *Ḥāwī*, vol. 9, pp. 59, 71.
93 Al-Rāzī, *Ḥāwī*, vol. 9, pp. 60–1, 59.

94 Al-Rāzī, *Manṣūrī*, p. 451.

95 Al-Majūsī, *Kāmil*, vol. 2, p. 427. See Green, 'Transmission', pp. 109–15, for al-Majūsī's reliance on Greek gynaecological ideas.

96 Al-Majūsī, *Kāmil*, vol. 2, pp. 427–9.

97 Ibid., p. 375.

98 Ibn al-Jazzār, *On Sexual Diseases*, pp. 153–60 (Arabic text), pp. 274–6 (English translation).

99 Al-Rāzī, *Ḥāwī*, vol. 9, pp. 56, 58, 67–8 and 72–3 (quoting Galen).

100 Ibid., p. 62 (quoting Paul of Aegina).

101 Ibid., p. 68.

102 *Hippocratic Treatises*, pp. 2–3. The description of women's and men's experience of pleasure in *On Generation* is discussed by Hanson, 'Medical Writers' Woman', 314–15; Dean-Jones, *Women's Bodies*, p. 157.

103 Hippocrates, *Kitāb al-Ajinna*, pp. 3–4 (English), pp. 36–8 (Arabic).

104 Galen, *Usefulness*, vol. 2, p. 643; Connell, 'Aristotle and Galen', p. 412.

105 Galen, *Usefulness*, vol. 2, p. 645.

106 Al-Majūsī, *Kāmil*, vol. 1, p. 235

107 Weisser, *Zeugung*, p. 119.

108 King, *Hippocrates' Woman*, p. 222.

109 Al-Majūsī, *Kāmil*, vol. 1, p. 117. This idea is also rendered by ʿAlī ibn Naṣr, *Jawāmiʿ al-Ladhdha*, MS Aya Sofya 3836, fol. 39b.

110 Al-Majūsī, *Kāmil* vol. 1, pp. 117, 390; Weisser, *Zeugung*, p. 147.

111 Ibn Sīnā, *Qānūn*, vol. 2, p. 557.

112 Ibid. pp. 560–1; Weisser, *Zeugung*, pp. 150–1.

113 Al-Rāzī, *Ḥāwī*, vol. 10, pp. 291, 340.

114 Pseudo-Ibn Qurra, *Dakhīra*, p. 119.

115 In Weisser, *Zeugung*, p. 152.

116 Gewargis (*Gynäkologisches*, p. 6) argues that pharmacology is the main contribution of Islamic medical authors to the field of gynaecology. Green ('Transmission', pp. 116–17) agrees but identifies 'Galenization' of gynaecology as the main contribution of Islamic medical thinkers, that is applying Galen's medical ideas on a field that he, in fact, wrote little about.

117 Ibn Sīnā, *Qānūn*, vol. 2, p. 569.

118 Ibid., p. 551.

119 Weisser, *Zeugung*, p. 152.

120 Sezgin, *Geschichte*, vol. 3, pp. 207–8; vol. 4, pp. 112–16; vol. 5, pp. 71–3; an incomplete note in Ibn al-Nadīm, *Fihrist*, vol. 2, p. 317. Four remedies for the vagina are taken from 'the book of Tayādūq', and one for tightening the vagina from 'anonymous' (*majhūl*); al-Rāzī, *Ḥāwī*, vol. 10, p. 309. For 'anonymous' (*majhūl*), see Ullman, *Medizin*, p. 92.

121 Al-Rāzī, *Ḥāwī*, vol. 10, p. 305.

122 Ibid., pp. 289–90. Some of these vaginal remedies are also included in al-Rāzī, *Manṣūrī*, pp. 275–6.

123 Al-Rāzī, *Ḥāwī*, vol. 10, p. 291.

124 Ibid., p. 305. According to the author of *Jawāmi ʿ al-Ladhdha*, al-Kindī claimed that he had read in old books that the mother's intake of celery while breast-feeding can make the daughter a lesbian; see p. 158.

125 Al-Rāzī, *Manṣūrī*, p. 274; *Ḥāwī*, vol. 10, pp. 288, 316.

126 Al-Rāzī, *Ḥāwī*, vol. 10, p. 288.

127 Al-Ṭabarī, *Firdaws*, pp. 591–4.

128 Ibid., pp. 592–3.

129 Levey and Souryal, 'Galen's On the Secrets of Women', p. 218; Sezgin, *Geschichte*, vol. 3, pp. 60–1. The manuscript that Levey and Souryal rely on, Aya Sofya 4838, is undated. The claim that the text was translated by Ḥunayn ibn Isḥāq is given at the end of the subsequent text, *Kitāb Asrār al-Rijāl* (*On the Secrets of Men*), fol. 88b.

130 Pseudo-Galen, *Kitāb Asrār al-Nisā ʾ*, MS Aya Sofya 4838, fols 55b–56a.

131 Ibid., fol. 59b.

132 The text has 'she will not be able to . . . shave it with *nūra*'. According to Lane (*Lexicon*, s.v. *nwr*), *nūra* is quick-lime or a lime-stone 'used as a depilatory for the pubes', or 'a mixture of quick lime with arsenic, or orpiment . . . and other things, used for removing hair'.

133 Al-Rāzī, *Ḥāwī*, vol. 10, p. 94.

134 See for example Weisser, *Zeugung*, p. 82.

135 Giladi, *Midwives*, p. 2.

136 Ibn al-Nadīm, *Fihrist*, vol. 2, p. 291. According to al-Qifṭī, it was instead dedicated to the mother of al-Mutawakkil; Abbou Hershkovits, 'Medical Services,' p. 129. A similar title is attributed to Hippocrates.

137 Abbou Hershkovits, 'Medical Services', 127.

138 See Musallam, *Sex and Society*.

139 Chapter 4, pp. 60–88, is on birth control in Arabic medicine.

140 Ibid., p. 62, and tables pp. 77–88.

141 Ibid., p. 88, table 9.

142 Musallam, *Sex and Society*, pp. 22–3.

143 Al-Majūsī, *Kāmil*, 2:440.

144 Ullmann, *Medizin*, pp. 250–1; quoted by Green, 'Transmission', p. 128, n. 107.

145 Weisser, *Zeugung*, p. 56.

146 Al-Ṭabarī, *Firdaws*, p. 39. He claims that he has this information directly from the 'head (*ra ʾīs*) of the *bimāristān* in Gondēshāpūr', using the Persian word for hospital that was common at this time. It had earlier been supposed that there was a hospital

in this now ruined town in south-west Iran since the fourth century, but that is a myth according to Pormann and Savage-Smith (*Medieval Islamic Medicine*, pp. 20–1).

147 Al-Rāzī collected nearly 900 case studies of male as well as female patients treated by him or under his supervision (Álvarez Millán, 'Graeco-Roman Case Studies', pp. 34ff). This collection, showing al-Rāzī's frequent contacts with real patients, complemented the theoretical writings for the benefits of students; ibid., pp. 34, 36. See Pormann, 'Female Patients', and Pomann and Savage-Smith, *Medieval Islamic Medicine*, pp. 103–8, for surveys of women in the field of Islamic medicine.

148 Goodman, 'al-Rāzī'. In Greek medical texts, 'the woman of experience' is a woman with awareness of her own body, who knows about its mechanism and how to heal disorders (Hanson, 'Medical Writers' Woman', 309–10).

## Chapter 2

1 The sanskrit erotic manual *Kāma Sūtra*, attributed to Vātsyāyana, was written in the third or fourth century CE, probably in North India.

2 ʿAlī ibn Naṣr, *Jawāmiʿ al-Ladhdha*, MS Aya Sofya 3837, fol. 27a and MS Fatih 3729, fol. 122a. 'At their first meeting' should probably be 'at their first sexual intercourse', as elsewhere, Ibn Naṣr cites 'the Indian', who advises men against having sexual intercourse with the woman at their first meeting; MS Aya Sofya 3837, fol. 37b.

3 Ibid.; MS Aya Sofya 3836, fols 1b–2a.

4 ʿAlī ibn Naṣr, *Jawāmiʿ al-Ladhdha*, MS Aya Sofya 3836, fol. 5b and MS Fatih 3729, fol. 5b.

5 Ibid.; MS Fatih 3729, fols 39b–40a; al-Majūsī, *Kāmil*, vol. 1, p. 116.

6 Galen, *Usefulness*, p. 630.

7 According to Ullmann (*Medizin*, p. 77) there is no definite proof of the existence of an Arabic translation of Soranus' *Gynecology*. Yet, his ideas as rendered in Late Antique encyclopaedias were influential; Green, 'Transmission', p. 80.

8 ʿAlī ibn Naṣr, *Jawāmiʿ al-Ladhdha*, MS Aya Sofya 3836, fol. 41a.

9 Kudlien, 'Cells of the Uterus' pp. 415–23.

10 ʿAlī ibn Naṣr, *Jawāmiʿ al-Ladhdha*, MS Fatih 3729, fol. 144a.

11 Ibid., fol. 146b.

12 Ibid., fols 149a–151b.

13 Al-Rāzī, *Ḥāwī*, vol. 10, p. 288. See Chapter 1.

14 Al-Rāzī, *Manṣūrī*, p. 275. *kirm-dāna* means 'a species of mezereon' or myrtle-seed according to Steingass, *Persian–English Dictionary*. See also 'kermidene', *Simon Online* (http://www.simonofgenoa.org/index.php?title=Kermidene), quoting Avicienna's Canon: 'in the Arabic text it says: it warms the *vulva*.'

15 Ibn Naṣr, *Jawāmiʿ al-Ladhdha*, MS Fatih 3729, fol. 153a.
16 Ibid., fols 152b–153a.
17 ʿAlī ibn Naṣr, *Jawāmiʿ al-Ladhdha*, MS Aya Sofya 3837, fol. 31b.
18 See Myrne, 'Discussing *ghayra*', for a few examples.
19 ʿAlī ibn Naṣr, *Jawāmiʿ al-Ladhdha*, MS Aya Sofya 3836, fol. 118a.
20 The word *māʾ* (water) may refer to semen already in the Qurʾan; Kueny, *Conceiving Identities*, p. 25, and see p. 257, n. 11.
21 ʿAlī ibn Naṣr, *Jawāmiʿ al-Ladhdha*, MS Aya Sofya 3837, fol. 31a. Notably, the word *nuṭfa* is used here for sperm; this is a word from the Qurʾan (verse 16:4) that is rarely used in this connection.
22 The discussion of Indian philosophers' view of female ejaculation corresponds roughly to *Kāma Sūtra* 2.1.10–2.30); MS Aya Sofya 3837, fols 111b–116a (ch 36); MS Chester Beatty ar4635, fols 190a–192b (ch 32); MS Fatih 3729, fol. 187b–191a (ch 35).
23 Ibid., MS Fatih 3729, fols 191a–192b: MS Aya Sofya 3837, fols 115b–119a; Chester Beatty ar4635, fols 193a–195a.
24 According to Ibn Sayyār al-Warrāq, author of a cookbook in the second half of the tenth century, sweet food increases semen; *Annals of the Caliph's Kitchen*, (English trs.) p. 100.
25 Green, 'Transmission', p. 49.
26 Ibn Sīnā, *Qānūn*, vol. 2, p. 563.
27 The water test in Aristotle, *Generation of Animals*, 2.7.747a: the fertile seed sinks in water and the infertile seed does not. Ibn Sīnā also mentions this method; Weisser, *Zeugung*, p. 152.
28 ʿAlī ibn Naṣr relates that he has found a similar book by an unidentificable author with the kunya al-Hindī; in MS Fatih 3729, fol. 191a: *Hrqṭ ibn Ṭsmn al-Hindī*; MS Aya Sofya 3837, fol. 115b: *Hrmṭ ibn Smṭn al-Hindī*; Chester Beatty ar4635, fol. 193a: *Hrwṭ ibn Ṭsmn al-Hindī.*
29 Ibn Naṣr, *Jawāmiʿ al-Ladhdha*, MS Fatih 3729, fol. 162b; MS Aya Sofya 3837, fol. 74b.
30 Al-Ṭabarī, *Firdaws*, p. 112.
31 Al-Kindī, *Kitāb al-Bāh*, p. 22. See Bos, 'Ibn al-Jazzār on Sexuality'; several of the examples Bos gives of the awareness of the importance of psychological factors for sexual stimulation are explicitly about male desire, none mentions women.
32 Al-Balkhī, *Maṣāliḥ*, p. 404. I owe this reference to Professor Hinrich Biesterfeldt, who kindly shared his translation of chapter 9, 'On the Regimen of Sex', with me.
33 Ibn al-Sīnā, *Qānūn*, vol. 2, p. 569.
34 ʿAlī ibn Naṣr, *Jawāmiʿ al-Ladhdha*, MS Fatih, fols 144a–b.
35 See Bos, 'Ibn al-Jazzār on sexuality', p. 251.

36 ʿAlī ibn Naṣr, *Jawāmiʿ al-Ladhdha*, MS Aya Sofya 3837, fol. 83a; MS Fatih 3729, fol. 168a. For the differentiation between free women and slave concubines, see Myrne, 'Slaves for Pleasure'.

37 MS Aya Sofya 3836, fols 103ff.

38 MS Aya Sofya 3836, fols 115a–116a; MS Fatih 3729, fols 116a–116b. The types in both MSS Aya Sofya (fol. 115b) and Fatih (fol. 116a) are: short, long, between long and short, plump, white-skinned, thin, dark blue-eyed (*shahlāʾ*) and brown-skinned.

39 MS Aya Sofya 3836, fol. 103b.

40 See Ghersetti, 'A Science for Kings and Masters', on physiognomy as a means to evaluate slaves according to al-Rāzī and other medieval Arabic authors. One of the authorities on physiognomy in *Jawāmiʿ al-Ladhdha* is Polemon; for him, see Ghersetti, 'Polemon in the Arab Tradition'.

41 For the currency of this genre see Ghersetti, ibid.

42 MS Aya Sofya 3836, fols 116a–b.

43 Ibid., fol. 109a.

44 Ibid., fols 116b–117a.

45 Al-Jāḥiẓ, *Ḥayawān*, vol. 7, p. 226. In the *Kāma Sūtra*, the deer and the elephant are females (2.1.1).

46 MS Aya Sofya, 3836, fols 110b–111b; *Kāma Sūtra*, 2.1.1–9. The paraphrase is illustrated in diagrams in the oldest extant MS; Aya Sofya 3836, fol. 111a. I thank Everett Rowson who first drew my attention to the paraphrases of the Kamasutra.

47 Ali, 'Padmaśrī's *Nāgarasarvasva*', pp. 41–2.

48 Ibid., pp. 45–6.

49 See van Bladel, 'The Bactrian Background of the Barmakids'.

50 ʿAlī ibn Naṣr, *Jawāmiʿ al-Ladhdha*, MS Aya Sofya 3837, fol. 108b. Bunyāfis al-Ḥakīm is the same as Bunyānnafs in Ibn al-Nadīm, *Firhrist,* vol. 2, p. 345.

51 Pseudo-Apollodorous, *The Library*, vol. 2, p. 367.

52 Ibn Ḥabīb, *Adab al-Nisāʾ*, p. 183.

53 Ansari and Umar, 'Aḥmad b. Muḥammad b. ʿĪsā'.

54 Al-Kulaynī, *Kāfī* vol. 5, pp. 338–9.

55 Al-Kharāʾiṭī, *Iʿtilāl*, p. 100.

56 Brown, *Canonization*, p. 61.

57 Al-Ṭabarānī, *Awsaṭ*, vol. 1, p. 178. Statements like this were collected by later scholars, and the Prophet's extraordinary potency became a theme in marriage manuals built on hadith; see Myrne, 'Women and Men.'

58 Ibn al-Nadīm, *al-Fihrist*, vol. 2, p. 345. The name Bunyāndukht is vocalized *Banyān dakht* by the editor Fuʾād Sayyid in *Jawāmiʿ al-Ladhdha*, but vocalized Bunyāndukht in MS Aya Sofya 3836. Likewise, Bunyānnafs is vocalized Banyān nafs by Fuʾād Sayyid.

59 ʿAlī ibn Naṣr, *Jawāmiʾ al-Ladhdha*, MS Aya Sofya 3836, fols 102b–103a, MS Fatih 3729, fols 104b–105a.

60 Ahriman in Zoroastrianism?

61 One out of a thousand women is like this woman, according to MS Fatih 3729. According to Aya Sofya 3836, of all women, not more than ten have this condition.

62 E.g. Ibn Manẓur, *Lisān*, s.v. *rbkh*; a *rabūkh* is a woman who 'faints when having sexual intercourse'.

63 ʿAlī ibn Naṣr, *Jawāmiʿ al-Ladhdha*, MS Aya Sofya 3836, fol. 103b and MS Fatih 3729, fol. 195b. The word translated 'sexual intercourse' and 'sex' here is *nayk*, which could, arguably be translated 'fucking', not the least as the anecdote is written in *mujūn* style. I have chosen the more neutral translation, as the word *nayk* has a wider semantic sphere than the vulgar 'fucking' in *Jawāmiʿ al-Ladhdha*; see also the discussion of the word on p. 9.

64 MS Aya Sofya 3836, fol. 1b.

65 See Bos, 'Ibn al-Jazzār on Sexual Diseases', p. 19.

66 ʿAlī ibn Naṣr, *Jawāmiʿ al-Ladhdha*, MS Aya Sofya 3837, fol. 110a, and MS Fatih 3729, fol. 187a,

67 MS Fatih 3729, fol. 187a; MS Aya Sofya 3837, fol. 110b.

68 MS Aya Sofya 3837, fol. 111b.

69 MS Fatih 3729, fol. 184b. MS Aya Sofya 3837, fols 107b–108a, is slightly different. It starts with زوج and ends with ببيوت, which is a better reading, but it changes from third to first person in the last sentence.

70 Whereas in anecdotes about the cultural scene of the Abbasids, *jāriya* usually refers to a female slave, in this case it is clearly an adolescent girl.

71 MS Fatih 3729, fols 159b–160b.

72 MS Aya Sofya 3836, fol. 87a. There are a two chapters that deal, more or less exclusively, with heterosexual anal intercourse in *Jawāmiʿ al-Ladhdha*. The author presents it as a better and safer alternative to sex with boys and men, which he treats in another chapter. Although he does not commend homosexuality, he recommends heterosexuality (most obviously, but not only, because it is legal).

73 MS Fatih 3729, fol. 138a; see Chapter 3 for the elaborations of the notion of *ghunj* connected to the Houris.

74 For the development and transformations of the Ḥubbā story, see Myrne, 'Who was Ḥubbā al-Madīniyya?'

75 MS Fatih 3729, fols 130b–131b; MS Aya Sofya 3837, fols 41a–44a.

## Chapter 3

1 ʿAlī ibn Naṣr, *Jawāmiʿ al-Ladhdha*, MS Aya Sofya 3836, fol. 53a; MS Fatih 3729, fol. 53b. For legal scholars' denial of the right for free women to have sexual relations with their male slaves, see Kecia Ali, *Marriage and Slavery*, pp. 176ff.

2 For the process of formal hadith defining Sunna and becoming an important legal source; see Hallaq, *Origins*, e.g. pp. 102–21.
3 Schacht, 'Nikāḥ'.
4 'With the emergence of legal theory by the middle of the fourth/tenth century or thereabouts, Islamic law can be said to have become complete', Hallaq, *Origins*, p. 150.
5 For the use of the term *milk* in legal discourses on marriage, see Kecia Ali, *Marriage and Slavery*, pp. 164–86.
6 Motzki, 'Bridewealth', p. 258.
7 Azam, *Sexual Violation*, pp. 24–5.
8 Ibid., p. 61–2.
9 Ibid., p. 62. Azam examines especially the Maliki and Hanafī schools of law, and argues that the latter was less favourable to the proprietary conception than the former.
10 Ali, *Marriage and Slavery*, p. 41.
11 Ibid., p. 65 and see ch. 2, 'Maintaining relations' for a thorough exploration of this exchange.
12 Ibid., pp. 40, 67. The jurists disagreed about whether male slaves could be coerced to marry; ibid., 40. In the case where the marriage was made willingly, the owner's consent was needed. For the conflicts between the owner's and the husband's rights over an enslaved wife, see ibid., pp. 67–72. The husband of an enslaved wife had, for example, no right to control his wife's movements; the owner decided on her mobility and domicile.
13 Ibid., p. 159; for divorce rights of slaves see pp. 154–60.
14 Ibid., pp. 153–4.
15 Abu-Zahra, 'Adultery', p. 28; Azam, *Sexual Violation*, pp. 67–8.
16 Azam, *Sexual Violation*, p. 72–4.
17 Azam exemplifies with hadiths from al-Bukhārī; *Sexual Violation*, p. 76, n. 31. Some claimed that slave women should never be stoned, based on Qurʾan 4:24; ibid., p. 82, n. 46.
18 Peters, 'Zinā'.
19 See Chapter 6 for Qusṭa ibn Lūqā on the temptation constituted by slave boys in the Abbasid cities.
20 For the husband's maintenance of his wife in exchange for her sexual availability, see Ali, *Marriage and Slavery*, pp. 64–96.
21 Ibn Māja, *Sunan*, vol. 1, p. 595; Ibn Abī Shayba, *Muṣannaf*, vol. 3, p. 553; al-Kulaynī, *Kāfī*, vol. 5, p. 507.
22 Al-Kulaynī, *Kāfī*, vol. 5, p. 508; a longer version by al-Bukhārī is in Bauer, 'Room for Interpretation', p. 81.
23 Al-Kulaynī, *Kāfī*, vol. 5, p. 513.

24 A hadith with some variants in al-Bukhārī, *Ṣaḥīḥ*, vol. 7, p. 93; Muslim, *Ṣaḥīḥ*, vol. 2, pp. 496–7; Ibn Abī Shayba, *Muṣannaf*, vol. 3, p. 553; Abū Dāwūd, *Sunan*, vol. 3, p. 476.
25 Al-Kulaynī, *Kāfī*, vol. 5, p. 493.
26 Ali, *Marriage and Slavery*, p. 71. There were some differences between the jurists in this regard, however. As for Ali's sources, al-Shāfiʿ, Mālik and their followers 'devoted more attention to the husband's right to take pleasure with his wife' than the Hanafī jurists; ibid., p. 65. See also Carolyn Baugh, *Minor Marriage in Early Islamic Law*, p. 212.
27 Al-Kulaynī, *Kāfī*, vol. 5, p. 508. In the same manner, the philologist and Qurʿan interpreter al-Wāḥidī (d. 468/1076) from Nishapur maintained that inattention to the things that enhance a man's pleasure is wifely disobedience (*nushūz*); such as when 'wives do not put perfume for their husbands' and 'stop doing the things which their husbands used to find delightful; translated by Bauer in 'Room for Interpretation', p. 157.
28 Al-Kulaynī, *Kāfī*, vol. 5, p. 507.
29 Ali, *Marriage and Slavery*, p. 83. The wife could, according to some, refuse sex if the husband did not fulfil his obligations, such as paying the dower.
30 In his exegesis of Qurʿan 4:34, al-Ṭabarī urges men not to punish their wives for not loving them as long as they obey them: 'do not oblige them to love you, for that is not in their hands'; translated by Bauer, 'Room for Interpretation', p. 162.
31 Muqātil, *Tafsīr*, vol. 1, p. 192.
32 Muqātil was accused of being unreliable by later scholars and his material influenced by the *qaṣṣāṣ*, the popular preachers and storytellers that flourished in early Islam; Armstrong, *Quṣṣāṣ*, pp. 97–110.
33 ʿAbd al-Razzāq, *Tafsīr*, vol. 1, p. 340.
34 Al-Bukhārī, *Ṣaḥīḥ*, vol. 6, p. 39; Muslim, *Ṣaḥīḥ*, vol. 2, pp. 495–6; al-Tirmidhī, *Jāmiʿ al-Ṣaḥīḥ*, vol. 5, pp. 199–200; Ibn Māja, *Sunan*, vol. 1, p. 620; al-Nasāʾī, *Tafsīr*, vol. 2, p. 255; Ibn Abī Shayba, *Muṣannaf*, vol. 3, p. 509; all on the authority of Jābir ibn ʿAbdullāh. See also al-Suyūṭī, *Al-Durr al-Manthūr*, vol. 2, p. 589.
35 ʿAbd al-Razzāq, *Tafsīr*, vol. 1, pp. 340–1.
36 Abū Dawūd, *Sunan*, vol. 3, pp. 292–3. Also quoted by Aḥmad ibn Ḥanbal, al-Tirmidhī, al-Nasāʾī. See al-Suyūṭī, *Al-Durr al-Manthūr*, vol. 2, p. 595. Al-Suyūṭī also quotes Ibn Rāhwayh (d. 238/852–3), al-Dārimī (d. 282/895) and later interpreters.
37 Al-Ṭabarī, *Tafsīr*, vol. 3, p. 757. See al-Suyūṭī, *Al-Durr al-Manthūr*, vol. 2, pp. 592–3, who quotes Ibn Abī Shayba (d. 235/849), Ibn Ḥanbal, ʿAbd ibn Ḥamīd (d. 249/863–4), al-Dārimī (d. 282/895–6), al-Tirmidhī, Ibn Abī Ḥātim (d. 327/938) and al-Bayhaqī (d. 458/1066). It is somehwat briefer in Ibn Abī Shayba, *Muṣannaf*, vol. 3, p. 509, and much briefer in al-Tirmidhī, *Jāmiʿ al-Ṣaḥīḥ*, vol. 5, p. 200, where it says nothing about the woman's refusal.

38 Al-Ṭabarī, *Tafsīr*, vol. 3, p. 745; for the section on this part of Q 2:223 see ibid., pp. 745–61.

39 Hūd ibn Muḥakkam, *Tafsīr Kitāb Allāh al-ʿAzīz*, vol. 1, pp. 211–12; al-Qummī, *Tafsīr*, p. 112.

40 Al-ʿAyyāshī, *Tafsīr*, vol. 1, p. 225.

41 Al-Tijānī, *Tuḥfat al-ʿarūs*, p. 129; see also al-Suyūṭī, *Nuzhat al-Mutaʾammil*, p. 39. *luʿab* can signify toys in general, but it is obvious from the contexts that the intention here is dolls. A prophetic hadith, which was more widespread, conveyed another metaphor with the same meaning, that women are glass vessels (*qawārīr*), and therefore have to be treated gently.

42 Al-Suyūṭī, *Al-Durr al-Manthūr*, vol. 2, pp. 589–618.

43 Burge, 'Scattered Pearls'.

44 ʿAbd al-Razzāq, *Muṣannaf*, vol. 6, p. 194.

45 According to Harald Motzki, ʿAbd al-Razzāq is 'extremely important for the study of early jurisprudence', as he includes older, lost sources in his writings; Motzki, 'ʿAbd al-Razzāq'.

46 Abū Yaʿlā, *Musnad*, vol. 7, pp. 208–9; Ibn ʿAdī, *Kāmil*, vol. 6, p. 150. The weak hadith transmitter is Muhammad ibn Jābir.

47 The small differences between the variants may be due to transmission.

48 Ali, *Marriage and Slavery*, pp. 118–19, and the Chapter 'Claiming Companionship', ibid., pp. 97–132.

49 Ibid., p. 119.

50 Ibid.

51 Musallam, *Sex and Society*, pp. 27, 31.

52 Mālik, *Muwaṭṭaʾ*, p. 596; Abū Yūsuf, *Āthār*, p. 155; al-Shaybānī, *Muwaṭṭaʾ*, pp. 171–2.

53 Al-Kāsānī, *Badāʾī*, vol. 2, p. 334.

54 Bauer, 'Room for Interpretation', p. 59.

55 Ibid., pp. 66–7.

56 Ibid., p. 68.

57 Ibid., 63–4. Bauer examines the development of exegesis of this segment on pp. 58–106. Al-Naysābūrī's comment is from his work *Aḥkām al-Qurʾān*.

58 Kueny, *Conceiving Identities*, p. 25; for further ideas from Greek medical wisdom in the Qurʾan, see ibid. p. 27.

59 Katz, *Body of Text*, p. 149. The crux of the matter was whether the verb *lāmasa* (as in Q 4:43 and 5:6) should be read literally or in a figurative sense, as a euphemism for sexual intercourse. The support for the literal interpretation is traced back to Ibn ʿAbbās; see ibid., p. 88.

60 For a summary of the practices in the area conquered or influenced by Islam and their assumed impact on the Islamic law of ritual purity, see Katz, *Body of Text*, pp. 3–13.

61 For ninth century collections, see al-Bukhārī, *Ṣaḥīḥ*, vol. 1, pp. 171–2; Abū Dawūd, *Sunan*, vol. 1, p. 172; ʿAbd al-Razzāq, *Muṣannaf*, vol. 1, pp. 283–5. The hadiths are also collected by Muslim and al-Nasāʾī.

62 The hadiths are obtained from three of his main sources, Ibn Jurayj, al-Thawrī and Maʿmar. For these sources, see Motzki, *Origins*, pp. 58–62.

63 ʿAbd al-Razzāq, *Muṣannaf*, vol. 1, pp. 283–5. This tradition is included already in Muwaṭṭaʿ by Māik ibn Anas (d. 795); see Kueny, *Conceiving Identities*, p. 54.

64 Motzki, 'ʿAbd al-Razzāq'.

65 Berkey, 'Circumcision', p. 22.

66 Salaymeh, *Beginnings*, p. 125. Lena Salaymeh argues that the historical accuracy of a tradition attributed to ʿĀ'isha, which has been taken as evidence for female circumcision in the earliest Muslim community, is questionable.

67 Al-Jāḥiẓ, *Ḥayawān*, vol. 7, pp. 28–9.

68 Ibid., pp. 27–8.

69 As pointed out by Berkey, 'Circumcision', p. 22.

70 Ibid., pp. 20, 22.

71 Ibid., pp. 25–6.

72 Ibn Qutayba, *ʿUyūn*, vol. 4, pp. 2, 4.

73 Ibid., p. 128.

74 Al-Kulaynī, *Kāfī*, vol. 5, p. 324.

75 Ibid., pp. 324–5.

76 Ibn ʿAdī, *Kāmil*, vol. 3, p. 1060; and also quoted by later scholars, such as al-Zamakhsharī and al-Suyūṭī.

77 Rustomji, *Garden*, p. 95.

78 Ibid.

79 Smith and Haddad, 'Women in the Afterlife', pp. 48–50. With an obvious male perspective, Ze'ev takes the presence of these heavenly wives who are 'unsullied by the various befoulments that plague the physiology of earthly women', as an example of a 'positive outlook' to sex; Ze'ev, *Virtues of the Flesh*, p. 14.

80 Quoted in Rustomji, *Garden*, pp. 112, 114.

81 Al-Ṭabarī, *Tafsīr*, vol. 22, pp. 323–8.

82 Quoted in al-Suyūṭī, *Shaqāʾiq*, pp. 64–9. In *Al-Durr al-Manthūr*, al-Suyūṭī adds the early exegetic Sufyān ibn ʾUyayna (d. 196/811–2 or 198/814); vol. 14, p. 202.

83 Quoted in al-Suyūṭī, *Al-Durr al-Manthūr*, vol. 14, pp. 201–6.

84 Al-Tūsī, *Ṭibyān*, p. 497.

85 Al-Ṭabarī, *Tafsīr*, vol. 22, p. 325.

86 Hallaq, *Origins*, p. 104.

87 *qaṭʿ al-ladhdha ʿan al-mawṭūʾa*; Ibn Qudāma, *Mughnī*, vol. 10, p. 228.

88 *ḥaqquhā fī al-istimtāʿ dūn al-inzāl*; al-Shīrāzī, *Muhadhdhab*, vol. 4, p. 235.

89 Al-Ghazālī, *Iḥyā*ʾ, vol. 2, p. 52. The reference is to al-Daylamī in ibid., n. 1. Translated by Madelain Farah, *Marriage and Sexuality*, pp. 106–7. Abū al-Manṣūr al-Daylami transmitted the hadiths from his father, Shīrawayh ibn Shahradār al-Daylamī (d. 509/1115), who was contemporary with al-Ghazālī, and whose *Firdaws al-Akhbār* was 'notoriously unreliable', according to Brown, 'Did the Prophet Say It or Not?', p. 270.

90 Al-Ghazālī, *Iḥyā*ʾ, vol. 2, p. 52. The translation differs somewhat from the translation by Madelain Farah, *Marriage and Sexuality*, p. 107. The edited text which this translation is based on has *fa'innā taḥṣīnahā wājib ʿalyhā*, 'protecting her chastity is his duty', whereas Farah has 'to satisfy her is his duty', for example.

# Chapter 4

1 For this study, I have consulted two editions of *Balaghāt al-Nisā*ʾ, Aḥmad al-Alfī's edition from 1908 and Habbūd's edition from 2000. Both editions are unsatisfying. The 1908 edition is based on two modern copies in Cairo (one of them copied in 1880), and later editions seem to be based either on the same manuscripts or on al-Alfī's edition, as is Habbūd's edition. Habbūd has compared al-Alfī's edition with other editions; unfortunately, he does not inform us which editions he has used and which manuscript they have used. Evidently, this important book is in need of a new, critical edition. The girl's name is spelt Dahnā and al-Dahnā in both editions but al-Dahnāʾ elsewhere. The poem is in Ibn Abī Ṭāhir, *Balaghāt* (ed. al-Alfī, 1908), p. 118 and (ed. Habbūd, 2000), p. 144, *qad zaʿamat Dahnā wa-ẓanna Misḥalu/ʾanna l-amīra bi-l-qaḍāʾi yaʿjalu / ʿan kasalātī* [so in Ibn Manẓūr, *Lisān*, s.v. *ksl* and *hkl* but written *kaslan lī* in *Balaghāt*] *wa-l-ḥiṣānu yuksilu / ʿani l-ḍirābi wa-huwa ṭirfun haykalu*. *Lisān* has *ʾaẓannat al-Dahnāʾ* instead of *zaʿamat*, and *al-sifād* instead of *al-ḍirāb*, which does not change the meaning.

2 In *Balaghāt al-Nisā*ʾ (the 1908 edition, p. 119; the 2000 edition, p. 144) the poem is rendered: *ʾaqsimu mā yumsikunī bi-ḍammin/ wa-lā bi-taqbīlin wa-lā bi-shammin/ wa-lā bi-ghazzin (should be bi-zaʿzāʿin) li-yusalliya ghammī/yaṭīru minhu fatḥī fī kimmī*. The last line is more correctly rendered *tasquṭu minhu fatakhī fī kummī*, as in Ibn Manẓūr, *Lisān*, s.v. *ftkh*, which also has *zaʿzāʿin* instead of *ghazzin*. I have chosen Ibn Manẓūr's version for the translation. The first line, *yumsikunī bi-ḍammin* probably refers to *imsākun bi-maʿrūfin* in Qurʾan 2:229, meaning retaining a wife after two pronunciations of *ṭalāq* 'in honour' (Pickthall), 'on reasonable terms' (Muhsin Khan). According to Szombathy, this Qur'anic passage was often cited in *mujūn* literature 'because of its obvious social relevance in matrimonial disputes', *Mujūn*, pp. 65–6. *zaʿzāʿ*, here translated as 'passionate motion', means 'vehement motion' and 'shaking', according to Lane, *Lexicon*, s.v. *zʿ*.

3 *Balaghāt* (the 2000 edition), p. 145: *wa-llāhi lawlā karamī wa-khayrī/wa-khashyatī ʿuqūbat al-amīri/ wa-rahbat al-jalwāzi wa-t-turtūrī / la-jultu ʿan shaykhi banī l-baʿīri/jawla qalūṣin ṣaʿbatin ʿasīri/ taḍribu ḥinway qatabin maʾsūri*. In the last line, *ḥinway qatabin*, refers to the two curved pieces of wood of the camel's saddle, more precisely, the anterior and posterior of the saddle, according to Lane, *Lexicon*, s.v. *ḥnw*. The *qalūṣ* is a young and youthful she-camel (ibid., s.v. *qlṣ*) and *ʿasīr* is a she-camel that was 'ridden before she was trained' or was 'taken in the first stage of her training, while yet difficult to manage' (ibid., s.v. *ʿsr*). The image suggests an unruly, young she-camel who attempts to get rid of the saddle.

4 The 'thing', *han*, often refers to the female genitalia.

5 Pellat, 'al-ʿAdjdjādj', states that al-ʿAjjāj died 97/715 and probably was born during the caliphate of ʿUthmān; Hämeen-Anttila, 'al-'Ajjāj', states only that he was born in the late seventh or early eighth century. He was present in Damascus in the year 69/688 (al-Ṭabarī, *History*, vol. 21, p. 161) and later appointed by ʿAbd al-Malik as governor of al-Yamāma.

6 Ali, *Marriage and Slavery*, p. 92.

7 See Salaymeh, *Beginnings*, for the chronology of wife-initiated divorce; pp. 172–9. In Late Antiquity, when this event purportedly took place, some jurists maintained that men did not have to pay full divorce settlement when the wife was considered recalcitrant, but from the ninth century on, most were in favour of full settlement; ibid., pp. 174, 177.

8 Heinrich, 'Ruʾba b. al-ʿAdjdjādj.

9 Ibn Manẓūr, *Lisān*, s.v. *ksl*.

10 Ibn Manẓūr, *Lisān*, s.v. *ftkh*; al-Jāḥiẓ, *Bayān*, vol. 3, p. 351, and *Ḥayawān*, vol. 3, 56: *allāhu yaʿlimu yā Mughīratu ʾannanī/qad dustuhā dawsa al-ḥiṣāni al-haykali/ wa-ʾakhadhtuhā ʾakhdha al-muqaṣṣidi shātahu/ʿajlāna yashwīhā li-qawmin nuzzali*.

11 Lammens, 'Mughīra'.

12 Ibn Manẓūr, *Lisān*, s.v. *ftkh*.

13 Ibn Abī Ṭāhir, *Balaghāt* (ed. 1908), p. 113; (ed. 2000), p. 136.

14 Al-Jāḥiẓ, *Bayān*, vol. 3, p. 207: *wa-llāhi lā ʾarḍā bi-ṭūli ḍammī / wa-lā bi-taqbīlin wa-lā bishammī / ʾillā bi-hazhāzin yusallī hammī / yasquṭu minhu fatakhī fī kummī / li-mithli hādhā waladatnī ʾummī*. The meaning of the word *hazhāz* is not entirely clear, but most probably it should be read as *zaʿzāʿ*, 'vehement motion', as in Ibn Manẓūr's rendering of al-Dahnāʾ's poem and Umm al-Ward's poem in *Balaghāt* (ed. 2000), p. 136.

15 ʿAlī ibn Naṣr, *Jawāmiʿ al-Ladhdha*, MS Fatih 3729, fol. 44b: *laysa bi-hādhā ʾamaratnī ʾummī/wa-llāhi lā tamlikunī bi-ḍammī/wa-lā bi-taqbīli wa-lā bi-shammī/lākinna bi-hazhāzin yusallī hammī/yasquṭu minhu khātamī fī kummī*. This is the most complete version of the poem in the three MSS of *Jawāmiʿ* that I have consulted. The other two quote the poem on the authority of Jaḥẓa, who also transmitted anecdotes about

ʿArīb. Their versions of the poem are incomplete, however, whereas both have line 1, MS Aya Sofya 3836 (fol. 44b) but lacks the second line and MS Chester Beatty 4635, fol. 54a lacks the second and fourth line. To make it clearer, the scribe of MS Aya Sofya has exchanged *hazhāz* with *nayk*.

16 According to later sources, he died 502/1108/1109, but there are indications that he lived in the Buyid era, and died in the early fifth/eleventh century, which makes him contemporary with the author of *Jawāmiʿ al-Ladhdha*.

17 The majority reading is فَتَخي في كُمّي but this reading is فَتْحِي في كِمّي. There are also several variants of the word *taṭīru*, 'fly', such as *taṭīḥu* and *tatīju*. The word *kimm* is vocalized *kumm* in the 2000 edition of *Balaghāt*.

18 Al-Alfī in Ibn Abī Tāhir, *Balaghāt*, p. 113, n. 8 and p. 119, n. 5; Habbūd in ibid., p. 136, n. 5, and p. 144 n. 6.

19 Both editions of *Balaghāt* that I have consulted have *fatḥī* instead of *fatakhī*. Unfortunately, I have not been able to consult manuscripts of *Balaghāt*, but the anecdote about Umm al-Ward also occurs in al-Suyūṭī's sex and marriage manual *al-Wishāḥ fī Fawāʾid al-Nikāḥ*, where it is explicitly attributed to Ibn Abī Tāhir and *Balaghāt al-Nisāʾ*. I have consulted four manuscripts and one edition (MS Lala Ismail 577, fols 53b–54a; MSS Paris, BnF Arabe 3066, fol. 39a, and 3067, fol. 54a; MS King Saud University 797, fols 66b–67a; and ed. Ṭalʿat Ḥasan ʿAbd al-Qawī, Damascus: 2001, p. 269). Only one manuscript has the intentional (i.e. vocalized) reading *fatḥī fī kimmī*, MS Lala Ismail, copied 973/1566; the rest have *fatakhī*.

20 Hammond, *Beyond Elegy*, pp. 61–2.

21 Ibid., pp. 71–98.

22 Ibid., pp. 115–28.

23 Kilpatrick, 'Women as Poets and Chattels'.

24 *Balaghāt al-Nisāʾ fī Munāzaʿāt al-Azwāj fī al-Madhḥ wa-l-Dhamm*; Ibn Abī Ṭāhir, *Balaghāt* (ed. 2000), pp. 92–147.

25 Van Gelder, 'Against Women', p. 65. The famous historian al-Madāʾinī (135–215/752–843) who wrote many works on women (see Myrne, 'Ladies and Lesbian's, pp. 204–5) also wrote about men who satirized their wives (van Gelder, 'Against Women', p. 65, n. 17).

26 See van Gelder, 'Against Women', who divides between downright *hijāʾ* against individual women, and *madhammat al-nisāʾ*, 'blaming women', which belongs – in Abū Tammām's Ḥamāsa – to the theme of *mulaḥ*, 'pleasantries'.

27 Ibn Abī Ṭāhir, *Balaghāt* (ed. 2000), p. 131.

28 Ibid., p. 129.

29 Ibid., p. 123.

30 Ibid., p. 124.

31 Roberts, 'Voice and Gender'.

32 Bray, 'Men, Women and Slaves', p. 138.

33 Ibid.

34 Abū al-Faraj al-Iṣbahānī, *Aghānī*, vol. 21, p. 83. The anecdote is told on the authority of the musician and poet Jaḥẓa (d. 324/936 or 326/938).

35 Ibn Abī Ṭāhir, *Balaghāt*, (ed. 2000), pp. 103–4.

36 See Myrne, 'Discussing *ghayra*'. Women as represented in Abbasid literature have different opinions as to whether jealousy is a good quality or not. In a tribal setting, it is more often considered a good masculine quality. When Hind bint ʿUtba, 'the *jahiliyya* woman par excellence', according to El Cheikh, chose a husband, she preferred Abū Sufyān as he was 'fiercely jealous' (*shadīd al-ghayra*), and quick to become suspicious, which the woman in the anecdote above did not like; Ibn Saʿd, *Ṭabaqāt*, vol. 8, pp. 170–2; El Cheikh, *Women, Islam, and Abbasid Identity*, p. 18.

37 Bernard, 'Abū l-Aswad'.

38 Ibn Qutayba, *ʿUyūn*, vol. 4, p. 122.

39 Ibid., p. 2.

40 In the introduction to biographical articles on women in *Kitāb al-Ṭabaqāt* by Muḥammad ibn Saʿd, their children are always introduced with a formula such as 'she gave birth to (a child) to him (her husband)'.

41 Hasson, 'Ziyād b. Abīhi'.

42 Ibn Abī Tāhir, *Balaghāt*, pp. 64–6.

43 The setting in Damascus makes this variant even less historically reliable, as Abū al-Aswad lived in Basra. Moreover, he seems to have had a restrained relationship with Muʿāwiya, as he fought with ʿAlī against him in the battle of Sittin and kept his loyalty to the Alids although he held an official position in Basra under the Umayyads. The anecdote is one of several in *Balaghāt al-Nisāʾ* about women who successfully brought their cases and complaints to Muʿāwiya; see Yazigi, 'Women Delegates', for reports about Alid women delegates to the caliph.

44 The last sentence is quoted by al-Jāḥiẓ in *al-Bayān wa-l-Tabyīn*, vol. 1, p. 408, as an example of good *sajʿ*, this time in an argument between a mother and her son.

45 Ibid., p. 408.

46 Frolov, *Classical Arabic Verse*, pp. 105–10.

47 Van Gelder, 'Against Women', pp. 64–5.

48 Ibn Qutayba, *ʿUyūn*, vol. 4, p. 97.

49 According to Lane, *rāmik* is a 'certain thing, black . . . that is mixed with musk', Lexicon, s.v. *rmk*.

50 Ibn Qutayba, *ʿUyūn*, vol. 4, p. 96.

51 Ibid., p. 25. Herakleios (d. 641) was the Byzantine emperor who lost a great part of his empire to the Arabs. The denarius was golden and considered beautiful. A girl was sometimes compared to a dinar.

52 Ibn Qutayba, ʿ*Uyūn*, vol. 4, p. 97.

53 For an interesting discussion of female poets' choices of literary forms, see Hammond, *Beyond Elegy*.

54 Ibn Abī Ṭāhir, *Balaghāt*, ed. 2000, pp. 92–9.

55 Rosenthal, 'Muslim Social Values and Literary Criticism', gives a short history of the hadith and its different recensions.

56 Ibid., pp. 48–9.

57 Ibn Abī Ṭāhir, *Balaghāt*, p. 102.

58 Ibid., pp. 134–5.

59 Ibid., p. 107.

60 Heinrich, 'Yazīd b. Miḳsam Ibn Ḍabba'.

61 Ibn Abī Ṭāhir, *Balaghāt*ʾ (ed. 2000), p. 133.

62 Gert Borg has translated some classical love poems attributed to lesser-known or anonymous women, from different time periods (Borg, 'Love poetry by Arab Women'). Borg arranges them in ten groups according to their predominant theme: 'love as concept', 'experience', 'the romantic escape', 'passion', 'vulnerability and fear of betrayal', 'conflicts with others', 'absence', 'memory', 'rejection of the candidate' and 'regret and separation'.

63 Malti-Douglas, *Woman's Body*, pp. 29–53. There is an extensive secondary literature on Abbasid slave courtesans, e.g. the recent volume edited by Matthew Gordon and Kathryn Hain, *Concubines and Courtesans*, and the monograph by Fuad Matthew Caswell, *The Slave Girls of Baghdad*, to mention just two.

64 Malti-Douglas, *Woman's Body*, p. 33.

65 See Meisami's criticism in 'Writing Medieval Women'.

66 Ibn Qutayba, ʿ*Uyūn*, vol. 4, p. 22.

67 Ibid., p. 85. A later variant of this anecdote is mentioned as an example of an anecdotal woman by Malti-Douglas, *Woman's Body*, p. 44.

68 I.e. during the pilgrimage ritual in Minā.

69 Ibn Qutayba, ʿ*Uyūn*, p. 29.

70 The joke about the dancer is particularly popular, and figures in ʿ*Uyūn al-Akhbār* by Ibn Qutayba, *al-Ajwiba al-Muskita* by Ibn Abī ʿAwn (p. 177), *Nathr al-Durr* by al-Abī, and *Muḥāḍarāt al-Udabā* by al-Rāghib al-Iṣfahānī, in addition to numerous post-Abbasid books.

71 Malti-Douglas, *Woman's Body*, pp. 33–6.

72 Cf. al-Abī, *Nathr al-Durr*, vol. 4, esp. pp. 247–64; Ibn Abī ʿAwn, *al-Ajwiba*, pp. 75–9.

73 According to Islamic law female slaves only had to display their face and hands; Raghib, 'Marchés aux esclaves', pp. 735–6.

74 Cf. ibid. Raghib concludes that luxury slaves often changed owners in private, without intermediates, but that owners sometimes put them up for public auction only to humiliate them or correct them, ibid., p. 724.

75 For example, the poet Faḍl was secured a high standing at the court of the caliph al-Mutawakkil, without being his concubine, by means of her quick and clever answers; Abū al-Faraj al-Iṣbahānī, *Aghānī*, vol. 19, p. 215. Al-Mutawakkil bought the slave-poetess Rayyā but not Ẓamyā, although she was equally talented, because she was freckled. She convinced him to buy her too, in spite of her minor blemish; Abū al-Faraj, *al-Imā ʾ al-Shawā ʿir*, pp. 115–16; see translation of the poems in Kilpatrick, 'Women as Poets and Chattels', pp. 165–6. Abū al-Faraj al-Iṣbahānī gives some accounts about successful presentations of individual *jawāri* other than those mentioned above; see, for example, his articles on Amal and Nabt in *al-Ima ʾ al-Shawā ʿir*.

76 Weipert, 'al-Aṣma ʿī'; Gibb, 'Abū ʿUbayda'.

77 See Bray, 'Men, Women and Slaves', pp. 126–7. For negative representations, see El Cheikh, *Women, Islam, and Abbasid Identity*.

## Chapter 5

1 Her name is spelt Dufāq in all manuscripts but one used for the Dār al-Kutub. edition of *Kitāb al-Aghānī*, but as her name is Duqāq in all other sources, the editors choose this name; Abū al-Faraj al-Iṣbahānī, *Kitāb al-Aghānī*, vol. 12, p. 282, n. 1; the biographical article, ibid., pp. 282–5.

2 For Aḥmad ibn Ḥamdūn; see Fleischhammer, *Quellen*, p, 76; Vadet, 'Ibn Ḥamdūn'. Aḥmad was a courtier of several caliphs from al-Mutawakkil to al-Mu ʿtamid. His father's identity is more obscure and his name is not mentioned in the article on Duqāq; Vadet concludes that Ḥamdūn is either his father or grandfather. However, elsewhere in *Aghānī*, it is stated that his father's name is Ḥamdūn.

3 A *mukhannath* was often an entertainer, a musician or a buffoon at the court. For the *mukhannathūn* in early Islamic society, see Rowson, 'Effeminates of Early Medina', and for their role in the ninth century, when they were generally supposed to be passive homosexuals, see Rowson, 'Categorization'.

4 Abū al-Faraj al-Iṣbahānī, *Aghānī*, vol. 12, p. 282

5 Ibid., p. 284.

6 Ibid.

7 His books are all lost; Rosenthal, 'al-Sarakhsī'.

8 Abū al-Faraj al-Iṣbahānī, *Aghānī*, vol. 12, p. 282. The term *futuwwa* literary means 'the qualities of young people'; for other meanings and interpretations, see Cahen and Taeschner, '*Futuwwa*'.

9 Wagner, ʿAbū Nuwās'.

10 Abū al-Faraj, *Aghānī*, vol. 18, p. 74.

11 For the date of Ḥamdūna's marriage, see al-Tabarī, *History*, vol. 30, p. 55.

12 Ibn al-Sā ʿī, *Nisā ʾ al-khulafā ʿ*, p. 53; translated in Ibn al-Sā ʿī, *Consorts*, p. 21.

13 Szombathy, *Mujūn*, p. 9.
14 See Feldman and Gordon, *Courtesan's Art*, p. 6.
15 Szombathy, *Mujūn*, p. 133.
16 Ibid. For al-Washshāʾ and *al-mutaẓarrifāt*, see Myrne, 'Of Ladies and Lesbians'.
17 Al-Marzūbānī was a scholar in Baghdad who was close to the Buyid ruler ʿAḍūd al-Dawla. His work on female poets had originally more than 500 folios, but only a fragment is extant: *Ashʿār al-Nisāʾ*; Sellheim, ʿal-Marzūbānī'.
18 Abū al-Faraj Al-Iṣbahānī, *Al-Imāʾ al-Shawāʿir*, p. 32.
19 ʿAlī ibn Naṣr, *Jawāmiʿ al-Ladhdha*, MS Fatih 3729, fol. 18a; MS Aya Sofya 3836, fol. 19a.
20 This distinction is made, in particular, for Abū Nuwās' erotic poetry; Wagner, 'Abū Nuwās'.
21 Rosenthal, 'Male and Female', p. 31.
22 The lines are from al-Nābigha, *Dīwān al-Nābigha,* pp. 41–2. Two lines are translated by Beatrice Gruendler: 'When you thrust your spear, you thrust it into a high target, rising to the touch and perfume-daubed. /And when you pull out, you pull out from a tight spot like a grown boy pulling on a twisted rope'; al-Sūlī, *Life and Times of Abū Tammām*, p. 25. The beloved woman is traditionally but probably wrongly identified as queen al-Mutajarrida, wife of al-Nuʿmān III ibn al-Mundhir (d. 602), the Lakhmid king of al-Ḥīra.
23 ʿAlī ibn Naṣr, *Jawāmiʿ*, MS Aya Sofya 3836, fol. 29a.
24 Ibn Abī Ṭāhir, *Balaghāt*, p. 93; Rosenthal, 'Muslim Social Values', p. 55.
25 Ibn Manẓūr, *Lisān*, s.v. *zrnb*.
26 ʿAlī ibn Naṣr, *Jawāmiʿ al-Ladhdha*, MS Aya Sofya 3836, fols 10b–11a, MS Fatih 3729, fols 10b–11a.
27 Ibid., MS Aya Sofya 3836, fol. 11a.
28 Ibid., fol. 18a.
29 ʿAlī ibn Naṣr, *Jawāmiʿ*, MS Fatih 3729, fol. 144a.
30 Al-Sūlī, *Life and Times of Abū Tammām*, p. 25 (Arabic text, p. 24).
31 The translation is from al-Suli, *Abū Tammām*, p. 25. The poem is in Ibn al-Rūmī, *Dīwān*, vol. 4, p. 1656, no 1286:58–60. A variant has *han* instead of *ḥir*; see *Abū Tammām*, p. 330, n. 17,
32 Ibid., p. 27; the poem is also in Abū al-Faraj, *Aghānī*, vol. 10, p. 162.
33 Abū Hilāl al-ʿAskarī, *Dīwān al-Maʿānī*, vol. 1, pp. 279–81. 'Abū Hilāl expected his books to be memorized and cited in learned conversation, with the purpose of social advancement in the reigning Arabic culture, fostered by the second generation of Būyid *amīrs* and ther *wazīrs*', Gruendler, 'al-ʿAskarī'.
34 Abū Hilāl al-ʿAskarī, *Dīwān al-Maʿānī*, vol. 1, p. 280; Ibn al-Rūmī, *Dīwān*, vol. 6, p. 116.
35 Abū Hilāl, *Maʿānī,* vol. 1, p. 281.

36 ʿAlī ibn Naṣr, *Jawāmiʿ*, MS Aya Sofya 3836, fols 10a–38a, MS Fatih 3729, fols 10a–38a, MS Chester Beatty ar4635, fols 10b–44a. The number of poems and their renderings differs somewhat between the manuscripts.

37 MS Fatih 3729 has *liḥya*, 'jaw', and Aya Sofya 3836 has *jabha*, 'forehead'. The vocabulary in this verse is obscure, with deviations between the extant manuscripts.

38 Ibn Naṣr, *Jawāmiʿ al-Ladhdha*, MS Chester Beatty, fols 39a–b. The readings of this poem differ somewhat in MS Aya Sofya 3836, fol. 34b and MS Fatih 3729, fol. 35a. The word 'noble' for example, comes from MS Chester Beatty (which has *nbl*); MS Fatih has *ml'* and Aya Sofya 3836 has *nayk*.

39 Ibn Qutayba, *ʿUyūn*, vol. 4, p. 101.

40 Lane, *Lexicon*, s.v. *ṣfw*.

41 Ibid., *ṣdʿ*.

42 Al-Marzūbānī, *Ashʿār*, p. 98.

43 Ibid., p. 99. The verse, *yā man yadullu ʿazaban ʿalā ʿazabin*, can also be translated 'who will guide a bachelor to a maiden', as *ʿazab* can be used for men and women alike. I have chosen to understand the second *ʿazab* as a verbal noun, meaning 'he went with [the sheep or goats] to a remote pasturage' (Lane, *Lexicon*, s.v. *ʿzb*). A similar verse, also attributed to Bint al-Ḥumāris (*Ashʿār*, p. 98) does not have the second verse ('to the daughter . . .') and the meaning seems to be 'Who will guide a bachelor to a maiden.'

44 I.e., the workhorse comes among the last animals in a *jalab*, which is a group of animals and possible slaves, driven from one place to another to be sold.

45 Marzubānī, *Ashʿār*, p. 99.

46 Rosenthal, 'Reflections', p. 56.

47 Al-Marzūbānī, *Ashʿār*, pp. 100–1.

48 *rābī al-majassa* is an image borrowed from al-Nābigha's famous poem, see above.

49 Ibn Abī Ṭāhir, *Balaghāt*, pp. 243–4.

50 Al-Marzūbānī, *Ashʿār*, p. 102.

51 Ibid., p. 100.

52 Ibn Abī ʿAwn, *Tashbīhāt* p. 234.

53 One verse is the same as in *Tashbīhāt* by Ibn Abī ʿAwn.

54 In the MSS Aya Sofya 3836, fols 19a–38a, and Fatih, 3729 fols 18a–38a. The poems are sometimes rendered differently in the different manuscripts and the sometimes large divergences between known poems here and in the poets' *dīwāns* points to the unstable transmission of the erotic texts.

55 Marzubānī, *Ashʿār,* pp. 68–70.

56 MS Aya Sofya 3836, fol. 32a; MS Fatih 3729, fol. 31a.

57 MS Fatih 3729, fol. 31b.

58 Papoutsakis, 'al-Farazdaq'.

59 Ibid.

60 Jorgensen, '*Naqa'id* Performance as Social Commentary,' p. 30.
61 Ibid., p. 75.
62 Ibid., p. 50.
63 van Gelder, 'Against Women.'
64 van Gelder, *The Bad and the Ugly*, pp. 64–6.
65 Ibid., p. 63.
66 Wagner, 'Abū Nuwās.'
67 Meisami, 'Arabic Mujūn Poetry', p. 9.
68 Rowson, 'Categorization,' p. 52.
69 Rowson, 'Mujūn,' p. 547.
70 For the vagina as sea, see Kennedy, *Abu Nuwas*, p. 47; Antoon, *Poetics of the Obscene*, pp. 96–8. For the *vagina dentata*, see Antoon, *Poetics of the Obscene* (diss.), pp. 96–9.
71 Shippers, '*Mujūn* genre,' p. 98.
72 Antoon, *Poetics of the* Obscene, p. 37.
73 Antoon, *Poetics of the Obscene* (diss.), pp. 96–8, 99.
74 Ibid., p. 155.
75 Antoon, *Poetics of the Obscene*, p, 131.
76 Ibn Qutayba, *ʿUyūn*, vol. 3, p. 156, and Ibn Abī Ṭāhir, *Balaghāt*, p. 176.
77 Told on the authority of ʿUmar ibn Bakīr, Hishām ibn al-Kalbī and Ibn Miskīn al-Madīnī; Balādhurī, *Ansāb*, 11:186.
78 Al-Tabari, *History*, vol. 21, p. 187.
79 Sezgin, *Geschichte*, vol. 2, p. 265. Abū al-Faraj al-Isbahānī devotes one article to him in *Aghānī*, vol. 21, pp. 179–92.
80 Al-Mubarrad, *Fāḍil*, pp. 766–7; Abū al-Faraj, *Aghānī*, vol. 21, pp. 188 and 190. The chain of transmitters in *Aghānī* is Ḥammād ibn Isḥāq–his father–Ibn Kunnāsa.
81 Ibid. pp. 200–1.
82 See Pellat, 'Al-Haytham b. ʿAdī,' and, especially, Leder, *al-Haiṯam ibn Adī*.
83 Jāḥiẓ, *Rasā'il*, vol. 2, p. 129.
84 Ibid. p. 131.
85 Ibn Abī Ṭāhir, *Balaghāt* (ed. 2000), pp. 194–5. See the translation of the anecdotes about Ḥubbā in Borg, 'Lust and Carnal Desire,' pp. 152–3.
86 For this book, see Gériès, 'al-Maḥāsin wa-'l-Masāwī.'
87 Pseudo-Jāḥiẓ, *Maḥāsin*, p. 221.
88 Al-ʿAskarī, *Jamharal*, vol. 1, pp. 562–3.
89 Hamza al-Iṣbahānī, *al-Durra al-Fākhira*, vol. 1, pp. 256–7.
90 She was more than *naṣaf*, which means, according to the editor, 45 or 50 years old; al-Jāḥiẓ, *Ḥayawān*, vol. 6, p. 75, n. 2.
91 See Malti-Douglas, *Women's Body*, pp. 45–7, for Ḥubbā as an *adab* character, and see Meisami's critique in 'Writing Medieval Women.'
92 Ibn al-Nadīm, *Fihrist*, vol. 1, p. 312.

93 Abū al-Faraj al-Iṣbahānī, *Imā'*, pp. 23–44, and *Aghānī*, vol. 23, pp. 84–91. For *al-Imā' al-Shawā'ir*, see Kilpatrick, 'Women as Poets and Chattels'.

94 See the biographical article on 'Inān in al-Isbahānī, *Aghānī*, vol. 23, pp. 84–91, and *Imā'*; pp. 23–44; al-Tawhidi, *al-Baṣā'ir*, vol. 5, p. 14; Ibn al-Sā'i, *Nisā' al-khulafā'*, pp. 48–53 (translated in Ibn al-Sā'ī, *Consorts of the Caliphs*, pp. 10–19); al-Suyūtī, *Mustaẓrif*, p. 39; Ibn 'Abd Rabbih, *'Iqd*, vol. 6, p. 61, Pseudo-Jāḥiẓ, *Mahāsin*, pp. 193–4, Ibn Jarrah, *Waraqa*, p. 41.

95 Ibn Mu'tazz, *Tabaqāt*, pp. 421–2.

96 The translation is from Ibn al-Sā'ī, *Consorts of the Caliphs*. Al-Nuṭṭāf is the same as al-Nāṭifī, Abū al-Faraj al-Iṣbahāni, *Imā'*, p. 37; the poem is in Abū Nuwās, *Dīwān*, pp. 293–4. Another opinion is that Hārūn al-Rashīd abstained from buying her when al-Nāṭifī requested a too high price; Pseudo-Jahiz, *Mahāsin*, p. 197; Al-Iṣbahānī, *Imā'*, p. 41, *Aghānī*, vol. 23, p. 89.

97 Al-Iṣbahānī, *Imā'*, p. 38. This is only the first part of the poem, which consists of 10 verses in *Imā'*, some of which, but not all, are quoted in Ibn Jarrāḥ, *Waraqa*, p. 44, and al-Suyūṭī, *al-Mustaẓrif min Akhbār al-Jawārī*, p. 40.

98 Abū al-Faraj, *Aghānī*, vol. 22, pp. 207–14. Slave courtesans were often accused of loose morals and falseness, most famously in al-Jāḥiẓ's epistle on the female singer, *Risālat al-Qiyān*. The slave singer became the archtype of the immoral woman; she associated freely with men and did not shun fornication.

99 The anecdotes are from Abū al-Faraj's article on her, *Aghānī*, vol. 21, pp. 53–91.

100 There is a variant of the poem in Ibn Qutayba, *'Uyūn*, vol. 4, p. 106, which differs slightly.

101 The banū al-Furāt was an important family of high officials; the Furāt brothers in this anecdote, Abū al-Ḥasan (d. 312/924) and Abū 'Abbās (d. 291/904) had important positions. Abū al-Ḥasan was *wazīr* under caliph al-Muqtadir.

102 *āla* is an instrument, a tool, and, according to Lane, used for the male sexual organ; *Lexicon*, s.v. *'wl*.

103 It is notable that al-Mu'tazz's son, Ibn al-Mu'tazz, who wrote a book about 'Arīb, is Abū al-Faraj's main source for this anecdote.

104 Abū al-Faraj al-Iṣbahānī, *Aghānī*, vol. 21, pp. 85–6.

## Chapter 6

1 Abū al-Faraj al-Iṣbahānī, *Aghānī*, vol. 4, p. 24, and vol. 15, pp. 277–8.

2 Rowson, 'Abu al-'Atahiya'; H. Kennedy, 'Ma'n'.

3 He also wrote invective verses against his rival, 'Abdullah ibn Ma'n, accusing him for being a passive sodomite; Rowson, 'Abu al-'Atahiya', p. 13.

4 For the translation of *nayk*, see Introduction.

5 Wāliba ibn al-Ḥubāb was also enaged in an exchange of invective poetry with Abū al-ʿAtāhiya; Rowson, 'Abu al-ʿAtahiya', p. 13; Wagner, 'Wāliba b. al-Ḥubāb'.
6 Rowson, 'Abu al-ʿAtahiya', p. 13.
7 Abū al-Faraj al-Iṣbahānī, *Aghānī,* vol. 17, p. 85. The anecdote is told on the authority of Aḥmad ibn Abī Ṭāhir Ṭayfūr, the author of *Balaghāt al-Nisāʾ*.
8 Ibid., p. 81.
9 Abū al-Faraj al-Iṣbahānī, *Aghānī*, vol. 21, p. 72.
10 In *Jawāmiʿ al-Ladhdha* and *Aghānī, saḥq* is used most of the time, whereas al-Samawʾal uses the term *musāḥaqa*. For more terms derived from the same root, see Juynboll, 'Siḥāḳ' and see Amer, 'Medieval Arab Lesbians', who discusses the meaning of *saḥq* and *saḥḥāqa* in *Jawāmiʿ al-Ladhdha* and later erotic manuals. For tribadism in the work of al-Tīfāshī (d. 561/1253), see Malti-Douglas, 'Tribadism/Lesbianism' and Habib, *Female Homosexuality*. The latter discusses different approaches to premodern homosexuality and compares modern discussions.
11 El-Rouayheb, *Before Homosexuality*.
12 Rowson, 'Categorization, p. 77, n. 36.
13 I owe this reference and the translation to Geert Jan van Gelder; I am very thankful for his help. Al-Jāḥiẓ's statement echoes a tradition from ʿĀʾisha, stating that 'if the two circumcised parts touch each other, ritual cleansing is necessary'; see Salaymeh, *Beginnings*, p.125
14 Ibn Naṣr, *Jawāmiʿ*, MS Fatih 3729, fols, 83b–84a.
15 Adang, 'Ibn Ḥazm on Homosexuality', p. 8.
16 Pickthall: 'As for those of your women who are guilty of lewdness, call to witness four of you against them. And if they testify (to the truth of the allegation) then confine them to the houses until death take them or (until) Allah appoint for them a way (through new legislation).'
17 See Juynboll, 'Siḥāḳ'.
18 Pickthall: 'And as for the two of you who are guilty thereof, punish them both. And if they repent and improve, then let them be. Lo! Allah is ever relenting, Merciful'.
19 Adang, 'Ibn Ḥazm', p. 9.
20 See Adang, 'Ibn Ḥazm', 9–10 and 10, n. 20.
21 ʿAbd al-Razzāq, *Muṣannaf*, vol. 7, pp. 334–5. See Juynboll, 'Siḥāḳ'.
22 Adang, 'Ibn Ḥazm', pp. 25–6.
23 Peters, 'Zinā'.
24 Juynboll, 'Siḥāḳ', and see Adang, 'Ibn Ḥazm', p. 26.
25 Adang, 'Ibn Ḥazm', p. 28.
26 Juynboll, 'Siḥāḳ'. Juynboll estimates that these hadiths go back to transmitters who lived through the Abbasid revolution. See also Adang, 'Ibn Ḥazm', p. 28.

27 Ibn Naṣr, *Jawāmiʿ*, MS Aya Sofya 3836, fol. 84b. I am thankful to Reuven Snir, who helped me translate some of the poems in this section.
28 See Myrne, 'Of Ladies and Lesbians'.
29 The translation of *tisʿīna ḥijjatan* is 'ninety years' but the meaning is 'many times' or 'for a long time'.
30 ʿAlī ibn Naṣr, *Jawāmiʿ*, MS Fatih 3729, fol. 85a. The English translation of *Jawāmiʿ al-Ladhdha*, glosses over the poems in this chapter, and parts of the text are abridged or omitted.
31 Or, 'refused a matter' (*amran*) I follow MS Fatih 3729, fol. 85a. The two other MSS that cover this chapter have *ayran*, 'a penis', instead of *amran*.
32 *lam yashʿar*, is more correctly translated 'has never had his hair grown long', but it is most probably beards, or men's body hair that is alluded to here.
33 *bīḍ* signifies white in the sense of light skinned, but also noble.
34 The falseness of the *qiyān* houses and the unfaithfulness of their female inhabitants are common literary motives, not the least in Abbasid poetry. It is also a main theme in al-Jāḥiẓ, *Epistle on Singing-girls*.
35 At least in al-Samawʾal, *Nuzhat*.
36 Ibn Naṣr, *Jawāmiʿ*, MS Fatih 3729, fol. 88a.
37 Al-Washshāʾ, *Muwashshā*; see Myrne, 'On Ladies and Lesbians'.
38 ʿAlī ibn Naṣr, *Jawāmiʿ*, MS Aya Sofya 3836, fol. 84b.
39 MS Fatih 3729, fol. 88a; MSS Aya Sofya and Chester Beatty have 'wrote to her girlfriend' instead of 'inscribed on her ring'.
40 Here, I follow MS Aya Sofya 3836, fol. 86b and MS Chester Beatty ar 4633, fol. 90b, which have *ṣādaqat*. MS Fatih 3729 has *ṣalaḥat rajulan*, 'reconciled with a man' (fol. 87b).
41 All MSS have *fḥlya*, which I do not find. Perhaps a *nisba* is added for the rhyme, or it should be *fiḥla*, as *baʿīr dhū fiḥla*, 'a camel chosen to be a stallion', from *fiḥla*, 'masculineness' and 'the state of being a stallion/male' (Lane, *Lexicon*, sv. *fḥl*).
42 ʿAlī bn Naṣr, *Jawāmiʿ*, MS Fatih 3729, fol. 88a.
43 Abū al-Faraj al-Iṣbahānī, *Aghānī*, vol. 12, p. 283. Religious imagery is also used in poems on male–male desire; see Rowson, 'Medieval Arabic Vice Lists', pp. 60–1.
44 MS Fatih 3729 has *ṣāḥibat al-baʿl* ('married woman'), fol. 87a. The version of this poem differs in Fatih; I have chosen the reading in MS Aya Sofya 3836.
45 ʿAlī ibn Naṣr, *Jawāmiʿ*, MS Aya Sofya 3836, fols 85b–87a.
46 Abū al-Faraj al-Iṣbahānī, *Aghānī*, vol. 2, p. 131.
47 Ibid., p. 132, Shahīd, 'Zarḳāʾ',
48 Other ingredients in the stories about these two women indicate that they lived three centuries or so apart; Shahīd, 'Zarḳāʾ'.
49 These poems and the anecdotes about the plotting of al-ʿĀdī and one of Hind's slaves are from the last part of the biographical article on al-ʿĀdī in Abū al-Faraj, *Aghānī*, vol. 2, pp. 31f.

50 Ibid., p. 128.

51 MS Aya Sofya 3836, fols 41b–42a. Her name was Hind bint al-Khuss, but she is sometimes called al-Zarqāʾ bint al-Khuss and quite commonly confused with Zarqāʾ al-Yamāma, according to Pellat, 'Hind Bint al-Khuss'.

52 Ibn al-Nadīm, *Fihrist*, vol. 2, pp. 329–30. See Ghazi ('La littérature d'imagination en arabe', p. 177) who argues that the women were chaste lovers.

53 Al-Washshāʾ, *Muwashshā*, pp. 61–2.

54 Ibid.

55 *Fihrist*, vol. 2, p. 345; and vol. 1, p. 468.

56 Abū Tammām, *Dīwān*, pp. 421–2. The translations of this and the other poems in the chapter on *madhammat al-nisāʾ* are found in van Gelder, 'Against Women and Other Pleasantries'.

57 Al-Ābī, *Nathr al-Durr*, vol. 4, p. 257.

58 Ibid., p. 260.

59 Ibid.

60 Al-Jurjānī, *Kināyāt*, has a short section on metonyms on *saḥq* which treats the practice more manifestly from a male perspective and also condemns it, pp. 140–2. See Rowson, 'Vice Lists', pp. 63–4.

61 Al-Rāzī devotes a tract to *ubna*, which he regards as a disease; Rosenthal, 'al-Rāzī', p. 49. Ibn Sīnā instead classifies it as a serious moral deficiency; Ibn Sīnā, *Qānūn*, vol. 2, p. 549. Medical authors also discuss the intersexed body (*al-khunthā*); al-Majūsī, *Kāmil*, vol. 2, p 488; Ibn Sīnā, *Qānūn*, vol. 2, p. 549. See also Qusṭā ibn Lūqā below.

62 ʿAlī ibn Naṣr, *Jawāmiʿ al-Ladhdha*, MS Fatih 3729, fol. 84b.

63 His name was Yuḥannā ibn Māsawayh, but is referred to as Yaḥyā in the extant manuscripts of *Jawāmiʿ al-Ladhdha*.

64 MS Fatih 3729, fol. 84a.

65 The idea that the sperm is hot goes back to Aristotle, who claimed that the male sperm is made up by pneuma (hot air) and water. According to his theory, female bodies are generally colder than men's; see Chapter 1.

66 Sbath, 'Le livre de caractères' (edition and translation of Qusṭā ibn Lūqā's treatise), p. 116 (Arabic edition), p. 146 (French translation).

67 Sbath, 'Livre', pp. 110–12.

68 Sbath, 'Livre', p. 132. This and the following line of reasoning came from a conversation Qusṭā ibn Lūqā had with the prince Abū al-ʿAbbās Aḥmad ibn al-Muʿtaṣim.

69 Al-Rāzī, *Ḥāwī*, vol. 10, p. 306.

70 Sbath, 'Livre', p. 136.

71 There is an English translation of al-Rāzī's treatise on *ubna* by Rosenthal ('Al-Rāzī'), pp. 54–5.

72 Ibn Sīnā, *Qānūn*, vol. 2, p. 549.

73 Ibid.

74 The anatomical model most widespread was that of Galen, the vagina was connected with the womb with a 'neck', corresponding to the cervix; see Chapter 1.

75 The term 'labia' is here understood as the external parts. Elsewhere, the author shows that he is aware of the clitoris. The anatomical description is somewhat blurry here, but it is obvious that ʿAlī ibn Naṣr was not very skilled in medical theory. He could have mixed it up, or the text could have been distorted during transmission. The available manuscripts show some significant variations. I follow the reading in MS Fatih 3729, fol. 83b with the help of MS Aya Sofya 3836, fol. 82b.

76 There is an edition based on two manuscripts (Gotha 2045 and Berlin 6381), which cover part one, sections six to eight of *Nuzhat al-Aṣḥāb*, edited by Taher Haddad, including the short chapter entitled 'The cause of some women's choosing tribadism (*saḥq*)', pp. 13–17. The main part of the Gotha manuscript is old, according to Pertsch (*Handschriften*, p. 78), but the Berlin manuscript was copied in the middle of the nineteenth century (Ahlwardt, *Handschriften*, p. 606). In addition to this edition, I have used MS Paris BnF ar 3054 (fifteenth century according to Slane, *Manuscrits arabes*, p. 543), fols 30a–32a, which sometimes has a slightly different reading that I found more accurate. The other available edition of *Nuzhat al-Aṣḥāb* lacks the chapter on lesbianism, as it is based on an incomplete manuscript (MS Escorial 830).

77 For the connection between *saḥḥāqāt* and *mutaẓarrifāt*, see Myrne, 'Ladies and Lesbians'.

## Conclusion

1 Ahmed, *Women and Gender*, p. 67.

2 Toorawa, *Ibn Abī Ṭāhir*, pp. 12–13.

3 Ibid., p. 12.

4 See Myrne, 'Life of a Jāriya'.

# Bibliography

## Primary sources

ʿAbd al-Razzāq al-Ṣanʿānī, *Muṣannaf*, 12 vols, edited by Ḥabīb al-Raḥmān al-Aʿẓamī, (Johannesburg, 1390/1970).

—— *Tafsīr*, vol. 1, edited by Maḥmūd Muḥammad ʿAbduh (Beirut, n.d.).

Al-Ābī, Manṣūr, *Nathr al-Durr*, vol. 4 (Cairo, 1985).

Abū Dāwūd, *Sunan*, 7 vols, edited by Shuʿayb al-Arnaʾūṭ and Muḥammad Kāmil Qurraballī (Damascus, 2009).

Abū al-Faraj al-Isbahānī, *Kitāb al-Aghānī*, 24 vols (Cairo, 1927–74).

—— *Al-Imaʾ al-Shawaʿir*, edited by Nuri Hamudi al-Qaysi and Yunus Ahmad al-Samirraʾi (1984, reprint; Beirut, 1406/1986).

Abū Hilāl al-ʿAskarī, *Dīwān al-Maʿānī*, 2 vols (Beirut, 1994).

Abū Nuwās, al-Ḥasan ibn Hāniʾ, *Dīwān* (*Der Dīwān des Abū Nuwās*), vol. 5, edited by Ewald Wagner (Beirut, 2003).

Abū Tammām, *Diwān al-Ḥamāsa*, 2 vols, edited by Muḥammad ʿAbd al-Qādir Saʿīd al-Rāfiʿī (Damascus, n.d., repr. from ed. Bulaq, 1879).

Abū Yaʿlā, Aḥmad ibn ʿAlī ibn al-Muthannā al-Mawṣilī, *Musnad*, 16 vols, edited by Ḥusayn Salīm Asad (Damascus, 1410/1989).

Abū Yūsuf, *Al-Āthār*, edited by Abū al-Wafāʾ al-Afghānī (Cairo, 1355/1936).

ʿAlī ibn Naṣr al-Kātib, Abū al-Ḥasan, *Jawāmiʿ al-Ladhdha*, MSS Aya Sofya, 3836, 3837, MS Fatih, 3729, Istanbul; MS Chester Beatty ar4635, Dublin.

—— *Encyclopedia of Pleasure*, translated by Adnan Jarkas and Salah Addin Khawwam (Toronto, 1977).

Pseudo-Appollodorous, *The Library*, 2 vols, translated by James G. Frazer (London, 1921).

Aristotle, *Generation of Animals*, translated by A. L. Peck (Cambridge, MA, 1942).

Al-ʿAskarī, *Kitāb Jamharat al-Amthāl*, 2 vols, edited by Muḥammad Abū al-Faḍl and ʿAbd al-Majīd Qaṭāmish (Cairo, 1384/1964).

Al-Ayyāshī, Muḥammad ibn Masʿūd, *al-Tafsīr* (Qom, 1421/2000).

al-Balādhurī, *Ansāb al-Ashrāf*, vol. 5, edited by Iḥsān ʿAbbās (Beirut, 1996); vol. 11 edited by W. Ahlwardt under the title *Anonyme arabische Chronik* (Greifswald, 1883).

Al-Balkhī, Abū Zayd Aḥmad ibn Sahl, *Maṣāliḥ al-Abdān wa-l-Anfus*, edited by Maḥmūd Miṣrī (Cairo, 1426/2005).

Al-Bukhārī, Muḥammad ibn Ismāʿīl, *The Translation of the Meanings of Ṣaḥīḥ al-Bukhārī*, translated and edited by Muḥammad Muhsin Khan, 9 vols (Medina, n.d.).

Farah, Madelain, *Marriage and Sexuality in Islam: A Translation of al-Ghazālī's Book on the Etiquette of Marriage from the Iḥyāʾ* (Salt Lake City, 1984).

Galen, Claudius, *On the Affected Parts*, translated and annotated by Rudolph E. Siegel, (Basel, 1976).

—— *On the Usefulness of the Parts of the Body*, 2 vols, translated by Margaret Tallmadge May (Ithaca, New York, 1968).

Pseudo-Galen, *Kitāb Asrār al-Nisāʾ*, MS Aya Sofya 4838, fols 55b–56a.

Al-Ghazālī, Abū Ḥāmid Muḥammad, *Ihyāʾ ʿUlūm al-Dīn*, edited by Badawi Tabana, 4 vols (Cairo, 1957).

Ḥājji Khalīfa (Katib Çelebi), *Kashf al-Ẓunūn ʿan Usāmī al-Kutub wa-l-Funūn*, edited by Şerefettin Yaltkaya and Rifat Bilge, 2 vols (Istanbul, 1941–3).

Hamza al-Iṣbahānī, *al-Durra al-Fākhira fī al-Amthāl al-Sāʾira*, edited by ʿAbd al-Majīd Quṭāmish, 2 vols (Cairo, 1971–2).

Hippocrates, *Kitāb al-Ajinna li-Buqrāṭ*, edited and translated from Arabic with introduction, commentary and glossary by M. C. Lyons and J. N. Mattock (Cambridge, 1978).

—— *The Hippocratic Treatises "On Generation" "On the Nature of the Child "Diseases IV"*, translated, with commentary, by Iain M. Lonie (Berlin and New York, 1981).

Hūd ibn Muḥakkam al-Huwwārī, *Tafsīr Kitāb Allāh al-ʿAzīz*, edited by Bālḥājj bin Saʿīd Sharīfī (Beirut, 1990).

Ibn ʿAbd Rabbih, *al-ʿIqd al-Farid*, edited by Muḥammad al-Tunji, 6 vols (2001, reprint, Beirut, 1427/2006).

Ibn Abī ʿAwn, *Al-Ajwiba al-Muskita*, edited by Mayy Aḥmad Yūsuf (Cairo, 1996).

—— *Kitāb al-Tashbīhāt*, edited by Muḥammad ʿAbdul Muʿīd Khān (London, 1950).

Ibn Abī Shayba, *Al-Muṣannaf*, 7 vols, edited by Muḥammad ʿAbd al-Salām Shāhīn (Beirut, 1995).

Ibn Abī Ṭāhir Ṭayfūr, *Balaghāt al-Nisā'*, edited by Aḥmad al-Alfī (Cairo, 1326/1908).

—— *Balaghāt al-Nisā'*, introduction by Barakāt Yūsuf Habbūd (Sidon and Beirut, 2000).

Ibn ʿAdī, ʿAbdullāh al-Jurjānī, *al-Kāmil fī Ḍuʿafāʾ al-Rijāl*, 7 vols (Beirut, n.d.).

Ibn Jarrāh, *Kitāb al-Waraqa*, edited by ʿAbd al-Wahhab ʿAzzām and ʿAbd al-Sattār Aḥmad Farrāj (Cairo, 1953).

Ibn al-Jazzār, *Ibn al-Jazzār on Sexual Diseases and their Treatment: A Critical Edition of Zād al-Musāfir wa-Qūt al-Ḥādir*, translation, introduction and commentary by Gerrit Bos (London and New York, 1997).

Ibn Ḥabīb, *Kitāb al-Ghāya wa-l-Nihāya aw Adab al-Nisāʾ*, edited by Abdel-Magid Turki (Tunis, 1992, repr. 2008).

Ibn Māja, Abū ʿAbdullāh Muḥammad, *Sunan*, 2 vols, edited by Muḥammad ʿAbd al-Bāqī (Cairo, 1952).

Ibn Manẓūr, *Lisān al-ʿarab*, 20 vols (Cairo, 1883–91).

Ibn al-Muʿtazz, ʿAbdullāh, *Ṭabaqāt al-Shuʿarā'*, edited by ʿAbd al-Sattar Ahmad Faraj (Cairo, n.d.).

Ibn al-Nadīm, Muḥammad, *Kitāb al-Fihrist*, edited by Ayman Fuʾād Sayyid, 2nd edition, 4 vols (London: Al-Furqān Islamic Heritage Foundation, 2014).

Ibn Qudāma, Muwaffaq al-Dīn Abū Muḥammad, *Al-Mughnī*, edited by ʿAbdullāh al-Turkī and ʿAbd al-Fattāḥ al-Ḥilū, 15 vols (al-Riyad 1417/1997).

Pseudo-Ibn Qurra, Thābit, *Kitāb al-Dakhīra*, edited by G. Sobhy (Cairo, 1928).
Ibn Qutayba, ʿAbdullāh ibn Muslim, *'Uyūn al-Akhbār*, vol. 4 (Cairo, 1930).
Ibn Saʿd, Muḥammad, *Kitāb al-Ṭabaqāt al-Kabīr*, edited by Eduard Sachau, 9 vols (Leiden, 1904–40).
Ibn al-Rūmī, Abū al-Haṣan ʿAlī ibn al-ʿAbbās, *Diwān*, edited by Ḥusayn Naṣṣār, 6 vols (Cairo, 1973–81).
Ibn al-Sāʿī, *Nisāʾ al-Khulafāʾ*, edited by Muṣtafā Jawwād (Cairo, n.d.). Translated as *Consorts of the Caliphs: Women and the Court of Baghdad*, edited and translated by Shawkat Toorawa et. al. (New York and London, 2015).
Ibn Sayyār al-Warrāq, *Annals of the Caliphs' Kitchens: Ibn Sayyār al-Warrāq's Tenth-Century Baghdadi Cookbook*, English translation with introduction and glossary by Nawal Nasrallah (Leiden, 2010).
Ibn Sīnā, *al-Qānūn fī al-Ṭibb*, edited by Idwārd al-Qashsh and ʿAlī Zayʿūr, 4 vols (Beirut, 1408/1987).
Al-Jāḥiẓ, Abū ʿUthmān ʿAmr ibn Baḥr, *al-Bayān wa-l-Tabyīn*, edited by ʿAbd al-Sallām Muḥammad Hārūn, 4 vols (Cairo, 1968).
—— *al-Ḥayawān*, edited by 'Abd al-Salām Hārūn, 7 vols (Cairo, 1945).
—— *Rasāʾil al-Jāḥiẓ*, edited by ʿAbd al-Salām Muḥammad Hārūn, 3 vols (Cairo, 1399/1979).
—— *The Epistle on Singing-girls by Jahiz*, translated and edited by A. F. L. Beeston (Warminster, England, 1980).
Pseudo-Jāḥiz, *Kitāb al-Maḥāsin wa-l-Aḍdād*, edited by Gerlof van Vloten (Leiden, 1898).
al-Jurjānī, Aḥmad ibn Muḥammad, *Kitāb Kināyāt al-Udabāʾ wa-Ishārāt al-Bulaghāʾ*, edited by Maḥmūd Shākir al-Qaṭṭān (Cairo, 2003).
Al-Kāsānī, Abū Bakr ibn Masʿūd, *Badāʾiʿ al-Ṣanāʾiʿ fī Tartīb al-Sharāʾiʿ*, edited by ʿAlī Muḥammad Muʿawwaḍ and ʿĀdil Aḥmad ʿAbd al-Mawjūd, 10 vols (Beirut, 1424/2003).
al-Kharāʾiṭī, Abū Bakr Muḥammad b. Jaʿfar, *Iʿtilāl al-Qulūb fī Akhbār al-ʿUshshāq wa-l-Muḥibbīn*, edited by by Gharīd al-Shaykh (Beirut, 1421/2000).
Al-Kindī, *Kitāb al-Bāh*, edited by Celentano, in Guiseppe Celentano, 'Due Scritti medici di al-Kindī, Instituto Orientale di Napoli', *Supplemento n. 18 agli Annali*, 39/1 (1979), pp. 11–36.
Al-Kulaynī, Abū Jaʿfar Muḥammad ibn Yaʿqūb, *al-Furūʿ min al-Kāfī*, vol. 5 (Beirut, 1401/1980–1).
Al-Majūsī, ʿAlī ibn al-ʿAbbās, *Kāmil al-Ṣināʿa al-Ṭibbiyya*, 2 vols (Cairo/Būlāq 1294/1877, repr. Frankfurt, 1996).
Mālik, ibn Anas, *Muwaṭṭaʾ Mālik*, edited by Fuʾād abū al-Bāqī, 2 vols (Beirut, 1406/1985).
Marzubānī, Abū ʿUbaydallāh, Muḥammad ibn ʿUmrān, *Ashʿār al-Nisāʾ*, edited by Sāmī Makkī al-ʿĀnī and Hilāl Nājī (Beirut, 1995/1410).
Al-Mubarrad, Muḥammad ibn Yazīd, *Fāḍil*, edited by ʿAbd al-ʿAzīz al-Maymanī (Cairo, 1956).

Mughulṭāy, ʿAlāʾ al-Dīn, *Al-Wāḍiḥ al-Mubīn fī Dhikr Man Ustushhida min al-Muḥibbīn* (Beirut, 1997).

Muqātil ibn Sulaymān, *Tafsīr*, vol. 1, edited by ʿAbd Allāh Maḥmūd Shiḥāta (Cairo, 1395/1975).

Muslim ibn al-Ḥajjāj, *Ṣaḥīḥ Muslim*, edited by Fuʾād ʿAbd al-Bāqī, 5 vols (Cairo, 1997).

al-Nābigha, al-Dhubyānī, *Dīwān al-Nābigha al-Dhubyānī*, edited by Karam al-Bustānī (Beirut, 1383/1923).

Al-Nasāʾī, Aḥmad ibn Shuʿayb, *Tafsīr*, 2 vols (Cairo, 1410/1990).

Al-Qifṭī, Jamā al-Dīn Abū al-Ḥasan, *Taʾrīkh al-Ḥukamāʾ*, edited by Julius Lippert (Leipzig, 1320/1903).

Al-Qummī, ʿAlī ibn Ibrāhīm, *Tafsīr al-Qummī* (Qom, 1435/2014).

Qusṭā ibn Lūqā, *Kitāb fī al-Bāh wa-mā Yuḥtāj ilayhi min Tadbīr al-Badan fī Istiʿmālilhi*, Edition Übertragung und Bearbeitung von Gauss Haydar (diss. med. Erlangen-Nürnberg, 1973).

—— *Kitāb fī al-Bāh*, Edition und Übertragung Najdat Ali Barhoum (diss. med. Erlangen-Nürnberg, 1974).

Al-Rāghib al-Iṣfahānī, *Muḥāḍarāt al-Udabāʾ*, 3 vols (Beirut, n.d.).

Al-Rāzī, Muḥammad ibn Zakariyyā, 'Kitāb fī al-Bāh', in *Thalāth Makhṭūṭāt Nādira fī al-Jins*, edited by Hishām ʿAbd al-ʿAzīz and ʿĀdil ʿAbd al-Ḥamīd (Cairo, 1999).

—— *Kitāb al-Ḥāwī fī al-Ṭibb*, 22 vols (Hyderabad-Deccan, 1955–74).

—— *Al-Manṣūrī fī al-Ṭibb*, edited by Ḥāzim al-Bakrī al-Ṣiddīqī (Kuwait, 1987).

Al-Samawʾal al-Magribī, *Nuzhat al-Aṣḥāb fī Muʿāsharat al-Aḥbāb*, chapters 6–8, edited by Taher Haddad, PhD diss. Erlangen, n.d.; MS Gotha 2045, MS Berlin 6381, MS Paris BnF ar 3054, MS Escorial 830.

al-Shaybānī, *Muwaṭṭaʾ al-Imām Mālik bi-Riwāyat Muḥammad ibn al-Ḥasan al-Shaybānī*, edited by ʿAbd al-Wahhāb ʿAbd al-Laṭīf (Cairo, 1994).

Al-Shayzarī, *al-Īḍāḥ fī Asrār al-Nikāḥ*, part 2, edited and translated by Krikor Amdha (Diss. med. Universität Erlangen-Nürnberg, 1976).

—— *Al-Īḍāḥ fī Asrār al-Nikāḥ*, edited by Aḥmad Farīd al-Mazīdī (Beirut, 2002).

—— *Rawḍat al-Qulūb wa Nuzhat al-Muḥibb wa-l-Maḥbūb*, edited by David Semah and George J. Kanazi (Wiesbaden, 2003).

Al-Shīrāzī, Ibrāhīm ibn ʿAlī Abū Isḥāq, *Al-Muhadhdhab fī al-Fiqh al-Imām al-Shāfiʿī*, edited by Muḥammad al-Zuḥaylī, 6 vols (Damascus, 1412/1992).

Al-Sūlī, Abū Bakr, *Life and Times of Abū Tammām*, translated by Beatrice Gruendler (New York, 2018).

Al-Suyūṭī, Jalāl al-Dīn, *Al-Durr al-Manthūr fī al-Tafsīr bi-l-Maʾthūr*, vol. 2, edited by ʿAbdullāh ibn ʿAbd al-Muḥsin al-Turkī (Cairo, 1424/2003).

—— *al-Mustaẓrif min Akhbār al-Jawārī*, edited by Ṣalāḥ al-Dīn al-Munajjid (n.p., 1963).

—— *Nawāḍir al-Ayk fī Maʿrifat al-Nayk*, edited by Ṭalʿat Ḥasan ʿAbd al-Qawī (Damascus, 2001?).

—— *Nuzhat al-Mutaʾammil wa-Murshid al-Mutaʾahhil*, edited by Muḥammad al-Tūnjī (Beirut, 1989).

—— *Shaqāʾiq al-Utrunj fī Raqāʾiq al-Ghunj*, edited by Ḥusayn ʿUmar Ḥamādah (Damascus, 2008).

—— *Kitāb al-Wishāḥ fī Fawāʾid al-Nikāḥ*, edited by Ṭalʿat Ḥasan ʿAbd al-Qawī (Damascus, 2001); MS Lala Ismail 577, Istanbul; MSS BnF Arabe 3066 and 3067, Paris; MS King Saud University 797.

Al-Ṭabarānī, *Muʿjam al-Awsāṭ*, 10 vols, edited by Ṭāriq ibn ʿAwaḍ Allāh (Cairo, 1415/1995).

Al-Ṭabarī, ʿAlī ibn Sahl, *Firdaws al-Ḥikma*, edited by Muḥammad Zubayr al-Ṣiddīqī (Berlin, 1928).

Al-Ṭabarī, Abū Jaʿfar Muḥammad ibn Jarīr, *The History of al-Ṭabarī*, vol. 21, 'The victory of the Marwānids', translated by Michael Fishbein (New York, 1990).

—— *Tafsīr al-Ṭabarī: Jāmiʿ al-Bayān ʿan Taʾwīl al-Qurʿān*, edited by ʿAbdullāh ibn ʿAbd al-Muḥsin al-*Turki,* 26 vols (Cairo, 1422/2001)

Al-Tawḥīdī, Abū Ḥayyān, *Al-Baṣāʾir wa-l-Dakhāʾir*, 10 vols, edited by Wadad al-Qadi (Beirut, 1408/1988).

Al-Tijānī, *Tuhfat al-ʿArūs*, edited by Jalīl al-ʿAṭīya (London, 1992).

Al-Tirmidhī, *Al-Jāmiʿ al-Ṣaḥīḥ*, edited by Aḥmad Muḥammad Shākir (Beirut, n.d.).

Al-Tūsī, Muḥammad ibn al-Ḥasan, *Al-Tibyān fī Tafsīr al-Qurʾān*, edited by Aḥmad Ḥabīb Qaṣīr al-ʿĀmilī, 10 vols (Beirut, n.d.).

al-Washshā', Abū Ṭayyib Muḥammad ibn Isḥāq, *Kitāb al-Muwashshā*, edited by Rudolphe Brünnow (Leiden, 1886).

## Secondary sources

Abbou Hershkovits, Keren, 'Medical Services and ʿAbbasid Ladies', *Journal of Women of the Middle East and the Islamic World* 12 (2014), pp. 121–36.

Abu-Zahra, Nadia, 'Adultery and Fornication', in Jane Dammen McAuliffe (ed.), *Encyclopaedia of the Qurʾān*, vol. I (Leiden, 2001), pp. 28–30.

Adang, Camilla, 'Ibn Ḥazm on Homosexuality, a Case-Study of Ẓāhirī Legal Methodology', *Al-Qanṭara*, XXIV/1 (2003), pp. 5–31.

Aerts, Stijn, 'Canon and Canonisation of Ḥadīth', in Kate Fleet et al. (eds), *Encyclopaedia of Islam, THREE.* Consulted online on 22 May 2019.

Ahlwardt, W., *Die Handschriften-Verzeichnisse der königliche Bibliotheken zu Berlin. Verzeichniss der arabischen Handschriften*, 10 vols (Berlin, 1887–99).

Ahmed, Leila, *Women and Gender in Islam: Historical Roots of a Modern Debate* (New Haven and New York, 1992).

Ali, Daud, 'Padmaśri's *Nāgarasarvasva* and the World of Medieval Kāmśāstra', *Journal of Indian Philosophy* 39/1 (2011), pp. 41–62.

Ali, Kecia, *Marriage and Slavery in Early Islam* (Cambridge, MA, and London, 2010).

Alvarez Millan, Cristina, 'Graeco-Roman Case Histories and their Influence on Medieval Islamic Clinical Accounts', *Social History of Medicine* 12/1 (1999), pp. 19–43.

Amer, Sahar, 'Medieval Arab Lesbians and Lesbian-Like Women', *Journal of the History of Sexuality* 18 (2009), pp. 215–36.

D'Ancona, Cristina, 'Greek into Arabic, in Kate Fleet et. al. (eds), *Encyclopaedia of Islam, THREE*. Consulted online on 7 November 2017.

Ansari, Hassan and Umar, Suheyl, 'Aḥmad b. Muḥammad b. ʿĪsā', in Wilfred Madelung and Farhad Daftary (eds), *Encyclopaedia Islamica*. Consulted online on 31 January 2019.

Antoon, Sinan, *The Poetics of the Obscene: Ibn al-Ḥajjāj and Sukhf* (New York, 2014).

—— 'The Poetics of the Obscene: Ibn al-Hajjāj and Sukhf' (PhD diss., Harvard University, 2006).

Armstrong, Lyall R., *The* Quṣṣāṣ *of Early Islam* (Leiden, 2017).

Azam, Hina, *Sexual Violation in Islamic Law* (New York, 2015).

Bauer, Karen, 'Room for interpretation: Qurʾānic Exegesis and Gender' (PhD diss., Princeton University, 2007).

Baugh, Carolyn, *Minor Marriage in Early Islamic Law* (Leiden and Boston, 2017).

Bearman, P., Th. Bianquis, C. E. Bosworth, E. van Donzel and W. P. Heinrichs (eds), *Encyclopaedia of Islam, Second Edition*, 12 vols with indexes (Leiden, 1960–2004).

Berkey, Jonathan P., 'Circumcision Circumscribed: Female Excision and Cultural Accommodation in the Medieval Near East', *International Journal of Middle East Studies* 28 (1996), pp. 19–38.

Bernards, Monique, 'Abū l-Aswad al-Duʾalī', in Kate Fleet et al. (eds), *Encyclopaedia of Islam, THREE*. Consulted online on 25 January 2018.

Blachère, R., 'al-Farrāʾ', in P. Bearman et al. (eds), *Encyclopaedia of Islam, Second Edition*, vol. 2, pp. 806–8.

van Bladel, Kevin, 'The Bactrian Background of the Barmakids,' in Anna Akasoy et. al. (eds), *Islam and Tibet: Interactions Along the Musk Routes* (Burlington, 2011), pp. 43–88.

Borg, Gert, 'Love Poetry by Arab Women', *Arabica* 54/4 (2007), pp. 425–65.

—— 'Lust and Carnal Desire: Obscenities Attributed to Arab Women', *Arabic and Middle Eastern Literatures* 3/2 (2000), pp. 149–64.

Bos, Gerrit, 'Ibn al-Jazzār on Women's Diseases and their Treatment', *Medical History* 37/3 (1993), pp. 296–312.

—— 'Ibn al-Jazzār on Sexuality and Sexual Dysfunction, and the Mystery of ʿUbayd ibn ʿAlī ibn Jurāja ibn Hillauf Solved', *Jerusalem Studies in Arabic and Islam* 19 (1995), pp. 250–66.

—— *Ibn al-Jazzār on Sexual Diseases and their Treatment: A Critical Edition of Zād al-Musāfir wa-qūt al-ḥādir (Provisions for the Traveller and Nourishment for the Sedentary)*, Book 6, translation, introduction and commentary by Gerrit Bos (London and New York, 1997).

Bosworth, C. E. 'Abu Saleh Mansur', *Encyclopædia Iranica*, I/4 (1983), p. 383; an updated version is available online at http://www.iranicaonline.org/articles/abu-saleh-mansur-b.

Bouhdiba, Abdelwahab. *Sexuality in Islam*, translated by Alan Sheridan (London, 1998). Originally published as *La sexualité en Islam* (Paris, 1975).

Bowen, H., '`Aḍud al-Dawla', in P. Bearman et al. (eds), *Encyclopaedia of Islam, Second Edition*, vol. 1, pp. 211–12.

Bowen, H. and Bosworth, C. E., 'Rukn al-Dawla', in P. Bearman et al. (eds), *Encyclopaedia of Islam, Second Edition*, vol. 8, pp. 597–8.

Bray, Julia, 'Men, Women, and Slaves in Abbasid Society', in Leslie Brubaker and Julia M. H. Smith (eds), *Gender in the Early Medieval World: East and West, 300–900* (Cambridge, 2004), pp. 121–46.

Brockelmann, Carl, *Geschichte der arabischen Litteratur*, 2 vols, 3 supps (Leiden, 1937).

Brown, Jonathan, 'Did the Prophet Say It or Not? The Literal, Historical, and Effective Truth of Hadiths in Early Sunnism', *Journal of the American Oriental Society* 129/2 (2009), pp. 259–85.

—— *The Canonization of al-Bukhārī and Muslim: The Formation and Function of the Sunnī Canon* (Leiden and Boston, 2007).

Browne, Edward Granville, *Arabian Medicine* (Cambridge, 1921).

Burge, Stephen R, 'Scattered Pearls: Exploring al-Suyūṭī's Hermeneutics and Use of Sources in *al-Durr al-manthūr fī'l-tafsīr bi'l-ma'thūr*', *Journal of the Royal Asiatic Society* 24/2 (2013), pp. 251–96.

Cadden, Joan, *Meanings of Sex Differences in the Middle Ages: Medicine, Science, and Culture* (Cambridge, 1993).

Cahen, Cl. and Fr. Taeschner, '*Futuwwa*', in P. Bearman et al. (eds), *Encyclopaedia of Islam, Second Edition*, vol. 2, pp. 961–9.

Caswell, Fuad Matthew, *The Slave Girls of Baghdad: The Qiyan in the Early Abbasid Era* (London and New York, 2011).

Cheikh-Moussa, Abdallah, 'L'Historien et la littérature arab médiévale', *Arabica* 43/1 (1996), pp. 152–88.

Connell, Sophia M., 'Aristotle and Galen on Sex Difference and Reproduction: A New Approach to an Ancient Rivalry', *Studies in History and Philosophy of Science* 31/3 (2000). pp. 405–27.

—— *Aristotle on Female Animals: A Study of the Generation of Animals* (Cambridge, 2016).

Cortese, Delia and Simonetta Calderini, *Women and the Fatimids in the World of Islam* (Edinburgh, 2006).

Crone, Patricia, *Meccan Trade and the Rise of Islam* (Princeton, 1987).

Dallal, Ahmad, 'Sexualities: Scientific Discourses, Premodern', in *Encyclopedia of Women and Islamic Cultures*, vol. III, *Family, Body, Sexuality and Health* (Leiden and Boston, 2006).

Dean-Jones, Lesley, *Women's Bodies in Classical Greek Science* (Oxford, 1994).

Dietrich, A., 'Māsardjawayh', in P. Bearman et al. (eds), *Encyclopaedia of Islam, Second Edition*, vol. 6, pp. 640–1.

Dols, Michael W., 'The origins of the Islamic hospital: myth and reality', *Bulletin of the History of Medicine* 61 (1987), pp. 367–90.

El Cheikh, Nadia Maria, 'In Search for the Ideal Spouse', *Journal of the Economic and Social History of the Orient* 45/2 (2002), pp. 179–96.

—— *Women, Islam, and Abbasid Identity*, (Cambridge, MA, 2015).

El-Rouayheb, Khaled, *Before Homosexuality in the Arab-Islamic World, 1500–1800* (Chicago, 2005).

Fancy, Nahyan, 'Womb Heat versus Sperm Heat: Hippocrates against Galen and Ibn Sīnā in Ibn al-Nafīs's Commentaries', *Oriens* 45 (2017), pp. 150–75.

Feldman, Martha and Bonnie Gordon (eds), *The Courtesan's Art: Cross-Cultural Perspectives* (Oxford and New York, 2006).

Fleet, Kate, Gudrun Krämer, Denis Matringe, John Nawas and Everett Rowson (eds), *Encyclopaedia of Islam, THREE* (Leiden, 2007).

Fleischhammer, Manfred, *Die Quellen des Kitāb al-agāni* (Wiesbaden, 2004).

Forcada, Miquel, 'ʿArīb b. Saʿīd al-Qurṭūbī', in Kate Fleet et al. (eds), *Encyclopaedia of Islam, THREE.* Consulted online on 31 January 2019.

Frolov, Dmitrij, *Classical Arabic Verse: History and Theory of ʿArūḍ* (Leiden, 2000).

Fück, J. W., 'Ibn al-Nadīm', in P. Bearman et al. (eds), *Encyclopaedia of Islam, Second Edition*, vol. 3, pp. 895–6.

Gacek, Adam, *Arabic Manuscripts: A Vademecum for Readers* (Leiden and Boston, 2012).

Gadelrab, Sherry Sayed, 'Discourses on Sex Differences in Medieval Scholarly Islamic Thought', *Journal of Medicine and Allied Sciences* 66/1 (2010), pp. 40–81.

van Gelder, Geert Jan, 'Against Women, and Other Pleasantries: The Last Chapter of Abū Tammām's Hamāsa', *Journal of Arabic Literature* 16 (1985), pp. 61–72.

—— *The Bad and the Ugly: Attitudes towards Invective Poetry (Hijāʾ) in Classical Arabic Literature* (Leiden, 1988).

Gériès, I., 'al-Maḥāsin wa-'l-Masāwī', in P. Bearman et al. (eds), *Encyclopaedia of Islam, Second Edition*, vol. 5, pp. 1223–7.

Gewargis, Albert Arkhim, *Gynäkologisches aus dem Kāmil al-Ṣināʿa aṭ-Ṭibbīya des ʿAlī ibn al-ʿAbbās al-Mağūsī* (Inaugural dissertation, Friedrich-Alexander Universität, Erlangen-Nürnberg, 1980).

Ghazi, Muhammed Ferid, 'La litterature d'imagination en arabe du II^e/VII^e au V^e/XI^e siecles', *Arabica* 4 (1957), pp. 164–78.

Ghersetti, Antonella, 'Polemon in the Arab tradition', in Simon Swain (ed.), *Seeing the Face, Seeing the Soul: Polemon's Physiognomy from Classical Antiquity to Medieval Islam* (Oxford and New York, 2007), pp. 309–25.

—— 'A Science for Kings and Masters: *firāsa* at the Crossroad between Natural Sciences and Power Relationships in Arabic Sources', in Eva Orthmann and Nader El-Bizri (eds), *The Occult Sciences in Pre-modern Islamic Cultures* (Beirut, 2018).

Gibb, H. A. R., 'Abū ʿUbayda', in P. Bearman et al. (eds), *Encyclopaedia of Islam, Second Edition*, vol. 1, p. 158.

Giladi, Avner, *Muslim Midwives: The Craft of Birthing in the Premodern Middle East* (New York, 2015).

Goodman, L. E., 'al-Rāzī', in P. Bearman et al. (eds), *Encyclopaedia of Islam, Second Edition*, vol. 8, p. 474.

Gordon, Matthew and Kathryn Hain (eds), *Concubines and Courtesans: Women and Slavery in Islamic History* (New York, 2017).

Green, Monica, 'The Transmission of Ancient Theories of Female Physiology and Disease Through the Early Middle Ages' (PhD diss., Princeton University, 1985).

Gruendler, Beatrice, 'al-ʿAskarī, Abū Hilāl', in Kate Fleet et al. (eds), *Encyclopaedia of Islam, THREE*. Consulted online on 31 January 2019.

Günther, Sebastian, 'Abū l-Faraj al-Iṣfahānī', in Kate Fleet et al. (eds), *Encyclopaedia of Islam, THREE*. Consulted online on 19 January 2019.

Gutas, Dimitri, *Greek Thought, Arabic Culture: The Graeco-Arabic Translation Movement in Baghdad and Early ʿAbbāsid Society (2nd–4th/8th–10th Centuries)* (London, 1998).

Habib, Samar, *Female Homosexuality in the Middle East: Histories and Representations* (New York and London, 2007).

Hallaq, Wael, *The Origins and Evolution of Islamic Law* (Cambridge, 2005).

Hambly, Gavin R. G. (ed.), *Women in the Medieval Islamic World: Power, Patronage, and Piety* (New York, 1998).

Hämeen-Anttila, Jaakko, 'al-ʿAjjāj', in Kate Fleet et al. (eds), *Encyclopaedia of Islam, THREE*. Consulted online on 12 May 2018.

Hammond, Marlé, *Beyond Elegy, Classical Arabic Women's Poetry in Context* (Oxford and New York, 2010).

Hanson, Ann Ellis, 'The Medical Writers' Woman', in David M. Halperin, John J. Winkler and Froma I. Zeitlin (eds), *Before Sexuality: The Construction of Erotic Experience in the Ancient Greek World* (Princeton, 1990).

Hasson, I., 'Ziyād b. Abīhi', in P. Bearman et al. (eds), *Encyclopaedia of Islam, Second Edition*, vol. 11, p. 312.

Heinrich, Wolfhart, 'Poetic, Rhetoric, Literaturkritik, Metrik und Reimlehre', in Helmut Gätje (ed.), *Grundriß der Arabischen Philologie*, vol. 2 (Wiesbaden, 1987).

—— 'Ruʾba b. al-ʿAdjdjādj', in P. Bearman et al. (eds), *Encyclopaedia of Islam, Second Edition*, vol. 8, pp. 577–8.

—— 'Yazīd b. Miḳsam Ibn Ḍabba', in P. Bearman et al. (eds), *Encyclopaedia of Islam, Second Edition*, vol. 11, pp. 312–13.

Hill, D. R., 'Ḳusṭā b. Lūḳā', in P. Bearman et al. (eds), *Encyclopaedia of Islam, Second Edition*, vol. 5, pp. 529–30.

Jorgensen, Cory, 'Jarīr and al-Farazdaq's *Naqa'id* Performance as Social Commentary' (PhD diss., The University of Texas, Austin, 2012).

Juynboll, G. H. A., 'Siḥāḳ', in Bearman et al. (eds), *Encyclopaedia of Islam, Second Edition*, vol. 9, pp. 565–7.

Kahl, O., 'Sābūr b. Sahl' in Bearman et al. (eds), *Encyclopaedia of Islam, Second Edition*, vol. 8, p. 694.

Katz, Marion Holmes, *Body of Text: The Emergence of the Sunnī Law of Ritual Purity* (Albany, 2002).

Kennedy, H., 'Maʿn b. Zāʾida', in P. Bearman et al. (eds), *Encyclopaedia of Islam, Second Edition*, vol. 6, p. 345.

Kennedy, Philip F., *Abu Nuwas: A Genius of Poetry* (Oxford, 2005).

Kilpatrick, Hilary, 'Women as Poets and Chattels. Abu l-Farağ al-Isbahānī's "al-Imā al-šawā'ir"', *Quaderni di Studi Arabi* 9 (1991), pp. 161–76.

King, Helen, *Hippocrates' Woman: Reading the Female Body in Ancient Greece* (London and New York, 1998).

—— *The One-Sex Body on Trial: The Classical and Early Modern Evidence* (Farnham and Burlington, 2013).

Kraemer, J. L., *Humanism in the Renaissance of Islam. The Cultural Revival During the Buyid Age* (Leiden, 1986).

Kudlien, Fridolf, 'Cells of the Uterus: The Doctrine and its Roots', *Bulletin of the History of Medicine* 39 (1995), pp. 415–23.

Kueny, Kathryn M., *Conceiving Identities: Maternity in Medieval Muslim Discourse and Practice* (Albany, 2013).

Lammens, H., 'al-Mughīra b. Shuʿba', in P. Bearman et al. (eds), *Encyclopaedia of Islam, Second Edition*, vol. 7, p. 347.

Lane, Edward, *Arabic–English Lexicon*, 2 vols (Cambridge, 1984) [first edition London, 1877–93].

Laqueur, Thomas, *Making Sex: Body and Gender from the Greeks to Freud* (Cambridge, MA, and London, 1990).

Leder, Stefan, *Das Korpus al-Haiṯam ibn Adī (st. 207–822): Herkunft, Überlieferung, Gestalt früher Texte der aḫbār Literatur* (Frankfurt am Main, 1991).

Levey, Martin and Safwat S. Souryal, 'Galen's On the Secrets of Women and On the Secrets of Men: A Contribution to the History of Arabic Pharmacology', *Janus* 55 (1968), pp. 208–19.

Malti-Douglas, Fedwa, *Woman's Body, Woman's Word: Gender and Discourse in Arabo-Islamic Writing* (Princeton, 1991).

—— 'Tribadism/Lesbianism and the Sexualized Body in Medieval Arabo-Islamic Narratives', in Francesca C. Sautman and Pamela Sheingorn (eds), *Same Sex Love and Desire Among Women in the Middle Ages* (New York, 2001), pp. 123–42.

Marín, Manuela, 'Women, gender and sexuality', in Maribel Fierro (ed.) *The New Cambridge History of Islam*, vol. 2 (Cambridge and New York 2010), pp. 335–80.

Marín, Manuela and Randi Deguilhem (eds), *Writing the Feminine: Women in Arabic Sources* (London, 2002).

Marlow, Louise, *Counsel for Kings: Wisdom and Politics in Tenth-Century Iran*, 2 vols (Edinburgh, 2016).

May, Margaret Tallmadge, 'Introduction', in *Galen; on the Usefulness of the Parts of the Body*, vol. 1, translated by Margaret Tallmadge May (Ithaca, New York, 1968), pp. 3–64.

Meisami, Julie Scott, 'Arabic Mujūn Poetry: The Literary Dimension', in Frederick de Jong (ed.), *Verse and the Fair Sex* (Utrecht, 1993), pp. 8–30.

—— 'Writing Medieval Women: Representations and Misrepresentations', in Julia Bray (ed.), *Writing and Representation in Medieval Islam: Muslim Horizons* (London and New York, 2006).

Mernissi, Fatema, *Beyond the Veil: Male–Female Dynamics in a Modern Muslim Society* (Cambridge, MA, 1975).

Meyerhof, Max, 'Alî at-Tabarî's "Paradise of Wisdom", One of the Oldest Arabic Compendiums of Medicine', *Isis*, 16/1 (1931), pp. 6–54.

Micheau, Françoise, 'ʿAlī b. al-ʿAbbās al-Majūsī', in Kate Fleet et al. (eds), *Encyclopaedia of Islam, THREE*. Consulted online on 6 November 2017.

Motzki, Harald, 'Bridewealth', in Jane Dammen McAuliffe (ed.), *Encyclopaedia of the Qurʾān*, vol. 2 (Leiden, 2001), pp. 257–8.

—— *The Origins of Islamic Jurisprudence: Meccan Fiqh before the Classical Schools*, translated from the German by Marion Katz (Leiden, 2002).

—— 'ʿAbd al-Razzāq al-Ṣanʿānī', in Kate Fleet et al. (eds), *Encyclopaedia of Islam, THREE*. Consulted online on 6 November 2017.

al-Munajjid, Salāḥ al-Dīn, *Al-Hayāt al-Jinsiyya ʿinda al-ʿArab* (Beirut, 1958).

Musallam, Basil F., *Sex and Society in Islam: Birth Control Before the Nineteenth Century* (Cambridge, 1983).

Myrne, Pernilla. 'Discussing *ghayra* in ʿAbbāsid Literature: Jealousy as a Manly Virtue or Sign of Mutual Affection', *Journal of Abbasid Studies* 1 (2014), pp. 46–65.

—— 'Who was Ḥubbā al-Madīniyya?', in Lutz Edzard (ed.), *Arabic and Semitic Linguistics Contextualized. A Festschrift for Jan Retsö* (Wiesbaden, 2015), pp. 328–44.

—— 'Pleasing the Beloved: Sex and True Love in a Medieval Arabic Erotic Compendium', in Michael Beard, Alireza Korangy and Hanadi al-Samman (eds), *Beloved: Love and Languishing in Middle Eastern Literatures* (London, 2017), pp. 215–36.

—— 'The Prospects of a *jariya* in Abbasid Baghdad', in Matthew Gordon and Kathryn Hain (eds), *Concubines and Courtesans: Women and Slavery in Islamic History* (New York, 2017), pp. 52–74.

—— 'Of Ladies and Lesbians and Books on Women from the Third/Ninth and Fourth/ Tenth Centuries', *Journal of Abbasid Studies* 4 (2017), pp. 187–210.

—— 'Women and Men in al-Suyūṭī's Guides to Sex and Marriage', *Mamluk Studies Review* 21 (2018), pp. 47–68.

—— 'Slaves for Pleasure in Arabic Sex and Slave Purchase Manuals from the Tenth to the Twelfth Centuries', *Journal of Global Slavery* 4/2 (2019), pp. 196–225.

Papoutsakis, Nefeli, 'The *Ayrīyāt* of Abū Ḥukama (d. 240/854): A Preliminary Study', in Ahmad Talib, Marlé Hammond and Arie Shippers (eds), *The Rude, the Bad and the Bawdy: Essays in Honour of Professor Geert Jan van Gelder* (Cambridge, 2014).

—— 'al-Farazdaq', in Kate Fleet et al. (eds), *Encyclopaedia of Islam, THREE*. Consulted online on 6 November 2017.

Peirce, Leslie, 'Writing Histories of Sexuality in the Middle East', *American Historical Review* 114/5 (2009), pp. 1325–39.

—— The Imperial Harem (New York and Oxford, 1993).

Pellat, Ch., 'al-ʿAdjdjādj', in P. Bearman et al. (eds), *Encyclopaedia of Islam, Second Edition*, vol. 1, pp. 207–8.

—— 'Abu ʾl-ʿAnbas al-Ṣaymarī', in P. Bearman et al. (eds), *Encyclopaedia of Islam, Second Edition*, suppl., fasc. 1–2, pp. 16–17.

—— 'Al-Haytham b. ʿAdī', in P. Bearman et al. (eds), *Encyclopaedia of Islam*, Second *edition*, vol. 3, p. 328.

—— 'Hind Bint al-Khuss', in P. Bearman, et al. (eds), *Encyclopaedia of Islam, Second Edition*, vol. 3, pp. 454–5.

Pertsch, Wilhelm, *Die arabischen Handschriften der Herzoglichen Bibliothek zu Gotha* (Gotha, 1878–92).

Peters, R. (2012). 'Zināʾ', in P. Bearman et al. (eds), *Encyclopaedia of Islam, Second Edition*, vol. 9, p. 509.

Pickthall, Muhammad Marmaduke, *The Meaning of the Glorious Koran* (New York, 1930).

Pormann, Peter, 'Al-Rāzī (d. 925) on the Benefits of Sex: A Clinician Caught between Philosophy and Medicine', in Arnoud Vrolijk and Jan P. Hogendijk (eds), *O Ye Gentlemen: Arabic Studies on Science and Literary Culture in Honour of Remke Kruk* (Leiden, 2007), pp. 24–54.

—— 'Islamic Medicine Crosspollinated: A Multilingual and Multiconfessional Maze', in Anna Akasoy, James E. Montgomery and Peter E. Pormann (eds), *Islamic Crosspollinations: Interactions in the Medieval Middle East* (Exeter, 2007), pp. 76–93.

—— 'Female patients and practitioners in medieval Islam', *The Lancet* 373 (2009), pp. 1598–9.

Pormann, Peter and Emilie Savage-Smith, *Medieval Islamic Medicine* (Edinburgh, 2007).

Rāġib, Yūsuf, 'Les Marchés aux esclaves en terre d'islam', in *Mercati e mercanti nell'alto medioevo: L'area euroasiatica e l'area mediterranea* (Spoleto, 1993), pp. 721–63.

Rapoport, Jossef, *Marriage, Money and Divorce in Medieval Islamic Society* (Cambridge and New York, 2005).

Richter-Bernburg, L., 'ʿAlī b. ʿAbbās Majūsī', in *Encyclopedia Iranica*, vol. I, fasc. 8, pp. 837–8.

Rippin, A., 'Tafsīr', in P. Bearman et al. (eds), *Encyclopaedia of Islam, Second Edition*, vol. 10, pp. 83–8.

Roberts, Nancy N., 'Voice and Gender in Classical Arabic *Adab*: Three Passages from Aḥmad Ṭayfūr's "Instances of the Eloquence of Women"', *Al-ʿArabiyya* 25 (1992), pp. 51–72.

Roded, Ruth (ed.), *Women in Islam and the Middle East: a Reader* (London, 1999).

—— 'Mainstreaming Middle East Gender Research: Promise or Pitfall?', *Middle East Studies Association Bulletin* 35/1 (2001), pp. 15–23.

Rosenthal, Franz, 'From Arabic Books and Manuscripts VI: Istanbul Materials for al-Kindī and al-Sarakhsī', *Journal of the American Oriental Society* 76/1 (1956), pp. 27–31.

—— 'Al-Râzî on the Hidden Illness', *Bulletin of the History of Medicine* 52 (1978, pp. 45–60.
—— 'al-Sarakhsī', in P. Bearman et al. (eds), *Encyclopaedia of Islam, Second Edition.*
—— 'Fiction and Reality: The Sources for the Role of Sex in Medieval Muslim Society', in A. L. Al-Sayyid-Marsot (ed.), *Society and the Sexes in Medieval Islam* (Malibu, 1979).
—— 'Muslim Social Values and Literary Criticism: Reflections on the Ḥadīth of Umm Zarʿ', *Oriens* 34 (1994), pp. 31–56.
—— 'Male and Female: Described and Compared', in J. W. Wright Jr. and Everett K. Rowson (eds), *Homoeroticism in Classical Arabic Literature* (New York, 1997), pp. 24–54.
Rowson, Everett K., 'The Categorization of Gender and Sexual Irregularity in Medieval Arabic Vice Lists', in Julia Epstein and Kristina Straub (eds), *Body Guards: The Cultural Politics of Gender Ambiguity* (New York and London, 1991), pp. 50–79.
—— 'The Effeminates of Early Medina', *Journal of the American Oriental Society* 111 (1991), pp. 671–93.
—— 'Mujūn', in Julie Scott Meisami and Paul Starkey (eds), *Encyclopedia of Arabic Literature*, vol. 2 (London and New York, 1998), pp. 546–8.
—— 'Gender Irregularity as Entertainment: Institutionalized Transvestism at the Caliphal Court in Medieval Baghdad', in Sharon Farmer and Carol Braun Pasternack (eds), *Gender and Difference in the Middle Ages* (Minneapolis, 2003), pp. 45–72.
—— 'Abu al-ʿAtahiya', in Michael Cooperson and Shawkat Toorawa (eds), *Dictionary of Literary Biography*, vol. 311: *Arabic Literary Culture, 500–925* (Detroit, 2005), pp. 12–20.
—— 'Arabic: Middle Ages to Nineteenth Century', in Gaétan Brulotte and John Phillips (eds) *Encyclopedia of Erotic Literature*, vol. I (New York, 2006), pp. 43–61.
Rustomji, Nerina, *The Garden and the Fire: Heaven and Hell in Islamic Culture* (New York, 2009).
Salaymeh, Lena, *Beginnings of Islamic Law: Late Antique Islamicate Legal Traditions* (Cambridge, 2016).
Savage-Smith, Emilie, 'Medicine in Medieval Islam', in David C. Lindberg and Michael H. Shank (eds), *The Cambridge History of Science*, vol. 2 (Cambridge and New York, 2013), pp. 139–67.
Savage-Smith, Emilie, F. Klein-Franke and Ming Zhu, 'Ṭibb', in P. Bearman et al. (eds), *Encyclopaedia of Islam, Second Edition*, vol. 10, pp. 452–61.
Sbath, Paul, 'Le livre des caractères de Qosta ibn Louqua', *Bulletin de l'Institut d'Egypte*, vol. XXXIII (1941), pp. 103–69.
Schacht, J., 'Nikāḥ', in P. Bearman et al. (eds), *Encyclopaedia of Islam, Second Edition*, vol. 8, pp. 26–35.
Scott Meisami, Julia, 'Writing Medieval Women: Representations and Misrepresentations', in Julia Bray (ed.), *Writing and Representation in Mediaeval Islam: Muslim Horizons* (London and New York, 2006).

Sellheim, 'al-Marzūbānī', in P. Bearman et al. (eds), *Encyclopaedia of Islam, Second Edition*, vol. 6, pp. 634–5.

Selove, Emily and Rosalind Batten, 'Making Men and Women; Arabic Commentaries on the Gynaecological Hippocratic Aphorisms in Context', *Annales Islamologiques* 48/1 (2014), pp. 239–62.

Semerdjian, Elyse, 'Rewriting the History of Sexuality in the Islamic World', *Hawwa* 4/2–3 (2006), pp. 119–30.

Sezgin, Fuat, *Geschichte des arabischen Schrifttums*, 13 vols (Leiden, 1967–84).

Shahīd, Irfan, 'Zarḳā᾿ al-Yamāma', in P. Bearman et al. (eds), *Encyclopaedia of Islam, Second Edition*, vol. 10, p. 460.

Shippers, Arie, 'The *Mujūn* Genre by Abū Nuwās and by Ibn Quzmān: A Comparison', in Ahmad Talib, Marlé Hammond and Arie Shippers (eds), *The Rude, the Bad and the Bawdy: Essays in Honour of Professor Geert Jan van Gelder* (Cambridge, 2014).

*Simon Online: a collaborative edition of Simon of Genoa's 'Clavis sanationis'* (University of London, 2003–) http://www.simonofgenoa.org/, accessed 21 January 2018.

Slane, W. M. de, *Catalogue des manuscrits arabes* (Paris, 1883–95).

Smith, Jane I. and Yvonne Y. Haddad, 'Women in the Afterlife: The Islamic View as Seen From Qur᾿ān and Tradition', *Journal of the American Academy of Religion* 43/1 (1975), pp. 39–50.

Spectorsky, Susan A., *Chapters on Marriage and Divorce: Responses of Ibn Ḥanbal and Ibn Rāhwayh*, translated by Susan A. Spectorsky (Austin, 1983).

Steingass, Francis Joseph, *A Comprehensive Persian-English Dictionary* (New Delhi, 1892, repr. 2008).

Strohmaier, Gotthard, 'The Uses of Galen in Arabic Literature', in Vivial Nutton (ed.), *The Unknown Galen* (London, 2002), pp. 113–20.

—— 'Ḥunayn b. Isḥāq', in Kate Fleet et al. (eds), *Encyclopaedia of Islam, THREE.* Consulted online on 10 November 2017.

Szombathy, Zoltan, *Mujūn: Libertinism in Medieval Muslim Society and Literature* (Cambridge, 2013).

Temkin, Owsei, *Galenism; Rise and Decline of a Medical Philosophy* (Ithaca and London, 1973).

Thomas, D., 'al-Ṭabarī', in P. Bearman et al. (eds), *Encyclopaedia of Islam, Second Edition*, vol. 10, pp. 11–15.

Toorawa, Shawkat, *Ibn Abī Ṭāhir Ṭayfūr and Arabic Writerly Culture: A Ninth-century Bookman in Baghdad* (London and New York, 2005).

Ullmann, Manfred, *Die Medizin im Islam* (= *Handbuch der Orientalistik*, 1. Abteilung, Ergänzungsband VI, 1) (Leiden and Köln, 1970).

—— *Islamic Medicine* (Edinburgh, 1978).

—— 'Radjaz', in P. Bearman et al. (eds), *Encyclopaedia of Islam, Second Edition*, vol. 8, pp. 375–9.

Vadet, J.-C, 'Ibn Ḥamdūn', in P. Bearman et al. (eds), *Encyclopaedia of Islam, Second Edition*, vol. 3, p. 784.

Wagner, Ewald, 'Wāliba b. al-Ḥubāb', in P. Bearman et al. (eds), *Encyclopaedia of Islam, Second Edition*, vol. 11, pp. 126–9.

—— 'Abū Nuwās', in Kate Fleet et al. (eds) *Encyclopaedia of Islam, THREE*. Consulted online on 10 November 2017.

Walzer, R., 'Aflāṭūn', in P. Bearman et al. (eds), *Encyclopaedia of Islam, Second Edition*, vol. 1, pp. 234–6.

Weipert, Reinhard, 'al-Aṣmaʿī', in Kate Fleet et al. (eds) in *Encyclopaedia of Islam, THREE*. Consulted online on 31 January 2019.

Weisser, Ursula, *Zeugung, Vererbung und pränatale Entwicklung in der Medizin des arabisch-islamischem Mittelalters* (Erlangen, 1983).

WHO (World Health Organization), *Defining Sexual Health: Report of a Technical Consultation on Sexual Health, 28–31 January 2002, Geneva* (Geneva, 2006). http://www.who.int/reproductivehealth/publications/sexual_health/defining_sexual_health.pdf?ua=1

Yazigi, 'Some Accounts of Women Delegates to Caliph Muʿāwiya: Political Significance', *Arabica* 52/3 (2005), pp. 437–49.

Ze'ev, Mahen, *Virtues of the Flesh: Passion and Purity in Early Islamic Jurisprudence* (Leiden, 2005).

# Index

CPSIA information can be obtained
at www.ICGtesting.com
Printed in the USA
LVHW080145120821
695139LV00008B/152

9 780755 644698